THE MEANING OF PROPERTY

THE MEANING
OF PROPERTY

Freedom, Community, and the Legal Imagination

Jedediah Purdy

Yale
UNIVERSITY
PRESS
New Haven & London

Published with assistance from the foundation established in memory of
Calvin Chapin of the Class of 1788, Yale College.

Set in Electra and Trajan types by Tseng Information Systems, Inc.
Printed in the United States of America.

Library of Congress Cataloging-in-Publication Data
Purdy, Jedediah, 1974–
The meaning of property : freedom, community, and the
legal imagination / Jedediah Purdy.
p. cm.
Includes bibliographical references and index.
ISBN 978-0-300-11545-1 (alk. paper)
1. Right of property—Philosophy. I. Title.
K720.P87 2010
346.04'3201—dc22   2009033259

A catalogue record for this book is available from the British Library.

This paper meets the requirements of ANSI/NISO Z39.48-1992 (Permanence of Paper).

10   9   8   7   6   5   4   3   2   1

CONTENTS

Contents

Acknowledgments

Thanks to Kerry Abrams, Bruce Ackerman, Gregory Alexander, Jessica Areen, David Barron, Kate Bartlett, James Boyle, Erwin Chemerinsky, Nestor Davidson, John Eden, Bob Ellickson, Chris Elmendorf, Dan Farber, Kimberly Fielding, Philip Frickey, Bill Frucht, Brandon Garrett, Robert Gordon, David Grewal, Paul Haagen, Hayley Horowitz, Greg Klass, Anthony Kronman, Douglas Kysar, Susan Laity, David Lange, David Levi, Nicholas Parrillo, Eduardo Peñalver, Philip Pettit, Robert Post, Jeff Powell, Carol Rose, Jed Rubenfeld, James Salzman, Chris Schroeder, Neil Siegel, Joe Singer, Henry Smith, Dennis Thompson, Lindsay Toland, Erin Trenda, Christina Tucker, Christian Turner, Laura Underkuffler, Caroleen Verly, Jonathan Wiener, Duke Law School, Yale Law School, Harvard Law School, the Harvard University Ethics Center, the Berkman Center for Internet and Society, the New America Foundation, and all my students.

Introduction: Blackstone's Sociability

The phrases are almost Shakespearean in their familiarity. Like Hamlet's dithering and Mark Antony's evasive call for insurrection, they belong to the canon of the imagination: "There is nothing which so generally strikes the imagination, and engages the affections of mankind, as the right of property; or that sole and despotic dominion which one man claims and exercises over the external things of the world, in total exclusion of the right of any other individual in the universe."[1] That, of course, is William Blackstone, the muse of the common law, setting out on his treatment of "property, in general." Blackstone's is the canonical image of classical liberal property: the power, good against all the world, to exclude others from a resource, to determine the uses to which it shall be put, and to transfer it, by sale or otherwise. In fact, it was Blackstone's image of "the right of property,"[2] as much as the institution itself, that seized the imagination, for ownership in practice has always been hedged around with duties to neighbors, obedience to government, and limits from custom. Blackstone brought his own picture into question as soon as he set it out, noting, "Pleased as we are with the possession, we seem afraid to look back to the means by which it was acquired, as if fearful of some defect in our title."[3]

Why should a piece of land belong to you rather than me? Why should my father's owning a precious jewel, oceanside estate, or copyright in his father's novel mean he has the power to transmit it to me at his death, extending "despotic dominion" from beyond the grave?[4] What was the source of the claim that, as if by magic, distinguished ownership from theft, occupation from trespass, good use from pillage? Blackstone's countrymen were already using these distinctions to claim—or usurp—"new" continents from their aboriginal inhabitants. Soon Pierre Proudhon would examine the same distinctions and reject them, concluding that *property* was just another word for theft.

With such questions in mind, Blackstone proposed to "examine more deeply the rudiments and grounds" of ownership.[5] He then delivered a little-read tour de force. Blackstone "anticipated," as we in the present condescendingly say, the major lines of argument that preoccupy property scholars to this day.

Economics-influenced students of property follow Ronald Coase in approaching the institution as a means of reducing "transaction costs" by enabling people to identify the owners of those things they most desire, or find most offensive, and propose an exchange to acquire them or put them out of business. So Blackstone wrote, with property rights clearly marked out, it "was found, that what became inconvenient or useless to one man was highly convenient and useful to another; who was ready to give in exchange for it some equivalent, that was equally desirable to the former proprietor."[6] Blackstone also saw how property can encourage owners to announce their claims unambiguously, providing information to others and further reducing transaction costs: he characterized original acquisition of property not as the exercise of a natural right but as a man's "declaration that he intends to appropriate the thing to his own use," information on which others could rely.[7] He used this information rationale to sidestep hoary disputes between followers of Hugo Grotius and those of John Locke, who advanced competing natural-law grounds for the power to acquire property by occupation.[8]

Economists also understand ownership as motivating improvement by ensuring that owners can keep the benefits of their effort and innovation. So Blackstone observed that without ownership, "no man would be at the trouble to provide" so much as basic clothing and shelter, "if, so soon as he walked out of his tent, or pulled off his garment, the next stranger who came by would have a right to inhabit the one, and to wear the other."[9] Indeed, without "a separate property in lands . . . the world must have continued a forest, and men have been mere animals of prey."[10] (While this argument would later end up almost verbatim in the Supreme Court's approval of the expropriation of Native American lands by Europeans, Blackstone denounced "invaders" for "seizing on countries already peopled, and driving out or massacring the innocent and defenseless natives.")[11]

Nor did Blackstone neglect other "grounds and rudiments" of property rights.[12] His evocation of "sole and despotic dominion" captures the kernel of libertarians' view of ownership as a bulwark against interference by others and by the state.[13] Blackstone also described ownership as "ennobling . . . the human species" by creating new opportunities both to master and to contemplate the world,[14] an argument with traces of both the "personhood" claims associated with Margaret Jane Radin and the "civilizing" thesis that Carol M. Rose has argued links early-modern property thought to today's discourse on the political economy of development and democracy.[15]

History sometimes tosses up this kind of synoptic anticipation, particularly

when a good mind has the great fortune to come early in a tradition-to-be, surveying the field and noting in passing the major alternatives. (Witness the often-
heard remark that all of Western philosophy is a footnote to Plato, or to Plato
and Aristotle.) My concern here, however, is not with how unoriginal the past
manages to make the present look. It is, rather, with what Blackstone did with his
own past. His "grounds and rudiments" do display strong utilitarian themes and
chords of libertarian and personhood rationales for ownership, but systematic
normative theory is not his game. He tells a story about how and why property
came to be. Even as sympathetic a reader as Rose is somewhat nonplussed by this
approach, referring to Blackstone's "pseudo-history,"[16] "concocted history,"[17] and
"just-so story"[18] as she surveys his arguments.

But Blackstone does not seem to have intended his history as a whimsical
vessel for more serious normative arguments. He gave an account of humanity's
passage from hunting and gathering through herding and agriculture to the complex commercial life of his own time. That story was peppered with classical and
biblical instances, which Blackstone treated as documentary evidence, and, just
as important, with examples of old ways of life that were still practiced among
American aboriginal peoples, who, on the geographic margins of the world, he
believed lingered somewhere near the beginning of historical progress. It was,
moreover, a story with a clear causal sequence. Societies adopted property rights
as their needs required, needs defined by scarcity and the functional characteris-
tics of the resources that people exploited to overcome that scarcity. Property in
land arose when population growth rendered gathering and herding infeasible
and only agriculture could ensure the needed food supply—requiring, in turn,
that farmers enjoy the security of "dominion."

The radicalism of Blackstone's account, and the way in which it seems to have
been not at all casual, was this: property came first among institutions, and all
else followed. Blackstone wrote: "Necessity begat property; and, in order to ensure that property, recourse was had to civil society, which brought along with it a
long train of inseparable concomitants; states, governments, laws, punishments,
and the public exercise of religious duties. Thus connected together, it was found
that a part only of society was sufficient to provide, by their manual labor, for
the necessary subsistence of all; and leisure was given to others to cultivate the
human mind, to invent useful arts, and to lay the foundations of science."[19] This
is not simply the argument that property creates an economic surplus which sus-
tains civilization. It is far stronger than the argument that property reinforces
social stability, making laws and customs more secure. It is a picture of the whole
web of social institutions, including sovereignty, law, and organized religion, as
the children of property.

Understanding how Blackstone came to this narrative helps us see how he conceived of what Rose regards as an essential gap in his story: how self-interested people manage to create institutions such as property that require reciprocal restraint on self-interest—particularly in the absence of explicit law or strong government. As Rose puts it, there is "a kind of mystery of 'niceness' and trust at the center of economic transactions."[20] A story in which property comes first really puts something else first: sociability, a human propensity to form attachments and cooperative relationships outside and preceding formal legal structures. Whether such sociability existed, and if so how strong and reliable it was, were questions that obsessed jurists and philosophers of the eighteenth and nineteenth centuries. Property came to figure centrally in one answer to these questions: natural human sociability was strong enough to account for the origins of society and to explain the nature and purpose of social life. Human coexistence, in this account, came to be seen as an originally and essentially economic phenomenon, a cooperative venture of mutual benefit to all its members, producing civilization, prosperity, and liberty out of the pre-political transactions of, not exactly *homo economicus*, but social man. As we shall see, this theory filled a yawning gap in the self-understanding of European societies torn by religious wars and shaken by encounters with the human diversity of new continents. It also formed the worldview, what I call the legal imagination, in which our ideas about property's purposes and limits took shape.

In this book I locate today's theories of property within these origins. In that light, I argue for a way of understanding the relations among the purposes property is now thought to serve. Legal thinking about the purposes of property is fractured, but it is not formless, and appreciating the relations among its values can help us to deepen our understanding of the institution. I approach those values as aspects of a single master value, which was at the heart of the theory just sketched and which that theory served in good part to articulate and vindicate as both the normative and the practical keystone of social life: human freedom. Freedom is itself a plural value, of course, and locating its plurality within property thought is a major part of my aim.

By illuminating the relations among values already recognized but not, perhaps, completely understood, we can move toward integrating those values more fully with one another. The integration I argue for has its model in the vision of social life that Blackstone saw property as both setting in motion and sustaining. For modern property theorists, as for Blackstone, this form of social life centers on markets and liberal society, the sort premised on the individuality of its members and the chosen character of their projects and commitments. Indeed, *property* in this book means, unless otherwise stated, liberal property, the kind that is intimately tied to markets and liberal society. Arguments about the excellences and demerits of property are often also about the value and limits of markets and liberal society because our conception and practice of property are deeply linked to these, and those debates are part of larger debates. Understanding a legal institution within that context of social practices is part of the reason for referring not just to law but to legal imagination, the image of common life in which the law is set.

I follow the early-modern originators of the liberal theory of property—and, for that matter, today's economic theorists—in treating its scope broadly, as one that defines and allocates rights in scarce and valued resources. This approach implies, for instance, treating human labor power—now firmly ensconced in the law of labor and employment—as part of the concern of property law, a classification that would have seemed obvious to theorists and jurists of the eighteenth and even the nineteenth century. This scope expresses the ambition to treat property as a centerpiece of political economy at large, part of a picture of economic life that is attentive to both the functional virtues of property and the qualitative values it carries.

Defining and allocating property rights is a way of making a choice among possible markets. Some—though hardly all—of the conventional analyses of property rights examine how they work once they are fully defined and allocated, or, alternatively, how their definitions may be adjusted at the margins, either formally by judicial interpretation or informally by social norms. I approach the question of institutional design instead as an aspect of political choice, addressing larger-grained and more open-ended questions about who shall have what, and on what terms. As we shall see, that choice is the one the freedom-promoting tradition in property arose to guide, exemplarily in the work of Adam Smith. By understanding liberal property as an answer to that question, we can focus on how to address contemporary choices about defining and allocating property rights by way of the same tradition of values.

Property, in ways the most familiar of our major legal institutions, took its modern form as the centerpiece of a new way of understanding society: as a semivoluntary, semi-spontaneous order of mutual benefit that people brought about to overcome brute material necessity and make themselves and others freer. Appreciating the novelty and radicalism of that vision can contribute to historical interpretation but also to today's legal and political judgment. An institution that we now often regard as intrinsically conservative is no inert inheritance but the achievement of a frequently radical tradition of imagination and reform that has perennially sought new ways to integrate with social order the multiple dimensions of human freedom. Properly inheriting that tradition means carrying it forward in the same spirit.

Part One

———◆———

ORIGINS

Property and the Legal Imagination

At its origin in the thought of eighteenth-century jurists and reformers, classical liberal property was imagined as having two unique and extraordinary virtues. Both were triumphs of integration, in which property appeared able to channel the sweeping and disruptive ideas and values that were then ushering in a new world, guiding them from conflict to mutual reinforcement. First, property bridged two epochal innovations: the recognition that cooperation among reasonably self-interested individuals could spontaneously produce complex and mutually beneficial social practices and institutions, and the discovery that collective action through the power of the state could remake the social world. Both innovations are foundational in modern life, and they are in obvious tension. Spontaneous social order can make the state seem merely intrusive, incidental, or nugatory. State action can inhibit, even obliterate, spontaneous order. Property promised to be what one nineteenth-century enthusiast called the perfect reconciliation of individual freedom and social order, a legal institution, defined and enforced by the state, in which spontaneous order could freely proceed and perpetually reinvent itself.

Second, property promised to integrate the most important qualities of personal freedom, the signal value of the modern world. For a person to be free means at least these things: first, the person is free from direct interference in decision making, whether from the state or from other individuals, by virtue of some guaranteed immunity from their intrusions. Second, in making decisions, the person enjoys a reasonably rich set of acceptable alternatives and is not forced simply to choose between one bad situation and another horrible one. Third, the individual has the psychological capacity to define and pursue the interests, projects, and commitments that guide those choices, without crippling self-doubt, self-loathing, or other impediments to clear and consistent judgment. While each aspect of freedom falls along a spectrum, obtaining more or less in any case, all are necessary: someone who lacked one could not make use of the other two. As these values became universal demands and the standard of modern legitimacy, property emerged as the keystone institution of a social order whose advocates believed it could integrate them—that is, make them not just compatible but mutually reinforcing in the institution's ordinary operation.

These ideas were at the center of vast developments afoot in the social imagination of the time. As Charles Taylor has argued, the eighteenth century ushered in the rise of "an appreciation of the way in which human life is designed so as to produce mutual benefit," a vision in which "humans are engaged in an exchange of services" and "one could begin to see political society itself through a quasi-economic metaphor."[1] This idea gradually replaced long-standing visions of society as the expression of a hierarchical natural law, in which social orders reflected a structure of complementary superiority and subordination.[2] In early modern thought the economic view of society stood as the main rival of a different alternative to the traditional view, a theory of naked hierarchy and command that stressed not so much the goodness of traditional political order as the grim consequences of life without it.[3]

Two innovations particularly marked the economic view. The first was the idea that social life arose from the constructive efforts of individuals and groups. The normative and practical order of society did not simply precede and frame individual activity; it also arose from that activity. In an ideal-typical sense there were two ways of conceiving of this development. One, which Hugo Grotius substantially initiated and John Locke perfected, portrayed individuals as bearing natural rights akin to legal rights, which they combined in contractual fashion to produce political society.[4] The other, which Samuel Pufendorf set in motion and Adam Smith completed, made less use of the tinker-toy apparatus of natural rights and instead portrayed humans as naturally social and self-interested beings whose activity produced society incrementally, without the unique origin of a social contract.[5] Despite their conceptual differences, these versions of social order tended to run together and complement each other. They share a deep methodological individualism and are both based in the conviction that such a picture of the individual can underlie an account of society.[6] By this logic, each contributed to the economic image of society as an interest-driven system of mutual benefit.

The second innovation was often in some tension with the first, and remains so today. This is the idea that the institutions in which mutual benefit occurs arise not just from the aggregation of bottom-up activity but also from collective action guided by political and institutional vision. The history of social life is therefore not simply a narrative of explanation, along the lines of natural history, it is also a story of collective choice, and the central place of choice in past developments implies a choice of futures now. Taylor argues that this dual quality means that the "modern grasp of society is ineradicably bi-focal," seeing on the one hand individuals as acting within contexts of mutual benefit and on the other politics as choosing and creating these contexts.[7] This duality, in turn, reflects the fact that "freedom as a central good is over-determined in the modern moral order: it is . . . one of the central properties of the humans who consent to and thus constitute society; and it is inscribed in their condition as the artificers who build their own social world, as against being born into one which already has its own 'normal' form."[8] Integrating the two sides of this duality, defining a mutually supportive relation between state power and private ordering, was the first extraordinary promise of classical liberal property.

These images of how social life arose and maintained itself were intimately connected with new ideas of what mattered most to human beings: their autonomous projects and judgments, their legitimate self-interest, their capacity for self-responsibility, and their power to contribute to the commonweal even as they pursued their own ends, which were arguably selfish and indisputably self-regarding. These features combined in the novel image of the free person, whose liberty, interests, and duties were not incidents of social status but the very premises of existence—not society's fruits but its elemental ingredients and building blocks. It was for such a person that freedom's three dimensions—choice without interference, a rich set of alternatives, and the subjective capacity to identify and pursue interests and projects—became the signal values of modern life. It was through the economic image of society that they came to be understood first as possible, then as inevitable sources of order and criteria of legitimacy in social life. In this new vision, property was the keystone institution.

These ideas form one of the major concepts of this book, a *social imaginary*. A social imaginary, as Taylor describes it, is "that largely unstructured and inarticulate understanding of our whole situation, within which particular features of our world show up for us in the sense they have."[9] This understanding is "both factual and 'normative'; that is, we have a sense of how things usually go, but this is interwoven with an idea of how they ought to go."[10] It is, in other words, an often implicit and widespread idea of how the world works and of what features of it are most important—and important in what ways—which "makes possible common practices, and a widely shared sense of legitimacy."[11] Because the motivation of this book is to offer an understanding of how the legal institution of property and its moral and political associations arose within a broader view of shared life, I use the term *legal imagination* to capture the part of the social imaginary that is especially germane here.

A social imaginary is not the same as an explicit theory. It typically influences more sectors of society, more powerfully defines the limits of the acceptable or plausible, and is made up more of presuppositions and perceptions than of propositions and their entailments. Its elements combine to form an incompletely articulate idea of how the world works and what in it matters most. We shall see several versions of the property-centered legal imagination in the course of this book, including the commercial republicanism of the early American jurist James Kent, the Free Labor thought of the middle and later decades of the nineteenth century, and the vision of imperial governance that helped guide British rule in India and informed Chief Justice John Marshall's account of the European expropriation of Native Americans in the infamous and seminal case *Johnson v. M'Intosh*.[12] Here it will be helpful to make the idea more concrete by setting out the foundational property-centered legal—and social—imaginary, the Scottish Enlightenment thought of Adam Smith.

PROPERTY IN THE SCOTTISH ENLIGHTENMENT

Adam Smith was the iconic advocate and theorist of the principle that each person's labor is personal property, which that individual may freely sell provided the contract of sale is limited by a right to exit—unlike apprenticeship, indentured servitude, and slavery. These principles form the prototype of what we have come to know as the free-labor economy, one in which time, talent, and energy can be freely sold on the labor market at retail but not, so to speak, at wholesale. Smith's account of an economy governed by these principles of "natural liberty," which channel the self-interest of each individual into socially beneficial courses, is the foundation of both classical and neoclassical economics.[13]

A list of Smith's principles is incomplete without a picture of the social life that he envisioned them as animating and, just as important, the alternative social visions he hoped his view would supplant. He pursued an economic world of commercial relationships founded on private property, mediated by contract, and bounded by the right of exit, without fixed obligations based in status or inheritance. His commitment to such a world was not based directly on the principles that would govern it. Rather, the principles arose from a picture of what life would be in that world. By diminishing the prerogatives of inherited status and requiring people to bargain over the terms of their cooperative enterprises, commerce brought the mighty low(er), elevated the poor, and created a new middle class, closing the cruel gaps of sympathy and respect that feudal hierarchy and slavery produced.[14]

This social dimension of Smith's commitments rested on two aspects of his thought. First, he regarded economic orders not just quantitatively, in terms of their efficiency or productivity, but also qualitatively. He believed that any system of economic relations presupposes, and produces, people of a certain kind. Any social and economic regime is thus also a regime of character. Put in the language of contemporary economics, Smith saw people's preferences—and, indeed, their values and commitments, their very identities—as endogenous to the economic regimes in which they engaged in production and exchange. The rise of free labor, with its new market negotiations, also marked the arrival of a new set of attitudes, which would reinforce the activity of market society.[15]

Smith's second distinctive belief was that the basic motive in all social relations, including economic transactions, was not the wish for wealth as such but rather a desire for esteem. He bluntly demoted wealth seeking to a derivative position: "It is chiefly from the regard to the sentiments of others that we pursue riches and avoid poverty."[16] In Smith's thought, admiration and emulation pervaded social relations, as did their near opposites, indifference and aversion (mostly toward the poor and powerless). Appreciating the qualitative, attitude-forming dimension of an economy therefore required understanding how esteem worked in that economy.

To this end, Smith argued for free labor by contrasting it with two other economic regimes, showing how treating personal labor as classical liberal property could make people at once freer and more fit to be free.[17] His first contrast was between free labor and a feudal courtly society, in which both wealth and esteem depended largely on status: positions were generally inherited, and each one carried with it inherent duties, privileges, and rank. In a courtly society, hereditary nobles and high gentry dominated in the distribution of esteem. As a result, those seeking esteem became courtiers—sycophants, dependent on the whim and favor of their nominal betters (what Smith called "the fanciful and foolish favour of ignorant, presumptuous, and proud superiors").[18] In this setting, "flattery and falsehood too often prevail over merit and abilities."[19] The search for esteem in a courtly society was thus a path to degradation. It created a form of domination in which subordinates, subject to the arbitrary whim of superiors, adopted tastes, manners, and attitudes to suit their perception of the superiors' wishes. Smith wrote that courtiers were "proud to imitate and resemble [their superiors] in the very qualities which dishonour and degrade them. . . . They desire to be praised for what they themselves do not think praiseworthy, and are ashamed of unfashionable virtues."[20] Feudal subordinates, in this sketch, could not even formulate and pursue their own interests and commitments without distortion by their material and psychic dependence.

Smith also contrasted free labor with slavery. This choice of contrast is striking for what it reveals about Smith's conception of the alternatives that confronted his time. While the contrast of a free-labor society to a feudal one set modernity against premodernity, the contrast with slavery involved versions of the future. Smith seems to have regarded slavery not as a vestige of premodern life but as a premonition of modernity as nightmare rather than emancipation. Moreover, contradicting his later (undeserved) reputation for believing that economic efficiency conquers all, he declined to argue that slavery was doomed because of what he considered its inferior productivity. Although Smith did think that slavery was less efficient than free labor because it failed to give slaves incentives to produce, he could not be sanguine about free labor's prospects for supplanting the system of human chattel. Instead, consistent with his belief that economic life was motivated by esteem, he interpreted slavery as a system of status and emulation and gave reasons to doubt that it would perish quickly. Slavery, Smith wrote, appealed to "the love of domination and authority and the pleasure men take in having every thing done by their express orders."[21] This pleasure of masters, the ultimate satisfaction of domination, was possible only when coupled with the subjection of a slave class.

Smith argued that slavery's psychological appeal might make it the organizing economic principle of a possible dystopian modernity, despite its inferior productivity. This version of modern life served as a negative pole in his thought. Slavery's persistence, even its growth, struck him as perfectly compatible with the defining political and economic trends of early modernity: republican government and increasing prosperity. Republics of slaveholders, he argued, were much less likely than monarchies to abolish slavery because the social standing of the slaveholding class depended on its continued "domination and authority" over its human property.[22] Monarchs, by contrast, did not rely on slaveholding for their power or status: they stood categorically apart from even their free countrymen. Indeed, a king might even wish to weaken wealthy and independent citizens by liberating their slaves. Slaves' prospects for freedom would thus grow worse as republican liberty advanced in a slaveholding society: "[L]ove of domination and tyrannizing, I say, will make it impossible for the slaves in a free country ever to recover their liberty."[23]

Smith also believed that prosperity would worsen the condition of slaves, for one simple reason and one that was more complicated. The simple reason was that a rich society could afford more slaves than a poor one, and thus, to avert the prospect of slave revolt, must become a police state, with slaves on the receiving end of the boot heel. The more complex reason was that the wealth of the master increased the social, and thus the psychological, distance between master and slaves. Smith imputed to the relatively poor slaveholder, who worked alongside his chattel, a sympathetic attitude to these bonded creatures who so resembled him. The wealthy master, however, would lead a life so removed from the experience of his slave that "he will hardly look on him as being of the same kind; he thinks he has little title even to the ordinary enjoyments of life, and feels but little for his misfortunes."[24]

This analysis of slavery's prospects in increasingly wealthy and self-governing societies led Smith to one of the most arresting passages in all his work: "Opulence and freedom, the two greatest blessings men can possess, tend greatly to the misery of this body of men [slaves], which in most countries where slavery is allowed makes by far the greatest part. A humane man would wish therefore if slavery has to be generally established that these greatest blessings, being incompatible with the happiness of the greatest part of mankind, were never to take place."[25] The most important word in the passage is *if*: "if slavery has to be generally established."[26] For Smith, the purpose of free-labor principles was to move a society from a world in which some people are property to one in which all have it and can transfer it freely. From that choice of worlds, founded in a property rule, all else flowed.

The contrasts highlighted Smith's affirmative vision of free labor and commercial society. In his view, the laborer's right of exit negated the social superior's prerogative of command that defined both feudal and slave relations. Rather than issue an order, one who sought to enter a bargain with a free laborer had to make an offer, which the offeree could refuse. That simple legal fact changed the everyday transaction of the society from command to negotiation. Despite inevitable differences in bargaining power, a society of negotiation was also a society of reciprocity, in which the one who made an offer had to address the other in light of that person's interests, projects, and identity, either being useful by those lights or persuading the other to change them. This in turn required an awareness that one inhabited a world of other persons, each with distinct interests and self-conceptions, encompassing goals, aversions, and bases of dignity. It meant recognizing the relativity of one's own interests and self-conception to those of others. Smith argued of the emblematic interaction of commercial society, "The offering of a shilling, which to us appears to have so plain and simple a meaning, is in reality offering an argument *to persuade one to do so and so as it is in his interest.* Men always endeavour to persuade others to be of their opinion even when the matter is of no consequence to them. . . . And in this manner, every one is practising oratory on others thro the whole of his life. —You are uneasy whenever one differs from you, and you endeavour to persuade [him] to be of your mind. . . . In this manner [people] acquire a certain dexterity and adress in managing their affairs, or in other words in managing of men. . . . That is bartering, by which they adress themselves to the self interest of the person and seldom fail immediately to gain their end. The brutes have no notion of this."[27]

Smith hoped that men of commerce and free labor, shaped by such inter-action, would develop a new paradigm of personality: not the haughty, domi-neering lord or master but the man of competence, sensitivity, and integrity. That is *competence* in the double sense of having only enough wealth to preserve basic dignity and being diligent and able: people of middling means earned the esteem of others not by fatuous pretensions to greatness but by steady and solid execution of their commitments. Sensitivity, awareness of others' interests and feelings, was essential in a society of negotiation, but it was not enough by itself. To win the trust and admiration of others, commercial men would have to ac-quire their own variety of charisma: this was integrity, the steadiness of a man who knew his own mind and could hold it even as he recognized and responded to the experience of others.

What Smith offered, then, was a picture of commercial society in which em-blematic interactions and personalities were wound around a founding choice about the nature and scope of ownership. This was a normative theory of prop-erty rights, but it was also a fully fledged social imaginary, one Smith offered as an alternative to other, less egalitarian visions of social order. The principles crys-tallized the moral logic of the social vision, but they could not stand in dogmatic isolation. They took their sense and force from a much broader image of how the world worked, what alternative futures were available in it, and which qualities in human life were most valuable and which most abhorrent.

PROPERTY AS THE KEYSTONE INSTITUTION

With a view of the social imaginary in which it was set, we can now understand the relation between the structure of classical liberal property and its role as the keystone institution of that social vision. Classical liberal property is marked by a set of powers in the owner that are good against all the world: exclusion of others except by consent, transfer of the property by sale or other means, and control over the use made of it.[28] To its early proponents, the structure of the institution seemed to underwrite an integration of values that, in turn, defined a whole vision of social order. The paramount feature of ownership in this vision was the power to exclude, which in practice meant the power to decline any proffered relationship or joint venture. As to whatever resources one owned—land, chattels, one's own time and labor—one would enter into a cooperative venture only upon consent, that is, one could choose to forgo the exclusion power in that instance. The exclusion power tied decisions about resource use ineluctably to interest-based persuasion because that, and that only, was the way to win free consent. The sharpness and universality of the exclusion power helped ensure such relations. Any abrogation of the power, in contrast, produced claims on resources that did not arise from persuasion and consent: neighbors with access to a plot of land, a feudal superior with a claim to part of a tenant's product, or a master (of an apprentice, a servant, or a slave) with the power to command another's time, talent, and energy.

The power of transfer, which legal theorists often call the power of alienation, played a similarly important part in this image of social life. The alienability of real property, in particular, subjected it to economic risk, meaning that the wastrels, fools, and unfortunates in each generation stood a fair chance of losing what they began with. Conversely, this implied a greater chance for those who began with modest means to acquire the wealth that traditional restraints on alienability could make difficult to pry from a dynastic heir. Alienability meant risk, risk meant circulation, and circulation meant opportunity and social mobility. The stasis that inalienable wealth could enforce was also a fixity of status: a power to command both resources and respect outside the reciprocal play of interest and persuasion that property's liberal admirers associated with the marketplace.[29]

The power to determine the uses of one's property, too, facilitated the development of free personality even as it contributed to social wealth. It made ownership a field for initiative and the affirmative expression of autonomy: not just exclusion of others from one's own space but command over the scope and character of activity there. Such command, in contrast to the subordinate's position of receiving orders and seeking favor, was a major training ground of the free personality. Within the market relations that ownership set in motion, this free activity was sufficiently subject to financial reward and punishment that it aligned substantially with social welfare.

In this social imaginary, then, there was an integral connection between what Henry Smith has called an "exclusion strategy" in resource governance—a classically liberal property regime—and the vision of a social life that could integrate distinct and potentially competing values: freedom from interference, the growth of wealth and the corresponding enjoyment of an enriched set of alternatives, and the rise of free personality in autonomous activity and social relations of reciprocity and dignity.[30] Property rights in classically liberal form were regarded as uniquely able to integrate these signal values of modern life.

LEGAL IMAGINATION AND NORMATIVE TRADITION

We still inhabit a version of legal imagination that owes its shape to the early-modern social imaginary just sketched. The major ways of understanding the purpose and value of property rights are partial accounts, principled fragments, of a larger social vision that is continuous, though not identical, with that of the Scottish Enlightenment and its immediate descendants. Today's major normative takes on property share in a legal imagination that is indebted to an inheritance of property thought. To better understand them we shall consider what it means to approach legal thought, particularly normative legal thought, through the lens of the legal imagination.

This approach reflects a decision to eschew the first-principles style of reasoning that might be called high normative theory, which begins from a master value or formula—individual liberty, welfare maximization, an account of distributive justice—and treats legal institutions as objects of diagnosis and reform according to the canons of normative theory.[31] Instead, I begin within the tradition of argument about property law itself, asking what values it has been understood to serve, what the consequences of that understanding have been, and how far the institution has succeeded in meeting the claims its defenders make for it.[32] One result of this approach is that the institution emerges as serving no master value at all but rather engaging several distinct values that are related through the structure of property itself and the social relations it sets in motion. If there is a master feature in this normative account, it is the capacity to integrate these distinct values, making them mutually reinforcing in the ordinary activity of the institution. As argued earlier, it is illuminating to understand property's distinct values as aspects of the modern master value of freedom, but that way of stating their significance does not magically unify them. Instead, it shows how closely the structure of property thought is tied to the most basic ideas about the purposes of modern social life in general. This is not surprising: one of my arguments, recall, is that the modern idea of social life, centered on a plural vision of freedom, emerged in critical part through the development of a new style of property thought and a social and legal imagination with property at its center.

This approach may seem to run together the descriptive and the normative, and, in fact, it does: it works from the premise that normative reasoning can claim no "view from nowhere" but takes place within traditions of principle, argument, and aspiration, which in turn take some of their coherence and force from the larger social and legal imagination in which they are related. Such traditions are themselves partly normative and partly descriptive: they build in moral principles, ways of adjudicating moral disputes, enduring disagreements, and presuppositions about how the world ordinarily works. I shall not attempt to defend the focus on normative traditions as a matter of meta-ethics or philosophical anthropology but instead adopt the more pragmatic criterion of asking how far the approach can illuminate property thought. In this respect, it might be understood as a kind of mid-level theory, between high normative theory and doctrinal description, grounded in the normative logic of institutions and the social visions in which they work.

What emerges from this way of engaging property thought is fourfold. The approach provides interpretations of two interrelated aspects of property thought: the descriptive (how the institution has been understood to work in the larger social world) and the normative (what values it has been understood to serve).[33] These interpretations, in turn, serve two further normative projects that operate deliberately within the normative tradition of property thought, rather than as high-theory intrusions from outside. One of these is critical, a picture of the cases in which the property-centered legal imagination has obscured conflicts among its organizing values and of other cases in which its way of integrating those values obscures important alternatives or competing considerations.[34] Another is aspirational: using the reconstructed picture of property as an integrating and freedom-oriented institution to guide a search for new ways of enabling social practices in which autonomy, prosperity, and flourishing are mutually reinforcing values.[35]

PROPERTY'S ASPECTS

Today's normative property thought has three focal points, three ways of celebrating property rights. Each seizes on one virtue of private-property regimes as the centerpiece of writing and thinking about the institution. It is convenient to describe them as camps, although that is inevitably simplifying. What is most striking is their continuity with the major concerns of early-modern property thought, the three aspects of freedom.

The first way of praising property belongs to the *libertarians*. From the libertarian standpoint, property rights secure what Isaiah Berlin called negative liberty, freedom from interference with one's own choices and projects.[36] The libertarian take often concentrates on preventing state intrusion, but it can consistently sweep in interference from other private individuals, who must answer to owners' right to exclude others from their property. When libertarians include protection against private interference in their praise of property, they align themselves with both Berlin, who included such protection in his definition of negative liberty, and Jeremy Bentham, who saw it as central to the value of property rights. Libertarianism aims at a world of autonomous choice, in which individuals need not justify their decisions or projects to their neighbors—whether *simpliciter* or gathered as a government—but can act undisturbed, on their own self-authorizing judgment.[37] Libertarianism also has a strong affinity with an idea of responsibility, that private ownership makes individuals in fair measure the authors of their own successes and failures.

Welfarists understand property as an institution superbly designed to promote material well-being. Two excellences of private property produce this benefit. The security that property rights establish encourages owners to improve and innovate in using what they own, turning deserts into fields and words into sonnets and songs. This is *dynamic efficiency*. Property rights also enable people to identify the owners of things they would like to own themselves and to acquire them if they can make the transfer worthwhile to the present owners. This is *static efficiency*.[38]

The normative vision of dynamic efficiency is a world of perennial expansion and improvement, in which the frontier, that icon of abundance and opportunity, never really closes but moves from the border of settlement to the edge of innovation. That of static efficiency is a world of satisfied desires, in which any wish for which there is, somewhere, a corresponding object can be fulfilled if the wisher can pay enough. Both are counterpoints to scarcity and constraint. Dynamic efficiency denies the reality of a zero-sum world, in which anyone's wealth must imply that others have less. Static efficiency seeks to overcome the arbitrariness of existing allocations of resources from the perspectives of both preference satisfaction and fairness.

The third register of celebration comes from the *personhood* camp. The personhood approach to property concentrates on what Berlin called positive liberty, the achievement of a particular conception of autonomy.[39] On this account, which is particularly associated with the work of Margaret Jane Radin, ownership enriches identity by enabling owners to identify with and express themselves through the external objects they control.[40] A variant of this view, recently developed by Eduardo Peñalver, emphasizes a different aspect of positive liberty: the capacity to enter into and cultivate social relations, which ownership helps to secure.[41] The personhood approach aims at a world where people enjoy the preconditions of a flourishing life. Like other conceptions of positive liberty, any variant of the personhood approach rests on some idea of what counts as such a life.

These differing approaches contain a fair amount of variety, such as the difference between libertarians who concentrate on bounding state power and those who are equally concerned with private interference, or that between schools

of personhood theorists. Moreover, property theorists are not blind to interconnections among these values. It is a commonplace that libertarians' autonomous
choices help promote welfarists' efficiency—up to a point. That efficiency, in
turn, makes the material preconditions of personhood available to more people
than could otherwise enjoy them—at least in many cases. Nonetheless, the three
approaches capture real differences in emphasis. Each approach informs a body
of scholarship, fairly characterizes a set of cases and doctrines, and marks a way
of teaching property.

Just as there are three dominant ways to praise property rights, there are three
leading ways to call them into question. Critical approaches to property fall into
realist, *romantic*, and *republican* veins. Each critical camp concentrates on a
feature of the conventional defenses of property in which it identifies a serious
intellectual or moral omission. Realism, which arose as a critical posture in response to the dogmatic laissez-faire jurisprudence of the late nineteenth and
early twentieth centuries, attacks alleged ideological blindness in defenses of
property. Realism's unifying theme is that property rights are created and enforced by the state. On this basis, realists attack the distinction between public
power, explicitly exercised by the state, and the private power of owners, backed
by the warrant of the state.[42] In the strongest version of the realist position, developed polemically by Robert Hale, all private economic relations emerge redescribed as relations of coercion.[43] Realists also set out a second line of attack,
this one against the alleged tendency to naturalize the forms of property rights as
if they had inherent content rather than being mutable instruments of political
choices.[44] A third line of realist criticism applies these principles to political decisions that allocate property rights, pointing out their distributive consequences
and arguing that these may be as important as their libertarian or efficiency-
enhancing benefits yet be obscured by neglect of property's political origins.[45]

Romantics—a term not intended as pejorative—present the critical edge of
the personhood view, and indeed are sometimes also personhood theorists. They
concentrate on how the market relations that property sets in motion shape the
experience of value, casting all things in light of their power to satisfy morally
arbitrary and psychologically fungible preferences. In the romantic account,
ownership of market property implies a certain attitude toward the objects
owned: they are instruments of will and desire, not integral to the owner's identity but detachable, readily exchanged for some more convenient or lucrative or
pleasurable alternative. Moreover, their value is simply their capacity to satisfy
preferences and thus is commensurable with the value of all other objects; it is
neither unique nor even qualitatively distinctive.

From the romantic perspective, a property regime that treats everything as a potential market commodity creates a corrosive paradox: to act effectively we must make some objects into instruments of our will, yet if we approach the objects, qualities, and relationships most closely related to identity as commodities, we shall change who we are.[46] Specifically, if we regard sex, body parts, friendship, and personal belongings such as wedding rings and family homesteads as nothing more than placeholders for their price tags, then we will no longer be the particular individuals who are shaped by our relations to these things. Imagine, for instance, someone who values personal belongings according to the prices they can fetch on eBay, whose sexual relations center on relentless efforts to "trade up," or who regards marriage and prostitution as substitutable ways of pursuing the same satisfaction. By mastering everything in commodity form, romantics suggest, we create a morally flattened kingdom with a hollow ruler. The romantic prescription is to preserve from the full complement of ownership rights certain things that are essential to qualitatively valuable relations: organs, sexual relations, children, and perhaps even family homes or culturally important areas of the natural world.

Republicans share in the romantic objection to market-oriented property: that it tends to foster a worldview in which individual preferences appear self-authorizing and beyond argument or reproach, and all values wind up being reduced to price, the measure of the power to satisfy preferences.[47] Republicans, however, object specifically to the elevation of market valuation over civic sources of value. Civic value might be a view that the community has reached through deliberation or political mobilization, rather than the aggregation and coordination of individual preferences, or it could be the idea that the fundamental values of the political community require a certain definition or distribution of property rights, such as a prohibition on owning human beings or a minimum distribution of resources to each citizen.

These lines of celebration and criticism track familiar distinctions in moral and political thought. Libertarian and welfarist positions, respectively, recall deontological and consequentialist accounts of ethics. The personhood perspective evokes Hegel's counterpoint to Kantian individualism. And both the romantic and the republican criticisms of market-oriented property conjure up that same contrast, recently recapitulated in the so-called liberal-communitarian debate in political theory. Anyone seeking an antecedent to the realist criticism of received property categories need look no further than Karl Marx's sulfurous attack on liberal conceptions of emancipation in "On the Jewish Question."

None of this should be surprising. Property is so central among the institutions of modern social and political order that the surprise would rather be if debates around it did not recapitulate basic arguments about the purposes of that order and the terms of its legitimacy. The debates express genuine and persistent differences in characterizations of modern life, as well as genuine difficulties in integrating distinct values. That said property is not simply an instance of those debates but an integrating mechanism in which contrasting considerations and perspectives can, as far as possible, work as complements rather than mutually exclusive alternatives.

Even as the alternative approaches to property display differences, they also bear profound family resemblances. These reflect the fact that they have emerged as partial secessions from a fairly unified vision of the place of property in social order. Libertarianism continues the central place of negative liberty, or freedom from interference, in the legal imagination of property, with its foundation in the exclusion power and requirement of consent. Welfarism extends the moral vision of a legal system in which individual decisions would produce growing social wealth: a world of increasingly broad alternatives in ordinary lives, made possible by riches of a kind new in the world. Personhood theory develops the idea that free and flourishing personalities could arise in the autonomy and reciprocal social relations that classical liberal property was envisioned as bringing into being. Moreover, as we shall see, they continue to have their greatest appeal not as competing master values, but as mutually reinforcing parts of an integrating property regime.

The critical positions, too, are best understood in relation to the integrating ambitions that defined property's normative tradition at the outset. The realist critique expresses the permanent and always vexed interaction between property's status as the institution of spontaneous ordering par excellence and its nature as a creature of state definition and enforcement—a collective creation of the context in which individual and social activity takes place. These two understandings of property emerge conceptually from key innovations in the modern social and legal imagination, and losing sight of either would be a serious mistake. Moreover, while property operates in imperfect harmony on the border between private ordering and the state, these two forms of modern social order are not intractably in conflict. On the contrary, the property rights that sustain private ordering are often the products of political vision and reform as much as of spontaneous order. While the political aspect of a successful property regime may become nearly invisible, that mark of success would undermine the success itself if it meant forgetting that politics and the state remain part of the story. Forgetting that would mean losing the recognition that property depends on political action. It would also cost us in political vision for approaching later reformist efforts in a spirit of integration.

The republican and realist complaint that private ordering occludes political vision by elevating selfish personal preferences over civic value may seem less persuasive in light of this book's project. In the tradition of property thought that this book traces, securing a domain for personal preferences and private ordering is itself a civic project, not just in the formal sense that it depends on state action but also because it is a way of promoting the values of reciprocity and dignity for all social members, and these are also civic values. The perceived opposition between liberal property and civic and political values, then, results at least in part from losing sight of the complex social values that property has long been thought to promote.

The romantic claim that ownership produces an instrumental and commodifying attitude toward things that should not be so viewed, particularly other people, is belied by a broader view of property's normative tradition. The social relations that early reformers regarded as the antithesis of liberal property orders—feudalism and slavery—rested on commanding others directly, as incidents of ownership, that is, treating them as things. Liberal ownership aimed at a world in which those who wished to enlist others' effort would have to address them as human beings. In this respect, the way of imagining the self that the romantic critique ascribes to liberal ownership—as an autonomous agent in a world of passive objects open to manipulation—is mistaken. A more accurate image would be of the self as an agent in a world of self-owning agents, a world not flattened into monotonic preference satisfaction but rich with the diverse perspectives of others.

From a more generous point of view, the romantic quarrel with the liberal property regime marks an important dispute between the vision of society as a system of mutual material benefit and a dissenting view that emphasizes the prerogatives of moral and aesthetic perfectionism. This alternative has long styled the emphasis on material benefit a form of enslavement to convention and small-spiritedness and sought to emancipate a distinct form of consciousness. There are a few things to say in favor of a productive relation between this aspiration and property's liberal, commercial integration of purposes. The most obvious is that libertarian autonomy sweeps in most forms of eccentricity: private ordering has provided the legal instrument of utopian communities throughout American history, which suggests that as a social form it includes more diverse aims than the romantic criticism suggests. Moreover, the increasingly qualitative and experience-oriented versions of welfare that people pursue through markets—meaningful careers, therapeutic reflection, unique travel, physical self-improvement—mark a partial convergence between the anti-instrumental tradition of romanticism and the ways existing markets have enabled people to pursue such aims. Such a convergence also finds programmatic expressions within the freedom-oriented tradition of property today, as we shall see in later chapters' discussions of voluntary and decentralized production, which involves as much sharing and play as accumulation and labor. These romantic aspirations, then, find support, not frustration, in a properly broad conception of property's purposes.

THE INTEGRATION OF VALUES IN THE
SCOTTISH ENLIGHTENMENT VIEW

To develop the idea of normative integration a little further, consider Adam Smith's view of property and commercial society in light of the preceding discussion. That view is remarkable for integrating so much of the field of competing values, then and now, and this integration qualifies it as a continuing touchstone for thought within the same normative tradition.

Calling his approach a touchstone does not mean that Smith or his contemporaries created a theory which we today could simply adopt to overcome the divisions in our property thought. Those divisions are best regarded not as marks of a deficient theory but rather as emblems of persistent and appropriate pluralism. The Scottish Enlightenment view is a touchstone because its integration of property's plural values provides a guiding ideal, not a blueprint. Its orientation to freedom offers help in developing a principled pluralism, rather than a merely eclectic one, for understanding the values instinct in property. Freedom is the leading value of modern social and political life, and it encompasses a wide range of moral visions and ambitions. For all its own pluralism, however, it also has a rough structure, a set of sometimes competing and sometimes mutually supportive values that can illuminate the relations among competing takes on property.

Smith's posthumous reputation reflects the libertarian commitment to "natural liberty" that was central to his conception of the property rules defining commercial society. It was one of his major points of justification for that society that its economic relations were organized around consent, an affirmative act always offset by the possibility of refusal or exit. The society Smith sought represented a considerable expansion of the protected domain of negative liberty.

As the preceding discussion has emphasized, Smith valued negative liberty for its power to produce relatively respectful and reciprocal relationships. He believed that these, in turn, fostered personalities at once self-respecting and respectful and aware of others—characters suited to a society built on persuasion and negotiation rather than hierarchy and command. This is very much a program of personhood. Negative liberty mattered to Smith because in his legal imaginary it was the linchpin for the construction of free personality. A critical difference between libertarians and personhood theorists is that libertarians tend to assume that negative liberty is sufficient protection for autonomy, while personhood theorists concern themselves with the quality of choices people are able to make, choices that may be impeded by fear, dependence, or solipsism. Although Smith was devoted to negative liberty, he clearly fell on the personhood side of this contrast, understanding negative liberty as a way of securing a version of self.

These commitments combine to give Smith a particularly interesting profile along the third dimension of property's theoretical defenses as a kind of welfarist. The metaphor of the invisible hand is the point of departure for classical and neo-classical welfare economists, with their arguments that voluntary exchanges will concatenate to maximize social wealth. The passages discussed earlier, however, make clear that Smith's view of what ultimately counted in evaluating an economic system was more diverse. His insistence that one should wish to give up wealth (and political liberty) rather than accept slavery was dramatic in a theorist of social wealth. Although Smith was greatly concerned with describing the conditions for the production of wealth, he did not regard it as the sole measure of an economy. Instead, he believed that an economy should be measured by its capacity to integrate three aims: personal liberty, the production of wealth, and the creation of the conditions for free personalities to flourish. This is not a contrast to welfarism but a version of it, a way of describing well-being. So understood, it has several distinctive features. First, in the language of contemporary welfare economics, its information base is diverse: it is concerned not just with wealth, nor with whether transactions are voluntary, but with a combination of prosperity, negative liberty, and flourishing. Because of its multifarious information base, Smith's version of welfarism would almost certainly defy formalization: it would have to be approached instead through a picture of the social life that property rules produced. Moreover, Smith's view of welfare was centrally concerned with distribution—of wealth, as well as of negative liberty and opportunities for flourishing. If slavery had proven more productive than the alternative, there is every reason to believe Smith would nonetheless have argued against it as an unjust restriction of the freedom of some for the convenience of the rest.

As we shall see, this way of integrating contrasting commitments gives Smith's thought much in common with that of the 1998 Nobel laureate in economics Amartya Sen. (Indeed, Sen identifies Smith as a predecessor.) Sen argues that what welfare economics should count is, abstractly stated, freedom, but that freedom is itself a plural value, including negative liberty, the positive capacity to achieve one's potential capabilities (particularly including the material preconditions of doing so), and the psychological ability to make choices and commitments lucidly.[48] This three-part division corresponds roughly but genuinely to

Smith's three welfare criteria. It also basically maps the values of the three major celebratory approaches to property. Smith's approach was an effort to integrate the competing values that then defined, and still define, assessment of property regimes.

Smith's approach also manages to acknowledge some of the animating concerns of the major critical approaches to property. Take the realist insistence that property rights are creatures of the state, and hence of political decision. As a reformer pressing against inherited institutions and recent innovations alike (feudal remnants were the first, New World slavery the second), Smith would not have mistaken "natural liberty" for anything other than a product of human choice. His *if,* the crucial word in his discussion of slavery, crystallized his belief that people make their own institutions. Indeed, his entire project of reform was intelligible only on that supposition.

Take next the romantic and republican arguments that values and personality are endogenous to legal and economic regimes. In the hands of critics, this insight has grounded an argument that liberal property flattens the experience of value and produces instrumental attitudes toward others and the natural world. Smith had a very different view of the substance of the issue: he believed that liberal property fostered personalities that were aware of their own interests and the identities and attachments of others—that is, were more rather than less sensitive to the world's range of value. He shared with his later critics, however, the belief that people's choices were endogenous to the systems in which they made them. The difference in substance marks the rift between the eighteenth-century moderate Enlightenment and twentieth-century inheritors of the Romantic revolution in consciousness, with its emphasis on the depth of identity, the priority of individuality, and the legitimacy of intense and irrational experience. Smith's ideal of a society of negotiation and persuasion is, indeed, anathema to those committed to these substantive counter ideals, at least if either approach tries to claim simple primacy. On shared premises about endogeneity, however, it would at least be possible to undertake a conversation about clashing values and the laws that promote them, rather than fall back on incommensurable axioms. Some of the motives are different, as one might expect across centuries, but the premises are much the same.

Smith's approach is also well-suited to serious engagement with the civic dimension of republicanism, the perception that some values instinct in a certain form of political community should weigh heavily in assessing property regimes. Smith was intensely concerned with forms of personality appropriate to reciprocal and respectful social relations—basically, those of liberal and, later, democratic society. He believed that property rights expressed political choices and that individuals' values and choices were formed partly by the influence of those rights. These are all the premises necessary to start a serious conversation with a republican critic of liberal property. Indeed, such views can even be understood as a kind of liberal republicanism, stressing individuality and reciprocity as social virtues and aiming at the institutional conditions that best foster these.[49]

New Visions of Order

"If we can agree where the liberty and freedom of the people lies," hazarded Colonel Thomas Rainborough in 1647, "that will do all."[1] That question was indeed at the heart of the dispute when the officers of the New Model Army convened in Putney, England, to debate their visions of political community; but there was little chance of agreement between radicals such as Rainborough and (relative) conservatives such as Oliver Cromwell and Henry Ireton. The entwined conceptions of property and freedom set out in the Putney debates express the tensions of the transition from a hierarchical, natural-law view of society to the individualistic theory of mutual benefit that Adam Smith expressed. The arguments of the debates show both the premises of the old order and the arrival of new, insurgent claims, whose advocates had not yet worked them into a whole theory of social order.[2]

The radicals at Putney argued for one of the major ingredients in the economic view of society: that individuals have natural rights in property and self-government, which are the building blocks of social order. This was the approach to social life that Hugo Grotius had recently developed and that John Locke—an ideological cousin of the Putney radicals—would later perfect.[3] The conservatives—an ironic term for them, as they were rebels and would soon be regicides—answered that this vision was incoherent and dangerous, and that taken seriously it "tends to anarchy, must end in anarchy."[4] The radicals also offered hints of the other major aspect of the economic view of society: that reasonably self-interested activity could generate complex, self-sustaining practices and institutions. To this the conservatives replied that an open market, the basic institutional form of spontaneous sociability, would destroy all "peace in the kingdom."[5] In other words, the two most basic and widely shared ideas of the economic view, well on their way to becoming commonplace by Smith's time, figured a mere 130 years earlier as the enemies of order. Why were these innovations so radical, and how did they came about?

The decade had begun in an established political and legal culture in which important issues were regarded as settled, even when they arguably were not. "Before 1642," writes Norah Carlin, "all the participants in political debate in England shared an ideology of tradition, order, and harmony."[6] In law as in politics, between 1550 and 1600 "there occurred a great hardening and consolidation of common-law thought" around the belief that both private law and English constitutionalism were indigenous in origin and continuous across time, carried forward from the ancient Saxons to contemporary pleading practice.[7]

This impression of stability was ironic, for in other respects the world was turning upside down. The opening of settlement in the Americas and trade with the Indies had changed the European vision of the globe, bringing home evidence of diversity that produced wonder and horror.[8] The Reformation and Wars of Religion had turned European Christendom into a fratricidal slaughterhouse, and religious disputes loomed large in the civil war the Putney debaters were fighting.[9] Partly in response to these developments, European humanism had taken a skeptical turn, away from the optimistic view of Aristotle and Cicero that political community ennobled humankind and toward the shadowed, ironic tones of Tacitus, emphasizing disunion, perversity, and ignoble violence.[10] Among the reactions to these crises was Hugo Grotius's development of his seminal account of political communities as assembled by consent from their subjects' inherent rights.[11]

Views of the natural world had changed, too. Francis Bacon had advanced a view of science that called for "extend[ing] the power and dominion of the human race itself over the universe . . . the empire of man over things."[12] In a saltier (and more overtly sexist) mood, he compared nature to "a common harlot," requiring firm direction to give satisfaction, hardly an idea calculated to inspire reverential contemplation of a harmonious universe.[13] Any idea of a Great Chain of Being, joining cosmology and social hierarchy in a single pattern, was at best under severe stress.[14]

Despite all this ferment, the ambit of political and legal argument had been narrow, perhaps the more so in response to the pressures of a time that was disruptive in so many other respects. This changed dramatically when conflicts between King Charles I and Parliament broke into open warfare over who governed England, and by what right. The deepening conflict called familiar customs and accommodations into doubt. Charles was personally rigid and unyielding, and he sometimes seemed to propound a theory of absolute royal power. The parliamentary forces included landowners and aristocrats who treasured their own role in the constitution—particularly the requirement that any proposed taxation win their consent—and commoners, many of them radical Protestants, who resented Charles's marriage to a Catholic and suspected him of plotting to establish a popish theocracy. In the winter of 1649, a faction of the increasingly radical parliamentary forces put Charles on trial for treason and executed him, an act that threw basic questions of English constitutional order wide open.

Of course, constitutional politics must already have been unsettled in important respects for the execution to have been widely intelligible as a lawful act. The English Civil War is notoriously a historiographic Slough of Despond, and it is not my intention to add to the legions of historians, beginning in the seventeenth century, who have argued over its origins in social and economic change (either widespread decadence or the rise of vital new commercial classes), religious conflict, proliferating antinomianism and social radicalism, the tensions of a growing empire, or the competing ideologies of English constitutionalism itself.[15] What is clear, though, is that the terms of political argument expanded vastly, often racing to make sense of fast-changing circumstances. Arguments that would previously have been unrecognizable as constitutional politics (as opposed to, say, utopian literature) took shape and came to the fore as earnest proposals.[16]

The occasion of the debate was a dispute over interpretation. The New Model Army, the most important of the parliamentary forces, had endorsed a proposal to reform the boroughs that selected members of the House of Commons. Many pocket boroughs were small, ancient places, often dominated by a single local landowner, while large populations elsewhere were scantily represented. The reform document urged that districts "be more indifferently proportioned according to the number of inhabitants," and the question at Putney was just what the officers of the New Model Army meant by that.[17] The debate rapidly turned to the more basic question of who should be able to vote in parliamentary elections and, in turn, to the nature of legitimate political power. The faction of the New Model Army that historians have come to call—along with their civilian allies—the Levellers (after the name their opponents gave them) made the case for something like universal manhood suffrage. Their opponents purported to show why this was practically reckless and theoretically incoherent, and, for both reasons, "must end in anarchy."[18]

Like their contemporaries, the participants used *property* and *propriety* interchangeably to mean on one hand wealth and land and on the other what was "one's own," a man's distinctive rights and privileges. The second sense was broad: it included claims that arose from particular social standing, such as that of a landowner or a member of the nobility; rights attaching to all freeborn Englishmen, such as the protection of the laws; and any concept of natural rights.[19] Such ideas had a tendency to be particularistic: historically, a "liberty" or "freedom" referred to a special right or power attaching to social status, membership in a guild, chartered market town, or corporation, or other distinction.[20] Well before the Civil War, however, the words had also acquired implications of more general, potentially universal values or interests, including security in one's person and possessions and ideas about "the special value of political independence and self-government."[21]

This equivocation was not just semantic. Rather, it expressed an idea that political membership and property rights were so integrally related that to hold property was to partake of political power, and to be without property was to fall outside the political community. Henry Ireton, deputy to Oliver Cromwell, pressed this conception hard against the Levellers. Only property holders, Ireton insisted, had "any permanent interest in the kingdom," and "taken together" they must "comprehend the whole, permanent, local [that is to say, not removable to another country] interest of the kingdom."[22] Clarifying the point later in the debate, he asserted that "the original of power of making laws, of determining what shall be law in the land, does lie in the people—but by 'the people' is meant those that are possessed of the permanent interest in the land."[23] Ireton did not strictly intend to identify the political community with those who owned the physical body of England: he accepted that members of chartered corporations or market towns could also share in political power.[24] But that power was co-extensive with property rights. He analogized those who did not hold property to foreign visitors, subject to the law and entitled to its protection but with no part in making it.[25]

In 1647 the English legal imagination envisioned political and social order in a way that came to seem deeply fragile. Two particular threats haunted this vision. The first was any idea of rights, whether political or in property, as inherent to human beings, preceding and existing outside the sanction of political society. The second, as we have already glimpsed and shall see in more detail in a moment, was the voluntary and spontaneous activity of individuals who order their own affairs and connections outside the requirements of formal law and inherited roles. Those signal threats of chaos are today's cardinal points of order. The idea of inherent and universal rights has been integral to property's place in the modern legal imagination, while the spontaneous sociability that appeared most ominous at Putney is precisely what we now think of liberal property as emerging from and enabling. The passage out of the fragile imaginary of Putney into a new vision, in which rights and sociability anchored rather than undermined political order, was an extraordinary transition.

NATURAL RIGHTS AND ANARCHY

The Levellers sought to characterize human beings in a way that would make intelligible an inherent "property" of political power. New Model Army colonel Thomas Rainborough described the individual human being, abstracted from social standing, as able to claim a property, freedom, or liberty (three largely synonymous terms) inherent in personhood. In the terms of the time, this was an attempt to move from property (in the double sense of rights of estate and rights of freedom) as a function of social position to property as a feature of individual existence—from *a* liberty to *liberty*, from *a* freedom to *freedom*. Because of the integral conceptual relation of these senses of property to the word's more concrete sense of ownership, this argument tended to imply a universalizing account of property as ownership.

Rainborough gave several versions of the nascent natural-rights position. One was the "gift of reason without other property," a "small thing" but universal.[26] Rainborough took this as support for general manhood suffrage: "[T]he main cause why Almighty God gave men reason . . . was that they should make use of that reason, and that they should improve it," drawing judgments on the laws and proposing to revise them.[27] Another formulation rested on something like equal dignity, intuited from the importance each man attached to his own existence and choices. In Rainborough's expression of the idea, "[R]eally I think that the poorest he that is in England has a life to live as the greatest he, and therefore truly, sir, I think it's clear that every man that is to live under a government ought first, by his own consent, to put himself under that government; and I do think that the poorest man in England is not at all bound in a strict sense to that government that he has not had a voice to put himself under."[28]

This was a radical conceptual inversion. Jurists had long recognized as a legitimate imperative self-preservation, which created a duty of charity in owners or even a limited right of theft for the indigent in times of extreme need.[29] Ireton acknowledged this principle several times during the debate, referring to each person's special claim on property "of necessity for the preservation of his being"[30] or "of necessity to sustain nature."[31] Rainborough's idea turned natural rights from what they had been, the basis of signal exceptions to legal obligation, toward a new role as the foundation of such obligation. It was because of natural liberty that legitimate law required "consent," by which Rainborough and the other Levellers seem to have meant, mainly, the chance to vote for representatives.[32]

Cromwell responded that this formula "must end in anarchy."[33] There were two parts to his argument. One was that natural rights had no conceptual bounds and thus threw open whatever domains they purported to govern to clashing antinomian claims. The second was that to claim natural rights in the *political* domain of "property" implied claiming such (boundless) rights in the domain of *ownership* as well. Thus, if the Leveller case for universal suffrage rested on "the right of nature," then, as Ireton argued, "I think you must deny all property too . . . by that same right of nature (whatever it be) that you pretend, by which you say that one man has an equal right with another to the choosing of him that shall govern him—by the same right of nature he has the same equal right in any goods he sees: meat, drink, clothes, to take and use them for his sustenance. He has a freedom to the land, to take the ground, to exercise it, to till it, he has the same freedom to anything that anyone does account himself to have any propriety in. . . . [I]f you do, paramount to all constitutions, hold up this law of nature, I would fain have any man show me their bounds, where you will end, and why you should not take away all property."[34]

The intelligibility of this argument depends on a strong identification between property rights and political rights as parts of a single concept. In this "most fundamental part" of England's "civil constitution," Cromwell and Ireton presented ownership and political jurisdiction as each giving shape reciprocally to the other.[35] When either was set free from that reciprocal relation, both must lose their "bounds" and become open-ended assaults on order. As an analytic matter, of course, it would be easy to contend that the two classes of rights are distinct and that a discrete right to participate in government bears no particular relation to an unchecked right to acquire or use whatever material goods one comes across. That the argument was available to Ireton in the form he used, however, highlights the power of the idea that political and property rights were parts of the same body of social order and that any "natural" right that originated outside that body would prove an enemy to order as such. It was for this reason, in the traditionalist account, that natural rights could not anchor either property or sovereignty but must instead destroy both.

THE SOCIAL ORDER OF PROPERTY AND COMMERCE

The traditionalists took the same view of what would later become the other side of property's coin, the theory of interest-based sociability. There came a moment at Putney when Ireton, noting the relation between the right to vote and membership in a chartered corporation or market town, offered a passing observation that contained the presuppositions of an entire worldview. By a "corporation," he noted, he meant "a place which has the privilege of a market and trading—*which if you should allow to all places equally, I do not see how you could preserve any peace in the kingdom*: and that is the reason why in the constitution we have but some few market towns."[36] Trade, then, figured in Ireton's legal imagination as a threat to order, a privilege to be closely regulated in the interest of harmony. We are a long way here from Smith's definition of "natural liberty" as the freedom to pursue the inherent "propensity to truck and barter."[37] That transition made possible new ways of thinking about the relation of economic life to the state. It also powered a theory of property and history that became integral to the law of Anglo-American imperialism, including important residues in the law of the United States.

Why did Ireton imagine commerce and order as nearly opposed principles, requiring strict political regulation to coexist? One reason was connected with his conception of the good subject as tied by "permanent, fixed interest" to the national community.[38] As discussed earlier, Ireton argued that only those with interests of this sort should participate in sovereignty rather than passively receive the laws. A man without such a tie to the nation would be "here today and gone tomorrow" with no "permanent interest" in the political community.[39] Merchants, as the baron de Montesquieu would note in a later and friendlier discussion, were mobile, inclined to pursue wealth wherever it led and to put their placeless personal interests above the general interest of the country.[40] Only by constituting their right to trade as a legal privilege—often tied to specific market towns—could governments artificially align their interests with those of the whole community.

But Ireton did not just argue that unregulated merchants would be unworthy of the vote. He said that if commerce were unregulated, "I do not see how you could preserve any peace in the kingdom."[41] That he made this claim in the midst of civil war at least suggests that he knew what a kingdom without peace might look like. If we assume that he did not mean the phrase lightly, what might have been involved in his regarding commerce as a threat of potentially equal weight with the very live and current problem of civil war? (Remember, he was imagining as a path to anarchy a general right to engage in buying and selling, presumably under regular laws of property and contract—exactly what Smith would later term natural liberty.)

One start toward an answer is to appreciate what Ireton did not have among his conceptual resources: a way to understand commerce as producing its own self-reinforcing forms of order, which could in principle extend peaceably across the kingdom. Instead he seems to have envisioned something like a violent cacophony of warring interests. Why should this be so?

Intellectual descendants of Aristotle had long insisted that human beings were naturally sociable: it was their character to seek the company of others and join together in both local and extended communities. Aristotle had identified the human species as *zoon politikon*, the political animal, and this idea anchored a belief that political community was the natural home of human beings.[42] The devastation of Europe's religious wars, the revival of interest in Tacitus's often bleak and bloody view of politics and history, and new awareness of global human diversity all seem to have contributed to—or at least resonated with—a skeptical idea, coming into prominence late in the sixteenth century, that Aristotle's premise was complacent and unscientific.[43] Were the inhabitants of the Americas also examples of the zoon politikon? When countries and even families divided into blood warfare over religious doctrine, was our inherent fellow feeling and attachment to political community in evidence? And did not history, viewed honestly, reveal more of the same: schism, cruelty, and the sheer puzzlement of human plurality?

The Putney debates were in some respects a constitutional convention in which property and sovereignty were mutually inextricable ideas, in others a microcosm of a larger crisis of authority in which events seemed to overwhelm the familiar intellectual resources for giving accounts of human community. Out of that crisis, jurists sought a formulation that could rebuild a picture of authority and social order after devastation. The emblematic extreme was Thomas Hobbes's view of the state of nature, which was both an intervention into the constitutional politics of the English Civil War and a reflection (by indirection) on that war's seeming lessons about human nature.[44] Hobbes rejected as unscientific any premise of human sociability, holding that people's relations to one another were instead directed by their own self-regarding passions and appetites: above all, the wishes for pleasure and glory (domination over others) and the fear of death.[45] The last was the decisive motive, giving individuals adequate reason to submit to a sovereign of virtually unlimited power in exchange for security from the incursions of other individuals. Hobbes, like Ireton (who was on the other side of the war), regarded commerce as a threat to sovereign order, a sphere in which the appetite for domination would sow discord unless regulated by the state.[46] He stressed, moreover, that property and commercial life would be impossible in the state of nature, that is, without the prior erection of political sovereignty.[47] Whereas most who engaged the issue wished to avoid Hobbes's conclusion that a scientific view of politics implied absolutism, the problem was how to do this without returning to a vision of natural sociability that had come to seem wishful. Otherwise the natural-rights theories that Rainborough and others advocated seemed to produce the unhappy result that people in the state of nature rationally should trade away their inherent rights to a sovereign in return for the safety that they could not give one another.

Into this gap stepped a novel approach to the problem of order. Adam Smith, who was to perfect it and begin its transformation into the discipline of economics, called it a middle way between two visions of human relations: a society of fear, which he associated with Hobbes, and a society of love, which he identified with the Aristotelians.[48] The simplest way of describing the middle term of Smith's account is that it was interest, and this has often been proposed as a way of understanding modern society: as an order founded on "interests" rather than "passions."[49] As we have already seen, however, there was a great deal more to his way of addressing the problem.

The most basic feature of an interest-based theory of social order is that people need one another: Aristotle, too, had seen this—it is hard to miss—and treated it as the basis of *oikonomia*, the life of nonpolitical social relations, of production and reproduction.[50] Samuel Pufendorf, who preceded Smith and whose writings helped guide Smith's reconstruction of natural sociability, had drawn on Aristotle's idea of need to argue that interdependence could in itself form the basis of a stable social life, held together by the webs of mutual reliance that constitute economic activity.[51] In principle, then, it would be possible to imagine the state as arising out of a more basic and spontaneous economic order, which would be the primary frame of human activity. Sociability, in the narrow and nonpolitical sense of *interest*, could be prior to sovereignty, both conceptually and in the course of history, rather than a potentially disruptive force needing discipline by sovereign constraint.[52]

The image of social order as based on sociability was one of two novel early-modern approaches to property that put the institution at the center of origin stories: accounts of how human beings came together and formed increasingly complex and wealthy societies. The other was the constructivist narrative, which concentrated on natural rights that individuals could voluntarily combine to produce sovereign government. This was the tradition of Grotius and Locke, represented at Putney by Levellers like Rainborough. Both approaches were attempts to understand social order in a manner that took account of new social facts: the demands for individual freedom and a role for consent in legitimate government on the one hand, the intensification and extension of commerce on the other. Both also responded to the deficit in legitimacy and intelligibility that afflicted social order after the Wars of Religion—of which the English Civil War, with its nearly hysterical religious animus, was a late outcropping even as it was an early instance of the new demand for political liberty. The two were distinct, though related, as rigorous theory and were deeply intertwined as sources of the legal imagination.

THE FOUR-STAGES ACCOUNT

The major eighteenth-century contribution to the theory of sociability was the view of human society as having developed in four stages, each characterized by a distinctive property regime. Striving to make sense of dramatic changes in their local histories, jurists developed templates for a universal history, theories of social development as such. As Istvan Hont has emphasized in his magisterial study of the intersecting economic and political thought of the period, this theory was "an outgrowth of the natural lawyers' attempt to legitimize the modern regime of private property."[53] The "natural" view of social life that these jurists drew upon was the innovative vision of property and exchange as the basic expressions of interdependence and the foundation of a society based on sociability. In Hont's expression, "The commerce of private property owners reconstituted a new society on the basis of the mechanisms offered by Pufendorf's basic utility-based sociability."[54]

Eighteenth-century jurists proposed that the historical diversity of societies across time and the geographic diversity of societies across space had the same logic—a single grammar uniting two fields of human variety. On this theory, the European historical experience, rendered in a highly stylized way, formed a master template of societal evolution, describing a passage from a hunter-gatherer existence through a nomadic herding economy to settled agriculture and culminating in the complex institutions of commercial society. Other contemporary societies were assumed to fall into stages in a typology of earlier European experience and could therefore be classified by their place on the civilizational timeline that Europe had defined.[55] Thus William Blackstone, in his introductory discussion of the law of property, illustrated the hunter-gatherer stage by reference to "the manners of many American nations when first discovered by the Europeans; and from the ancient method of living among the first Europeans themselves, if we may credit either the memorials of them preserved in the golden age of the poets, or the uniform accounts given by historians of those times."[56] He similarly explained that the basic principle of real property for the stage of nomadic herder societies—the right to move one's stock onto unoccupied land—"is still retained among the wild and uncultivated nations that have never been formed into civil states, like the Tartars and others in the east; where the climate itself, and the boundless extent of their territory, conspire to retain them still in the same savage state of vagrant liberty, which was universal in the earliest ages."[57] This practice, "Tacitus informs us[,] continued among the Germans till the decline of the Roman Empire."[58] From this perspective, then, the present lives of non-European societies were way stations along the history of Europe.

Expressing the same idea, Adam Smith maintained that the laws of property

vary according to the periods of human society. The four states of society are hunting, pasturage, farming, and commerce. . . . The age of commerce generally succeeds that of agriculture. As men could now confine themselves to one species of labour, they would naturally exchange the surplus of their own commodity for that of another of which they stood in need. According to these stages occupation must vary. . . . Among savages property begins and ends with possession, and they scarce seem to have any idea of any thing as their own which is not about their own bodies. Among shepherds the idea of property is further extended. . . . When it first became necessary to cultivate the earth, no person had property in it, and the little plot which was dressed near their hovels would be common to the whole village, and the fruits would be equally divided among the individuals. . . . Private property in land never begins till a division be made from common agreement, which is generally when cities begin to be built. . . . An Arab or a Tartar will drive his flocks over an immense country without supposing a single grain of sand in it his own.[59]

The law of property formed the institutional keystone of this theory of history. Property rights were the exemplary indicators of a stage of civilization, corresponding to modes of social order and productive activity. In the earliest stage, property meant a right of exclusive use in personal possessions—those things one had appropriated or made—and a general, nonexclusive right of occupation and use of all other resources. The herding stage brought a *collective* right of exclusive use in grazing grounds, coupled with a right to expropriate unoccupied land for one's own herds. In the third stage, settled agriculture, came the first appearance of the classical private ownership of land. Then came commercial society marked by liberalized land markets and the new treatment of labor as a market commodity on free-labor principles of contract and the right of exit. Property regimes were not only diagnostic: they also provided an Archimedean lever by which reformers could induce change from one stage of civilization to another. By breaking the power of elites wedded to old regimes and reordering incentives to induce dynamic efficiency, it was possible to move an entire society forward in history—that is, along the timeline marked out by the historical experience of Europe.

This narrative of history came to have unintended importance for the law of imperial governance. It proved valuable in arranging sovereigns along a spectrum that corresponded to each society's stage of progress, which imperial jurists used to specify the powers that a "civilized" country could legitimately take over from a less advanced sovereign. The "earlier" the stage, the farther the less advanced sovereign fell from full sovereign self-sufficiency, and the greater was the prerogative of the relevant "civilized" sovereign. Beginning from an account of social order as arising without government, the four-stages theory culminated in a blueprint and legitimating theory for state power as comprehensive as any that preceded it.[60]

THE CONSTRUCTIVIST ACCOUNT AND
THE LEGAL IMAGINATION

John Locke's thought expresses a mature flowering of the natural-rights theory of social and political order. Viewed strictly in terms of its theoretical structure, this approach to the problem of order is distinct from the sociability-based view of Smith and his predecessors.[61] Viewed as an aspect of a legal imaginary, as an image of the world in which property rights are envisioned as emerging and operating, Locke's thought falls much nearer Smith's tradition. Locke's theory of rights is also an account of property in a society of mutual benefit, organized by the desires of self-interested but reasonably cooperative individuals. This connection underlies Charles Taylor's claim that a common vision tightly connects Smith's thought to the "Grotian-Lockean idea of order."[62] When the aim is to understand the development of the legal imagination, rather than the doctrines of political theory, Taylor's take is more apt than is a more formalist classification of the views as distinct.

It is widely appreciated that Locke's formula for the original acquisition of property was a response to Robert Filmer's attack on the constructivist theory of sovereignty.[63] Filmer, making the case that all political power was necessarily absolute and arbitrary at bottom, had attacked Grotius's account of the emergence of humanity from the state of nature into political society by the consensual joining of natural rights (inherent self-sovereignty) into a government.[64] Filmer denied that the kind of consent that Grotius's theory required could ever have taken place.[65] Grotius's rights theory posited an individual right to use resources for self-preservation but not a right to acquire property without receiving the consent of the rest of humanity, who all shared the natural right of use: rights to resources which could be carved from the original global commons only by the consent of all.[66] The same threshold applied to sovereignty: people could form a government only by a universal act of consent, which Filmer argued was too demanding ever to have happened. Sovereignty was the real game for Filmer: he meant to show that government by consent was impossible, and so consent could not provide the criterion for legitimate government. Within a style of rights theory that drew property and jurisdiction very near to each other, the paired targets drew a common attack from Filmer and inspired a common conceptual defense from Locke.

Locke's ultimate aim in answering Filmer was to establish the coherence of constitutionally limited government based on the original consent of the governed. He also, however, gave an answer to Filmer's charge that property could not arise in a consent-based theory of society. In positing a natural power to acquire property by enclosing, cultivating, or otherwise systematically improving unowned land, Locke articulated a pre-political right to property that did not, as Grotius's had, require the consent of all others for original acquisition.

As he set out the operation of original acquisition, Locke intended to protect it from the objection that "any one may ingross as much as he will," the settler's equivalent of claiming a continent by planting a flag.[67] He explained that the right of acquisition was limited by the amount one could fruitfully use.[68] Hoarding what one could not use would be taking more than one's "share" and what "belongs to others."[69] "Nothing," Locke continued, "was made by God for man to spoil or destroy."[70] This latter principle—the prohibition on waste—was essential to the political as well as the property aspects of Locke's theory, for it included a divine prohibition on suicide (self-destruction), which Locke used to deny that a people could consent to an absolute government because such consent would give the ruler unchecked power over their lives, the equivalent of their committing suicide.[71] As for limiting ownership, this proviso ensured that "enough, and as good" would remain for others after a man had acquired his own property.[72] In Locke's account, however, the proviso was annulled with the introduction of money, which, as a token of value, enabled owners to "store" great wealth without its spoiling.[73] Money marked the juncture between a world where most goods are held in common until someone takes them for personal use and a world parceled out in rights of property.

Once the latter world has come into being, Locke's thesis of what property does falls near that of the commercial theorists: property produces utilitarian fruits in an order of mutual benefit that marks the achievement of a higher form of civilization. Locke used North America to illustrate the contrast between the natural stage of property, in which it is governed by rights of original acquisition, and the social stage, in which it is a legal instrument for utilitarian ends. The second, developed form, and not the primordial form, is the heart of Locke's understanding of property and illustrated for him, as for the commercial theorists, why European claims to North America were superior to those of its native inhabitants.

Locke presented Native Americans as the paradigm of a culture without permanent, fixed property apart from personal goods—what would become Smith's first stage of society. He explained that day-to-day subsistence figured as the chief concern of pre-monetary peoples, "as it doth the Americans now."[74] "Where there is not something both lasting and scarce" to serve as money, he wrote, "there Men will not be apt to enlarge their Possessions of Land. . . . What would a Man value . . . An Hundred Thousand Acres of excellent Land, ready cultivated, and well stocked too with Cattle, in the middle of the in-land Parts of America, where he had no hopes of Commerce . . . to draw Money to him . . . ?"[75] With a famous sentence, he perfected his identification of seventeenth-century America with the historical stage of common property: "[I]n the beginning all the World was America."[76] Under these circumstances, for Native Americans to deny Europeans the right to occupy and cultivate land would be a naked denial of another's natural right to acquisition. Native Americans would be trying to take more than they could use, and in turn would be "liable to be punished" like a man who "invaded his Neighbour's share, for he had no right, farther than his Use called for[.]"[77]

This rights-based account interacted with a second, more nearly utilitarian basis for Locke's distinction between Native American and European claims to land. This basis was itself composed of two elements: an account of property's wealth-creating benefits and a claim that divine prescription instructed humans to improve the God-given earth. Locke explained, "God and [man's] Reason commanded him to subdue the Earth, i.e. improve it for the benefit of Life. . . . He that in Obedience to the Command of God, subdued, tilled and sowed any part of it, thereby annexed to it something that was his Property."[78] Elaborating the relation between divine purpose and improvement, Locke added a telling distinction between property-making and property-less cultures: "God gave the World to Men in Common; but since he gave it them for their benefit, and the greatest Conveniencies of Life they were capable to draw from it, it cannot be supposed he meant it should always remain common and uncultivated. *He gave it to the use of the Industrious and Rational* (and Labour was to be his Title to it;) *not to the Fancy or Covetousness of the Quarrelsom and Contentious.*"[79] The status of "industrious and rational" belonged to settlers who could improve "the wild woods and uncultivated wast[e] of America,"[80] while whoever disputed their claim counted as quarrelsome and contentious. A theory of rights, an account of property's purpose, and a view of divine command coincided in Locke's property theory to generate a vivid distinction between settler claims and those of aboriginal populations.

The vision of property as a social institution anchoring an economic order of mutual benefit bridges the distinct but related views of social and political order that Locke and Smith exemplified. It was within this widely shared framework that Smith developed his integrated view of property as an institution that incorporated important libertarian, welfarist, and personhood values while taking seriously the endogeneity of personal choices to institutions and the political underpinnings of legal rights. That vision was a particularly well-elaborated response to a general crisis in the project of theorizing social and political order, a crisis which marked the thought of the seventeenth and eighteenth centuries. In Smith's view, but also in the larger vision of order in which Smith plays a key part, property is the core institution in the creation and legitimacy of social and political order. In that vision, human beings belong to no inherent hierarchy but instead are alike in their essential situation: needy but capable, self-interested but sociable enough to band together and solve basic problems through collective action, and, especially, able to generate institutions that promote security and prosperity. Property is the foremost of these, the most basic institutional expression of our double character as needy and vulnerable beings who are able to rework the world in a way that makes provision for our limitations and enables us to flourish together.

VARIETIES OF PROGRESS:
AMERICAN WASTE DOCTRINE AND
PROPERTY IN REPUBLICAN FREEDOM

The version of legal imagination traced in this book is not restricted to the grand strokes of political theory and the philosophy of history. Its shaping influence extends to a very different scale of issue, the common law of waste, which historically governed (and to some extent still does) the rights of tenants and subsequent owners in using real property. This legal imagination informed both the legal culture in which American waste doctrine took shape and the thought of a great judge who participated in the seminal American case on waste law, New York's chancellor James Kent. Although waste law nowadays is understood in rather dry economic terms, it arose at a time and place in which economic relations were pregnant with ideas about the balance of hierarchy and equality in social life, the nature of political community, and visions of progress in an opening continent. It bears the marks of all of these.

The study of waste doctrine in context also suggests something general about modes of historical explanation. When I first began to look at waste, I thought it would provide an opportunity to arbitrate between two narratives of what motivated historical changes in property law—and thus what counted, historically, as the purpose of property. One of those narratives would have been an "economic" explanation, concentrating on how the rational maximization of legal actors' preference satisfaction motivated movement in the common law toward a regime of rights that fostered wealth production. The alternative would have comprised "noneconomic" explanations—motives arising from ideas about civic order, individual dignity or personality, visions of national purpose, and other such qualitative goods. These plural motives might have found expression in explicit pronouncements or doctrinal developments difficult to explain in economic terms alone—or, ideally, since talk is sometimes cheap and conventional economic ends sometimes motivate ineffectual means, in both.

For the sake of fixing ideas, I still set out some of my analysis by way of this contrast. One of the most interesting points to emerge from the discussion, however, is that the contrast would have seemed false to those historical actors whose motives I am trying to understand. Precisely because visions of economic order—particularly those derived from the Scottish Enlightenment—were attempts to integrate multiple dimensions of freedom within a legal regime, they constantly overran and rendered artificial any distinction between the economic and noneconomic purposes of property law. Although my reliance on the distinction acknowledges its usefulness for certain purposes, therefore, its artificiality is equally relevant.

THE LAW OF WASTE

Waste law comprises a set of default rules governing the changes that tenants, for term or for life, may make to the estate they occupy. A tenant who uses the estate in prohibited ways is said to have "committed waste" in violation of the rights of the reversioner or remainderman,[1] to whom the estate will pass in fee simple when the tenant's claim expires. The crux of the law is therefore the definition of *waste*—that is, the actions tenants may not commit—and conversely, the set of actions they may commit without permission from the reversioner.

In the United States, it is generally said that a tenant may "make changes in the physical condition of the . . . property which are reasonably necessary in order for the tenant to use the . . . property in a manner that is reasonable under all the circumstances."[2] The touchstone of this reasonableness standard is the type of use contemplated in the creation of the tenancy: changes such as harvesting timber, erecting new buildings, and extracting minerals are permissible to the extent that they are reasonably necessary to conduct the activities that the parties understand the tenant may undertake.[3]

From an economic perspective, waste law addresses the problem that tenants are motivated to use land inefficiently. An efficient management strategy for an estate will maximize the present discounted value of its entire expected earnings stream.[4] Tenants, however, will have an incentive to maximize the value of earnings from the estate *during their tenancy*.[5] This incentive will lead them to harvest renewable resources like timber and nonrenewable resources like minerals prematurely, and to neglect resources whose gradual decay does not affect their earnings prospects but will affect the long-term value of the estate, such as soil, fences, and buildings.[6] Richard Posner has suggested that an efficient solution to this problem would be to assess tenants *as if they were owners*, authorizing them to do only what a rational owner would have incentive to do, no more, no less.[7]

Indeed, this was the solution offered by American waste law in the early and middle decades of the nineteenth century. The doctrine had two formulations, which state supreme courts repeated across the country: first, the standard of husbandry, or of the prudent farmer, which held that a tenant's action was not waste if it was consistent with the actions a prudent owner would take;[8] and second, the standard of material injury, which held that a material or "permanent injury to the inheritance," that is, to the reversioner's legitimate interests, would count as waste.[9] Both assessed tenants by the standard of an economically rational owner to ensure that they passed to the reversioner an estate managed in a way consistent with its efficient exploitation.[10]

To the extent that scholars and commentators pay attention to the law of waste, Posner's efficiency-enhancing account accords with the mainstream view. Morton J. Horwitz has argued that the evolution of waste law was part of a general development in nineteenth-century American law toward treating land exclusively as a commodity, freeing it from social controls and the inconvenient claims of smallholders, in order to make it available as a capital-generating resource for the economic development of the continent.[11] John G. Sprankling has taken a similar tack, although his concerns are driven by ecological conservation rather than the Marxian account of history that motivated Horwitz.[12] Sprankling contends that an "instrumentalist" view of the natural world, coupled with a perceived imperative to bring the new continent under the ax and plow, led to the good husbandry standard, which allowed tenants to clear and develop land in the interests of advancing cultivation.[13]

Neither Horwitz's nor Sprankling's account is incompatible with the conventional economic view of waste law that Posner propounds. However, both are distinguished by their distaste for Posner's efficiency-enhancing doctrine. Horwitz would think that Posner's doctrine tends to reflect the interests of the capitalist class,[14] while Sprankling sees in waste doctrine a lack of proper regard for the intrinsic worth of land in an unspoiled state.[15]

Against this background, I contend that U.S. courts refashioned the English law of waste for several reasons: to promote efficient use of resources that the English law would have inhibited; to advance an idea of American landholding as a republican enterprise, free of feudal hierarchy; and because of a belief that the cultivation of wild land underlay the Anglo-American claim to North America. These values were parts of a single logic in the legal imagination traced in this book. They figured not as alternatives but as elements of a single vision of property in social order.

THE ENGLISH LAW OF WASTE

The English law of waste, part of the common law of real property, was focused on the prerogative of landowners. The first statement of waste law came in 1267, when the Statute of Marlborough set forth the following default rule: "[Farmers], during their terms, shall not make waste, sale nor exile of [house,] woods, men, nor of any thing belonging to the tenements that they have to [farm] without special licence had, by writing of covenant, making mention they may do it."[16] As the meaning of the term *waste* developed, the English doctrine remained a close constraint on the actions tenants could take without the express permission of the reversioner.[17] A successful legal action in waste resulted in treble damages and forfeiture,[18] and an injunction on conduct constituting waste was available in equity.[19]

The most abstract account of the law had much in common with the direction American doctrine would take: "Whatever does a lasting damage to the freehold or inheritance is waste,"[20] wrote William Blackstone, who elsewhere termed it "a spoil and destruction of the estate . . . by demolishing not the temporary profits only, but the very substance of the thing; thereby rendering it wild and desolate."[21] Both Blackstone and Edward Coke, however, made clear that the law was much more narrowly drawn in its specific requirements. The more abstract formulation enabled courts to avoid punishing tenants for trivial actions brought by landlords or reversioners to harass them, actions that the narrow and exacting requirements of the doctrine made possible.[22] The main lines of the law in its more specific rendering were as follows: Unless explicitly authorized, tenants could take from the land only the timber that was necessary for maintaining buildings, making tools, and warming themselves in winter, called respectively "house bote," "tool bote," and "fire bote."[23] Tenants were required to use deadwood for these tasks unless none was available,[24] in which case they could take living trees in ascending order of their quality as timber: beech and maple first, then oak, ash, and elm.[25] In places where finer woods grew widely, tenants might be free to take poorer trees like beech at will, but nowhere in England could they harvest oak, ash, or elm outside the strict limits of waste doctrine.[26] Lesser trees, including willows and aspens, might be protected where they served as windbrakes, shade trees, or ornaments but were otherwise susceptible to the tenant's ax.[27]

Waste law restricted tenants' power to change patterns of land use. They could not erect new buildings or fences without permission but were only allowed to repair what they received with the land:[28] traditionally, it was no defense that a new building increased the value of the property.[29] Tenants also committed waste if they opened new mines on the land to search for hidden minerals,[30] but they could use open mines for their own consumption.[31] They could not allow arable land to grow up into forest, transform a meadow into a garden or the reverse, or otherwise change the uses the landowner had established.[32] Two reasons were given for this restriction. First, changes in land-use patterns could cause confusion where deeds listed land according to its use rather than by its more enduring metes and bounds (a consideration that itself reveals the pervasive expectation of stability in land use). Second, tenant initiative would "change the course of . . . husbandry" without the permission of the landlord.[33] To do so was "an injury to the title of the reversioners," that is, to their claim on the land, and thus "a present damage to them."[34]

Well after the transformation of waste doctrine in the United States, English courts seized on the flexibility in the phrase "injury to the inheritance" to uphold tenants' building industrial structures on previously open land.[35] This embrace of the dynamism of manufacturing, though, came for distinct reasons, long after American law had completed its break from English doctrine.[36] Moreover, the English industrial cases rhetorically displayed great regard for the old principle of stability in agricultural practice.[37] At the time the American law began diverging from it, English waste law supported a system in which tenants' initiative was closely constrained, their decisions susceptible to veto, and their role on the land nearer that of a custodian than a freeholder.

What sort of rule was the English law? It was, to begin with, a default rule, always susceptible to contractual revision. Scholars have identified several kinds of default rules, the most commonly discussed of which is the gap-filling or problem-solving default, in which incomplete agreements are filled out by embedding a term to which the parties would have agreed under optimal bargaining conditions.[38] Where waste law prevented a tenant from taking actions that the parties would have agreed to forbid under optimal bargaining conditions, as was surely the case with the most destructive or opportunistic acts, it had this function. Also much discussed is the equilibrium-inducing default, or bargaining default, in which a term is suggested that focuses the attention of the parties on a specific issue and induces them to agree to another term if the default term is not optimal.[39] Where the strict requirements of waste doctrine induced parties to bargain expressly over a tenant's power to exploit the reversioner's land, the doctrine had this function. For example, the default rule of waste law authorizing tenants to exploit minerals from mines already open, which was potentially ruinous to a reversioner, directed the landlord or testator to that issue, providing a strong incentive to define that right explicitly.

These two types of default rules have the same aim: to enhance the efficiency of agreements by leading bargainers to welfare-maximizing terms. However, the two embody different strategies. In the gap-filling default, terms are provided to which the parties would optimally have agreed, while in the bargaining default the parties are motivated to specify those terms themselves. Moreover, the gap-filling default rule expresses a substantive idea of rationality—what it is the bargainers would have wanted—while the bargaining default is more formal in simply drawing attention to the issue so that the resulting contract will embody whatever preferences motivate the parties.

Another function of default rules came to the fore when reversioners used waste doctrine to preempt or punish actions that did not reduce the value or productivity of the land, and to which they might plausibly have agreed beforehand, but which nonetheless fell afoul of their prerogative. Alan Schwartz has identified a "normative default" as one directing a result that "the decision maker prefers on fairness grounds but is unwilling to require."[40] Schwartz's definition requires a bit of adjustment to encompass the hierarchical character of the English property relations that waste law governed. *Fairness* suggests a standard for individualistic bargainers who merit the equal solicitude of the law; this was not the model of relations envisioned between tenants or widows in dower and their reversioners. If we instead take *normative* in a broader sense, encompassing, among other things, normative ideas about the basic character of social structure,[41] we can see that such a default is normative in the specific sense that it is *status-confirming*: it underscores the reversioner's superior claim to the land and corresponding superior social status. In its status-confirming function, waste law also tended to meet Schwartz's definition of a "transformative default," which "is adopted to persuade parties to prefer the result the rule directs"[42]—in this case, a pattern of social relations of prerogative and deference, partly organized around claims to land. Corresponding to the broad understanding of *normative* that I have proposed is a broad sense of *transformatory*:[43] not just inducing bargainers to adopt a specific term within a particular transaction but educating parties in the structure of social authority in which the prerogative of reversioners played a dominant role. In bargaining, wrote Adam Smith, we practice oratory on one another, proposing views of interest and purpose to others and absorbing their proposals in return. As Smith emphasized, these exchanges take place in hierarchies of status in which the weaker may internalize self-limiting ideas of themselves, and the transactions can reinforce or undermine these hierarchies.

JACKSON V. BROWNSON AND THE
TRANSFORMATION OF AMERICAN WASTE LAW

In 1810, the Supreme Court of New York[44] decided *Jackson v. Brownson*,[45] the key case in the transformation of American waste law. The plaintiffs, heirs of the landholder Philip Schuyler,[46] were lessors seeking to repossess the land of a tenant for life who had allegedly violated a covenant in his lease forbidding him to "commit any waste."[47] The defendant, Brownson, had leased the land in 1790, at which time it was "wild and uncultivated, and covered throughout with a forest of heavy timber."[48] By 1796, when he sublet the northern portion of the land to another farmer, Brownson had cleared all but 35 of the original 133 acres, leaving 12 acres of forest on the land he continued to lease.[49] Between then and the time of the suit, Brownson did not clear more land, although he cut timber for fuel, to build fences, and to raise a building on his farm.[50] The trial court ruled in Brownson's favor on a technicality, and the plaintiffs appealed to the New York Supreme Court to determine whether Brownson's clearing was waste as a matter of law.[51]

Philip Schuyler, a general in the Continental Army and the father-in-law of Alexander Hamilton, was a scion of one of the great landholding families of the Hudson River valley; together these families' tenant-inhabited property represented an attempt to create a landed aristocracy in North America.[52] In a country that saw itself as a nation independent smallholders,[53] the plaintiffs, heirs of Schuyler, were proposing to exercise a landlord's prerogative to repossess a small farmer's land. Facing a conflict between landlord and tenant that was reminiscent of English social relations, the court had to decide what form a doctrine of hierarchy and prerogative would take in American land law. The result was a three-to-two split in favor of the plaintiff in which James Kent, whose *Commentaries on American Law* would later belong to the American legal canon, joined the majority in creating a new and distinctly American doctrine of waste.[54]

The plaintiffs contended that clearing forest constituted waste under the English rule, while the defendant denied that cutting timber to make way for cultivation could be waste.[55] Although the majority ruled in favor of the plaintiffs, the justices adopted the defendant's interpretation of the doctrine, seizing on Blackstone's formulation that waste was made up of actions that did "a permanent injury to the inheritance."[56] In English common law, harvesting timber or changing patterns of land use was deemed such an injury; a rule, in other words, lent its crystalline lines to the nominal standard. In the United States the doctrine would henceforth take its shape from the standard alone, which became a source of considerable latitude for tenants. Despite applying the more flexible standard, the *Jackson* court found that the clearing was waste as a matter of law because Brownson had cut nearly all the wood on the estate and did not leave enough to supply timber for farm maintenance.[57]

The dissenting justices recognized the significance of the movement from rule to standard and reproached the majority for their embrace of vagueness.[58] Justice Spencer, joined by Justice Yates, recited the specific rights of bote that English waste law preserved for tenants, and continued, "I insist that, according to the common law of *England*, no tenant can cut down timber, &c. or clear land for agricultural purposes; and that the quantity of timber cut down never enters into the consideration whether waste has or has not been committed; but that it is always tested by the act of cutting timber, without the justifiable excuse of having done it for house-*bote*, fire-*bote*, plough-*bote* or fence-*bote*. A single tree cut down, without such justifiable cause, is waste as effectually as if a thousand had been cut down; and the reason is this, that such trees belong to the owner of the inheritance, and the tenant has only a qualified property in them for shade and shelter."[59]

The dissenters did not propose that the English rule, in all its particulars, would be desirable in America; indeed, they pointed out that the rule was "inapplicable to a new, unsettled country"—meaning by *inapplicable* not powerless but unsuitable.[60] The dissenters' point, rather, was that the form of the common-law rule, with its clear prerogatives and prohibitions, alerted all parties to their rights, while a standard required courts to engage in the uncertain business of distinguishing between appropriate and inappropriate uses of land. "The criterion set up by the plaintiff"—and adopted by the court—they argued, setting out a familiar objection to standards, "is altogether fanciful and vague; and the case shows, that men differ very widely as to how much woodland ought to be left for the use of a farm."[61] By contrast, the "rule furnished by the common law is fixed and certain."[62] That certainty created clear background conditions for bargaining: "If the parties before us intended that a sufficient quantity of timber should be left for the use of the farm, it was very easy to have inserted a covenant to that effect."[63] Replacing a clear rule with a "fanciful and vague" standard created undesirable uncertainty: "[I]f a covenant not to commit waste is hereafter to be considered as a covenant to leave a sufficient quantity of land in wood, no lessee is safe" from the shifting opinions of courts and juries on a matter better left to freely contracting parties.[64] Both sides, then, described their motive as being to protect the lessee from unfair expropriation; however, they identified opposite doctrinal instruments for that aim.

Whatever their motive, the dissenters had lost. The standard of "permanent injury" or "material prejudice" to the inheritance soon became the American law of waste.

Jackson v. Brownson was the progenitor of a line of state supreme court cases that adopted the same standard, with some variation in the wording of the formula. The Massachusetts Supreme Court held that in the United States, "it is difficult to imagine any exception to the general rule of law, that no act of a tenant will amount to waste, unless it is or may be prejudicial to the inheritance, or to those entitled to the reversion or remainder."[65] In Tennessee, when determining whether a widow with a life estate had committed waste, the supreme court asked, "[D]id she materially injure the dower estate thereby?"[66] In Rhode Island, to succeed in an action of waste, the supreme court held, "it is necessary to show that the change is detrimental to the inheritance."[67] In North Carolina, "the cutting down of timber" was not waste, unless it did "a lasting damage to the inheritance, and deteriorate[d] its value; and not then, if no more was cut down than was necessary for the ordinary enjoyment of the land."[68] Under Vermont law, the tenant could act freely, but "not so as to cause damage to the inheritance."[69]

The *Jackson* majority did take care to connect their interpretation of the doctrine to the English common-law rule, and they tried to show that their articulation of the doctrine did not vary from the motivating principle behind the rule. The majority made much of the doctrinal latitude created by ecological variation in the English law, which protected trees in timber-poor areas that would have been free for cutting in regions with better stocks.[70] Because "[w]hat kind of wood in *England* is deemed to be timber depends upon the custom of the country," and wood "which in some counties is called timber is not so in others," the court concluded that the prohibition on cutting timber in England "in principle, extends no further . . . there than it does here."[71] The principle which joined the two continents in this formulation was "whenever wood has been cut in such a manner as materially to prejudice the inheritance, it is waste."[72]

Bolstered by American precedent, the cases that followed displayed none of *Jackson's* argument that the American standard simply perpetuated the principle of the English rule. Instead, the opinions insist on the distinctness of the American approach. They are studded with such phrases as "the law must necessarily be varied in this country from the English doctrine. . . . [as] it would be absurd to apply the rigid principles of the English law to a state of things wholly variant from theirs";[73] "whatever may be [the] law of England, it is not in this Commonwealth waste, unless it may be prejudicial to the plaintiff";[74] and "[w]hile our ancestors brought over to this country the principles of the common law . . . [i]t would have been absurd to hold that the clearing of the forest, so as to fit it for the habitation and use of man was waste."[75] While courts could as easily have followed *Jackson*'s approach, they instead insisted that American law was unlike that of the old country.

What did it mean, in the words of *Jackson*, "materially to prejudice the inheritance?"[76] The rule could not be so simple as to require that the property go to the reversioner worth as much as or more than its value at the time the tenant occupied it, for that would be both over- and under-inclusive. On the one hand, tenants could commit waste while increasing the value of the land if they compromised the capacity of the reversioner to provide for the needs of the place from its own soil. In *Jackson*, the cleared land was worth considerably more than the land as wild timber,[77] yet the court found waste as a matter of law because the tenant had left less timber than was necessary for the upkeep of the property.[78] On the other hand, even under the English rule a tenant who cut timber for firebote and then ended the tenancy would have diminished the value of the land but not committed waste. A reduction in the value of the estate, then, was not always a necessary condition of waste, nor was it sufficient to constitute waste. Whether waste had occurred depended more on a concept of *appropriate* use than on whether the estate's value had increased, decreased, or held constant.

Despite some sallies toward ambitious theoretical formulation,[79] the principle of sustainable use tended in practice to remain abstract and vague, while courts resolved waste cases by another standard, which they presented as either synonymous or conjunctive with the prohibition on "permanent injury" or "material prejudice." This was the standard of husbandry or the prudent farmer.[80] By this standard, a tenant's actions were not waste if they comported with the hypothetical behavior of a prudent fee-owner who was using the land for profit. This standard appealed not to objective agronomic principles but to the custom of the area where the dispute took place.[81] To a substantial degree, it was treated as a question for juries rather than courts.[82]

What was the character of the American standard? What were its motives, the purposes it served? The core mischief the doctrine addressed was the negligent, opportunistic, or larcenous act of a tenant, inconsistent with the interest of the reversioner. The question was how to mediate between the reversioner and the tenant in a setting in which land use was dynamic and land-use patterns could be expected to change from decade to decade.

DEFAULT RULES AND THE AMERICAN STANDARD

The argument that the American standard was a problem-solving default—one that fills gaps in contracts with welfare-maximizing terms—runs this way:

Tenants are interested in maximizing their profit from the estate during their tenure, while reversioners are interested in maximizing the value of the estate when they get it back. The overlap of these interests lies in any improvements made to the land that both increase the tenants' profit and increase (or at least do not "materially" diminish) the value of the estate upon its transfer to the reversioner. The American standard is designed to embrace such improvements—whose paradigm is the clearing of wilderness for cultivation—while preserving the English rule's prohibition on tenant activity that diminishes the estate's value through action or neglect. Under optimal bargaining conditions, tenants and reversioners should agree on what activity falls in this zone of overlap. So far as this is true, the American standard should serve as an effective problem-solving or gap-filling default.

American courts envisioned this flexibility in contrast to the fixity of the English rule, which they portrayed as threatening to lock tenants into existing land-use patterns and forbidding the mutually beneficial activity that the American standard embraced. Some courts asserted that retaining the English rule might impose stasis on land-use patterns, even tying up portions of the country in wilderness.[83] This view, however, neglects the distinction between a default rule, which is susceptible to contractual revision, and a mandatory rule, which withdraws certain questions from the discretion of the contracting parties.[84] As a default rule, the English law locked no one into anything; it simply served as a backdrop to bargaining. Parties incorporated the rule into their agreements only by declining to specify alternative terms.

Despite its rhetorical currency, the image of a continent tied up in primeval forest was always a chimera; no one seems to have argued seriously that the clearing of frontier land should be regarded as waste. The jurists who defended the reform of American waste doctrine were protecting a westward movement of clearing and settlement that needed no protection. Moreover, a rationally self-interested reversioner would not insist on keeping a plot of land in wilderness unless relative property values shifted so that at least some of the land had become more valuable in timber than after clearing. Any economically rational invocation of the English rule would have been either to prevent a tenant's clearing a plot of land in a manner that jeopardized future productive use, which the doctrine of husbandry tended also to forbid in the American context, or as an opportunistic device to expropriate wealth from the tenant (a possibility which I discuss shortly).

Moreover, there is some reason to believe that the American standard, despite its initial promise to deal with the zones of overlapping interest between tenant and reversioner, functioned rather poorly as a gap-filling or problem-solving default. As Alan Schwartz has suggested, a problem-solving default should be assessed by three related considerations: whether it (a) solves a problem that a reasonable portion of contractors will face (b) in a way that is acceptable to those contractors and (c) in a manner that is guided by accessible or determinable information.[85] A default that does not address an actually occurring problem is either superfluous or wasteful; one that addresses problems in a way not acceptable to the parties will not survive in the marketplace; and one whose application is not guided by accessible information cannot determine a solution that fulfills its problem-solving purpose.[86]

Here I concentrate on the first criterion. Could the problem be expected to arise in a way that the American standard was particularly well suited to address? The problem of opportunistic tenants would arise anywhere, but the American standard was not superior to the English rule in controlling those tenants; its special capacity was meant to be distinguishing between such tenants and others whose land-use changes were neutral or beneficial to the reversioner.[87] On the assumption that the parties negotiated rationally, however, there is every reason to expect that they would agree beforehand to changes they regarded as mutually beneficial, such as clearing wilderness or changing cropping patterns, and revisit the agreement to pursue mutually beneficial opportunities that arose afterward. This is the sort of bargaining the *Jackson* dissenters envisioned as *induced* by keeping the English rule.[88] On this account, the American standard may actually have tended to produce the problem it was meant to solve by lulling inattentive parties into accepting its indeterminate principle rather than bargaining up front. That courts applying the standard had no special expertise in solving such problems would only have exacerbated the difficulty.

The *Jackson* dissenters were not alone in recognizing the value of the English rule in this respect and the disutility of its American replacement. American courts retained the English law of waste for minerals, apparently as a bargaining default, just as the *Jackson* dissenters proposed to do with the law of waste for renewable resources. In 1852 plaintiffs invited the Pennsylvania Supreme Court to apply the same standard to mining that American courts had adopted for other forms of land use: that tenants' use "cannot seriously impair the inheritance," as determined by "the nature and condition of the estate, and the circumstances of the parties."[89] The court declined the invitation and preserved the English rule, not on grounds of tradition, but as a basis for bargaining among free parties.[90] The testator might not have envisioned that the tenant for life would exhaust the coal mine in question, the court noted, and its unexpected exhaustion might disadvantage the reversioner, but "when the donor did not see proper to restrain the gift, how shall it be done? Surely courts have no such control over the arrangements which people choose to make of their affairs. . . . And [this court] cannot see how the enterprise of the citizen is to be restrained by judicial process."[91] The court continued by urging that "we . . . get ourselves freer from the notions derived from feudal subordination,"[92] which evidently was how some exponents of free contract had come to regard the doctrine of waste, with its judicial imposition of a standard of appropriate land use.[93] The Pennsylvania court's means of advancing free contract, ironically, was through preservation of the older English rule as a bargaining default for a society in which free agreement should be the governing principle.[94] I have found no American jurisdiction in which the English rule of waste for minerals underwent significant change. In sum then, reasons both general to defaults and specific to the development of waste doctrine give cause to doubt that the American standard was any improvement on the English rule as a problem-solving or gap-filling default.

A related economic explanation exists, however, which falls somewhat farther from courts' account of the American standard but is facially plausible all the same. The standard might have worked to avoid certain transaction costs and unconsummated bargains that the English rule threatened to produce.[95] The English rule created bilateral monopolies in which both tenants and reversioners enjoyed a veto over improvements to the estate. The tenant could simply refuse to make an improvement. The reversioner could refuse to approve an improvement, then institute a waste action if the tenant made it anyway. Even though a veto would reduce the value of the estate, tenant and reversioner might reach an impasse in bargaining over how to distribute the income from the proposed improvement.[96] The American standard theoretically fixed that problem by replacing the reversioner's veto with a trump for the tenant, who could make the improvement, collect the resulting income, and resist an action for waste on the ground that the change would not materially diminish the expected value of the estate to the reversioner.

One case seems to exemplify this thesis. In *Pynchon v. Stearns*, the Massachusetts Supreme Court found no waste in the activity of a tenant who had cut drainage ditches, dug cellars, and filled in wetlands.[97] The reversioner's action sought to terminate the tenant's lease. The court remarked that preventing such action, though it would accord with the "ancient doctrine of waste," would "greatly impede the progress of improvement, without any compensating benefit."[98] The court's language suggests that it understood its decision in this case as preventing the reversioner from imposing a productivity-reducing veto on tenant improvements. In this case, however, the practical result was somewhat different: it prevented the reversioner from opportunistically expropriating the value of the tenant's improvements and taking full ownership of the property prematurely by means of a waste action.

That point suggests that courts may have had in mind both productivity in general—the "progress of improvement"—and the distribution of gains from increased productivity. An exercise of the landlord's prerogative in those cases where the remedy was forfeiture is a particularly harsh instance of the opportunistic redistribution of gains via waste actions that courts might have wished to prevent. Moreover, the respective vetoes on improvements by the tenant and reversioner would not be symmetrical in a situation in which the tenant could not make an adequate living from the land without installing the improvement in question—for instance, in the initial clearing of forest for cultivation. Because the *Pynchon* court had such a situation in mind, it may have deliberately made a distributive choice in favor of the tenant by removing the landlord's power to force a strapped tenant to hand over, say, any income from the sale of cleared timber. If courts had this distributive issue in mind, that would suggest a somewhat different version of the "bilateral monopoly" explanation from the one I sketched earlier, one concerned at least as much with fairness as with welfare maximization. Of course, fairness of this sort would also feed back into ongoing productivity improvements, because tenants' confidence that they could keep the gains from their land-use innovations would provide an incentive to dynamic efficiency that the threat of a waste action would otherwise dampen.

Much of early-modern liberal political economy envisioned efficiency gains and egalitarian changes in status relations as complementary: generating reciprocal rather than hierarchical bargaining situations (and avoiding prerogative-based preemptions of bargaining) would induce efficient use of resources while also training people to treat one another as (relative) equals. That kind of complementary consideration would be a natural explanation for decisions that both produce internalization of gains from improvements and block expropriating or otherwise opportunistic demands by status superiors.

REPUBLICAN SOCIAL RELATIONS

While the second efficiency-enhancing explanation, concerned with bilateral monopolies, has some force, particularly in the version focused on distributive issues, there is good reason to believe that it was not the whole story and that distinct, complementary purposes also motivated the courts. Recall the status-confirming function of the English rule in its aspect as a normative default and its corresponding educative function as a quasi-transformative default. In light of the recognition that self-interested negotiators would tend to focus on the same area of overlapping interests that the American standard sought to define and secure from interference by reversioners, consider the circumstances under which the English rule would be invoked in practice. In addition to spoilage by an opportunistic or neglectful tenant, which the English and American defaults equally prevented, and cases of impasse or abuse arising from bilateral monopoly, reversioners would tend to invoke waste law as an expression of prerogative — to block changes in land use which did not comport with their aesthetic or other noneconomic preferences, or to underscore their social superiority to an ambitious or excessively self-regarding tenant.

Consider how the judges in *Jackson* might have viewed such use of the doctrine. As noted, the plaintiffs were the heirs of Philip Schuyler, a member of the land-holding aristocracy of the Hudson River valley,[99] where the landlords' relations to their tenants were characterized by pervasive social and political hierarchy.[100] In the seventeenth century, some set up manorial courts in the style of English lords.[101] Well into the nineteenth century, they controlled their tenants' votes as blocs and confounded the newly introduced secret ballot by distributing pre-marked ballots and instructing tenants to fold the ballots into distinctive shapes for instant identification.[102] The classic form of the Hudson River valley deed was the oxymoronic "lease-in-fee," which combined payment of periodic rent with the heritable right to remain a tenant.[103] Until its judicial abolition in the nineteenth century, this deed form required a tenant who transferred the lease to pay the landlord one-quarter the price it fetched.[104] Annual rent sometimes included such feudal remnants as one day's labor with a horse and cart or a tribute of "four fat fowl."[105] Although the record in *Jackson* does not contain the term "lease-in-fee," the majority noted that Brownson's lease was for life and that "the lessee covenants for himself, *his heirs* and assigns," strongly suggesting that it was such a deed.[106] In the decades after *Jackson*, the heritable rental estate became the flashpoint of sustained legal, political, and sometimes paramilitary conflict in New York.[107]

Consider these quasi-feudal property relations from the point of view of what is sometimes called the republican strain in early American politics. Although *republicanism* has been put to varied uses by theorists, historians, and polemicists,[108] the broad strokes of the early American view are clear. In politics, American republicanism signified rejection of monarchy, aristocratic government, and the dominance of dynastic families in favor of the equal basic political rights of each citizen (or each landholding citizen) and a vision of authority as ultimately founded on the consent of the governed.[109] In economics, republicanism repudiated feudal relations of authority and subordination in favor of personal independence, which was variously identified with the condition of the free laborer, the yeoman landholder, or the merchant or entrepreneur.[110] Finally, in culture, republicanism embodied a regard for ordinary individuals, combined with a belief (in some cases half a tenuous hope) that they would prove to be the true repository of virtues long identified with aristocracy: honor, dignity, and courage.[111] As this brief sketch suggests, the antithesis of republicanism was often clearer than the idea itself: that antithesis was, above all, the unchecked power of tyranny and absolutism, and, by analogy, of all forms of arbitrary power over others. Against these, republicanism defended the dignity and capacity of ordinary people. Ideas about the institutional arrangements necessary to secure republican liberty ranged from the civic to the commercial. "Commercial republicanism" is an apt term for the position of James Kent; under the influence of Adam Smith, Kent's position formed one of many American extensions of Smith's view.

Kent, a conservative Federalist and member of the *Jackson* majority,[112] later set out core commercial-republican ideas, with special emphasis on the place of real property in ordering social and political relationships.[113] According to Kent, property in England had a double character: on the one hand, the English freeholder was the archetypal figure whose common law and constitutional rights formed the model of the liberty of the American citizen.[114] On the other, the prerogatives of landlords in relation to their tenants, along with legal devices for keeping land in powerful families, formed the backbone of a quasi-feudal system that the United States had rejected.[115] American liberty rested partly on a process of stripping away feudal privileges and constraints on the transfer of property, thus doing away with aristocracy and extending the status of freeholder, at least potentially, to every white male citizen—every man a landowner, voter, and juror.[116]

Kent's vision of republican property had much in common with Smith's commercial, sociability-based anti-domination commitments. Kent was far from an egalitarian visionary: he mocked proposals for equal distribution of property as likely to be ruinous to economic initiative.[117] Nor did he have any sympathy for austere republican visions of frugal and upright citizens[118] maintaining their equality against the blandishments of luxury.[119] Instead, he believed the marketplace was the arena where free men should exchange labor and acquire land.[120] In contrast to feudal England, he argued, "Every individual has as much freedom in the acquisition, use, and disposition of his property, as is consistent with good order and the reciprocal rights of others."[121] (One sees here hints of what would become the rationale for a strong, judicially protected right of contract later in the nineteenth century.) Land made a person substantial, and it was in the marketplace that each man had an equal chance, in principle, of increasing and securing his substance.[122] Kent envisioned the formal equality of the marketplace as supplanting both the tangled hierarchy of feudal relationships and the abject servitude of slavery, which he termed "a great public evil."[123] In all these respects, his template was also Adam Smith's.

From Kent's commercial-republican perspective, the American standard of waste law would have been superior to the English rule in both its expressive significance and its preclusion of certain exercises of prerogative. The English doctrine enforced the presumptive veto of the reversioner against any initiative of the tenant, unless the reversioner explicitly surrendered that prerogative. In short, it made tenants answerable in their major economic and agricultural decisions to social superiors whose status was marked by their superior estate in land.

In contrast, the American doctrine put the two estates on equal footing in a critical sense: reversioners no longer exercised ongoing authority over use of the land and could not invoke waste doctrine in its status-confirming aspect. Instead, their right was to receive, at the end of the tenancy, a property commensurate in value to the one surrendered to the tenant. That said, the property might have been timbered, rearranged in its cropping patterns, or equipped with new fences and buildings. In principle, tenants were sovereign over the land for as long as they held it, their liberty bounded solely by the requirement that they pass on, in Locke's pregnant words, enough and as good at the end of their occupation.[124] This revision in waste doctrine removed its feudal echoes and placed tenants and reversioners within a new logic of status: a formally egalitarian vision of market relations, in which each individual had, as Kent observed, an equal right and opportunity to acquire, use, and dispose of property.[125]

Two aspects of the American standard are particularly striking in this regard. First is the symbolic matter of its expression: through the standard of husbandry, tenants were modeled as owners in fee and held to a corresponding standard. On the one hand this was simply an expression of the expectation that the owner in fee would use the land rationally, and that governing the tenant by that standard would avoid suboptimal land use. On the other, in a fashion suggestive of the egalitarian implications of marketizing relations in land, this expression of the American standard eliminated hierarchy from the language and the imagery of waste law. Tenants were *envisioned* as owners in fee, and their behavior was appropriate inasmuch as they lived up to that standard. This is far from the imagery of the English default—a tenant who collects wood for maintenance under quasi-feudal rights, persists in inherited patterns of cropping, and seeks the permission of the socially superior reversioner for any undertaking outside these bounds.

Another aspect of republicanism in the American standard is more concrete, but its imaginative significance is equally poignant. The power to assess a proposed land use under the English rule belonged predominantly to the reversioner. The American standard placed determination of what constituted a permanent injury to the land in the hands of jurors, that is, citizens. Under the English rule, the decision reflected a prerogative evocative of feudal authority. Command ran up the ladder of obligation, culminating in the crown, seat of power and theoretical owner of all land.[126] The American standard reflected, by contrast, a horizontal and republican image of political authority in which all citizens equally possessed the power of consent that founded the legitimacy of government. By indicating the will (and custom) of the citizenry, a jury trial confirmed the political community's status as the source of authority and checked the reversioner's prerogative with the judgment of that political community.

PROGRESS AND LAND USE

We have already referred to the importance of these property-centered ideas of social order and progress in justifications of European colonialism in the Americas. Discussing the seminal American land case of *Johnson v. M'Intosh*, Kent drew the same connection: "[O]ur colonial ancestors. . . . seem to have deemed it to be unreasonable, and a perversion of the duties and design of the human race, to bar the Europeans, with their implements of husbandry and the arts, with their laws, their learning, their liberty, and their religion, from all entrance into this mighty continent, lest they might trespass upon some part of the interminable forests, deserts, and hunting-grounds of an uncivilized, erratic, and savage race of men."[127] The specific "destiny and duty of the human race" as conceived by the first American settlers was, Kent explained, "to subdue the earth, and till the ground."[128]

Most state courts adopting *Jackson*'s rationale gave an account of the change from the English rule to the American standard that comported with these themes. These courts observed that North America was substantially uncleared, and a westward-moving population had to rework the landscape to settle it. Despite finding waste in the defendant's clearing of timber, the *Jackson* majority insisted, "The lessee undoubtedly had a right to fell part of the timber, so as to fit the land for cultivation."[129] The dissenters did the majority one better, conceding that the "doctrine of waste, as understood in England, is inapplicable to a new, unsettled country."[130] Even before *Jackson*, the Pennsylvania Supreme Court noted that "[l]ands in general with us are enhanced by being cleared," adding that it would be "an outrage on common sense" to call such enhancement waste.[131] North Carolina's highest court concurred: "It would have been absurd to hold that the clearing of the forest, so as to fit it for the habitation and use of man was waste."[132] America was "a new and opening land, covered largely with primeval growth. . . . [H]ere, the clearing of the forest growth, and fitting the virgin soil which it covers for cultivation, is ordinarily an improvement most valuable to the property."[133]

Complementing these courts' insistence on the distinctiveness of American conditions was an explicit anxiety about what it would mean for continental development to maintain English waste doctrine. The Massachusetts Supreme Court ruled that the old rule must be discarded because the "ancient doctrine of waste, if universally adopted in this country, would greatly impede the progress of improvement, without any compensating benefit. To be beneficial, therefore, the rules of law must be accommodated to the situation of the country."[134] In New York, the chancery court concluded that "to apply the ancient doctrines of waste to modern tenancies, even for short terms, would in some of our cities and villages, put an entire stop to the progress of improvement."[135] Progress and improvement were the courts' aims, and westward movement across the continent was synonymous with betterment. The contrasting, and anxiety-producing, image was of arrested movement, stasis, land tied up as forest, and the development of the continent brought to a halt.

Why anxiety? There is little reason, either in economic theory or historical evidence, to believe that the English rule of waste risked forcing any part of the country to remain wilderness. Nonetheless, the productive use of land had a special historical claim on Americans: whether it was everywhere and at all times the destiny of humankind, it was the destiny Americans had staked out for themselves. To indulge or encourage stasis, even symbolically or in a handful of exemplary cases, might have signified a break with American purpose. Much like republican values, values of progress and dynamism in land use shaped American waste law into the symbolic endorsement of an instrumental attitude toward the natural world, an attitude to which the country's public and legal culture was committed.

Any hint of embracing stasis might also have suggested an erosion of the commercial-republican spirit of liberty. Kent argued that a decent measure of equality in commercial societies came from the constant vicissitudes of the market: "When the laws allow a free circulation to property by the abolition of perpetuities, entailments, the claims of primogeniture, and all inequalities of descent, the operation of the steady laws of nature will, of themselves, preserve a proper equilibrium, and dissipate the mounds of property as fast as they accumulate."[136]

Social equality, in the sense of equal in-principle opportunity, depended in part on the dynamic operation of markets, which in turn depended on treating land as a commodity, so that it would move to its highest-value use and user. In this respect, economic dynamism and the commercial-republican version of egalitarianism seemed mutually reinforcing principles. Thus, the same normative considerations that encouraged a default against hierarchical land relations also encouraged a default against any legal enshrinement of stasis in land use.

A study of the American transformation of waste law reveals three classes of values shaping the doctrine. One is the social interest in the economically efficient use of resources. The other two are less widely recognized, and much of the analysis in this chapter has aimed at confirming their existence and illustrating their character. One comprises the organizing values of political society—in the instance of waste doctrine, rejection of hierarchical social relations founded on unequal claims to land and the embrace of a market in property which makes land a vehicle for opportunity and mobility. The other is the idea of an appropriate relation to the natural world and the role of settlement in progress. The integration and interplay of these values expressed a debt to the vision of property and social order that James Kent shared with Adam Smith, which deeply informed the legal imagination of the time.

Part Two

CRISES

The first part of this book dealt with the rise of the vision of property as a uniquely integrating institution for the values of liberal, commercial modernity, exploring the context of ideas and events in which it arose and providing a sketch of its application in early American jurisprudence. In the next part I treat signal failures of that vision. As a guide to imperial practice in India and, most dramatically, in the United States, the property-based social and legal imaginary proved vexed. It provided a comforting rationale for the exercise of power where comfort was the last thing needed. The vision traced in this book also failed to provide any simple answer to the question of how to reconcile freedom and equality in the jurisprudence and political economy of the nineteenth-century United States, despite the vivid promises of free-labor thought to extend Adam Smith's principles into the industrial economy. Had thinkers of the time been more attentive to the content of Smith's thought, they would not have imagined it as a source of simple and universal principles, or, perhaps, imagined that such principles could solve their problems. Nonetheless, some believed just that.

4

4

HAZARDS OF PROGRESS:
JOHNSON V. M'INTOSH AND PROPERTY
IN THE IMPERIAL IMAGINATION

The thesis that ideas matter, which is one of the arguments of this book, cannot be proven by a survey of ideas. These ideas must figure in the ways legal actors understand and resolve problems. To say that ideas matter is to say that they count in life's concrete tasks, including the tasks of the law, by framing perceptions of what those tasks are, what alternatives exist to address them, what each alternative is likely to produce, and what is good and bad in that result. The idea of the legal imagination traced in this book shows its power in the ways that its vision of legal order shaped legal doctrines, both momentous and small.

Johnson v. M'Intosh involved a dispute between two claimants to a tract of Northwest Territory. The land had been sold twice, first by its Native American occupants, then by the federal government, and the two litigants derived their claims from these two incompatible sources.[1] One of the seminal American property cases,[2] *Johnson* is also among the stranger opinions in all of American law. Chief Justice Marshall ruled that Native American tribes did not own their land in full and therefore could not sell it except to the federal government,[3] which in turn had the sole power to create full ownership in its purchasers. The opinion's strangeness lay not in the holding, but in the tone: Marshall was elegiac, triumphal, and recurrently ambivalent toward his own reasoning. He acknowledged that the principle of his holding, denying Native Americans full ownership and sovereignty over their own land, "may be opposed to natural right and to the uses of civilized nations"[4] but, in one of those moments of judicial candor that might convince a vulgar Legal Realist to declare (Pyrrhic) victory and go home, insisted, "Conquest gives a title which the Courts of the conqueror cannot deny."[5] He also spun a narrative tapestry of dicta, describing an ethnic cleansing free of human agency, in which Native Americans "necessarily receded," along with the deer and the unbroken forests, before the ax and plow of the American frontiersman.[6] By the end of the opinion, the European American expropriation of North America emerged as (1) lawful and (2) inevitable, even though the basis of its legality was "opposed to natural right" and the inevitability of the displacement gave only "excuse," not "justification," to the tribes' expulsion.[7]

As in the passages from Blackstone that open this book, Marshall's story in dicta is not incidental to the overall argument but essential to holding its parts together. *Johnson* is both a property case and a leading American opinion in the law of imperialism. The Anglo-American account of the legitimacy of imperialism depended essentially on a vision of property that made it, as it was for Blackstone, the linchpin of social order, progress, and sovereignty. Progress, as figured in *Johnson*, arises from an order of commerce and sociability in which the institutions of modern governance emerge in answer to increasingly complex economic relations. This story enabled imperial governors and jurists to identify, to their satisfaction, the legal changes that would foster social complexity, stable government, and growing personal freedom. This tapestry of progress was thought to justify the imperial powers' rule over subject peoples.

In a paradox that has marked modern imperialism, the same ideas also encouraged blindness to its human costs. With this paradox in mind I examine both jurisprudence and an issue of moral psychology: the contrast between those who rationalized imperial power and those who denied that it deserved any justification. Marshall's opinion in *Johnson* displays both attitudes. The capacity to hold both at once may be valuable wherever the legitimacy of power is in question, not just in foundationally unjust relations such as imperial rule.

THE LEGAL LOGIC OF IMPERIALISM

In saying that *Johnson* deals with a problem of imperialism, I mean that it concerns the competing claims of representatives of two political societies, one dominant, the other subordinate, within an extended system of such domination.[8] The courts of the dominant society enjoy ultimate say over the competing claims because of the imperial relationship. Therefore the issue is not which society will prevail but what concessions the dominant society will make to the subordinate one and for what reasons. This type of relationship formed the pattern of imperial rule throughout the age of empire, from the Spanish conquest of the Americas in the fifteenth century to the independence of India and the colonies of Africa after World War II.[9] In much of Anglo-American imperial thought, both jurisprudence and larger-scale normative reasoning developed by way of the property-centered legal imaginary I have been examining. These are essential to making sense of Marshall's reasoning and tone in *Johnson*.

The jurisprudential, political, and philosophical developments of the imperial period had no simple relation to empire.[10] Ideas about progress, rights, and the rule of law interacted with imperial practice in various and complex ways. The great liberal reformers John Stuart Mill and his father, James Mill, were enthusiastic partisans of what they themselves termed British "despotism" in India.[11] The moderate and humane conservative Alexis de Tocqueville strongly supported French rule over Algeria.[12] But Adam Smith, the jurist, economist, and philosopher of commercial society, resisted imperial projects, while the radical legal reformer and founder of utilitarianism (and muse to the Mills) Jeremy Bentham denounced them.[13] The conservative Edmund Burke was the greatest British enemy of imperial abuses in the second half of the eighteenth century.[14] The arch-liberal philosophe Denis Diderot could claim the same honor in contemporary France.[15] These examples are enough to suggest the complexity of the phenomenon and the various and nonobvious relations between general ideas and attitudes toward empire.

Nonetheless, there was a consistent logic in the questions or problems that imperial law posed. In assessing the claims of subject peoples within the legal system of the dominant society, jurists and theorists had to develop an account of the relation between the legal and the broadly normative cultures of the two societies.[16] Were they symmetrical, so that the role of the dominant society's courts, or of normative reasoning generally in the dominant society, would be to adjudicate between competing claims and interests in the manner of modern choice-of-law reasoning?[17] Was the subordinate society regarded as inferior, not just in power but in the quality of its normative claims, so that such claims would have no effect on the reasoning of the dominant society but would instead be regarded as symptoms of barbarism presenting themselves for management and correction?[18] Or was the subordinate society's normative order eligible for legal recognition in some respects but in others disregarded as primitive, in which case the interpreter's task was to distinguish between eligible and ineligible features of the subordinate society?

Addressing such questions necessarily involved representatives of the dominant society in interpretation of their own society and of the subordinate one. Did they envision the subordinate society as a more primitive version of their own, a living specimen of the past awaiting a determinate future? Did they understand it as genuinely different, not just a distinct link on a single chain of development, but nonetheless inferior according to some universal standard?[19] Or did they treat the two societies as incommensurable, embodying irreducibly distinct combinations of familiar values and even, perhaps, values that were unrecognizably different to outsiders?[20] These divergent attitudes presupposed beliefs about the nature of history and the degree to which human societies are bound by universal commonalities or are truly unlike one another.[21]

Two tendencies persisted in the ways that members of dominant societies interpreted subordinate ones. Broadly speaking, one attitude was *ironic*, attentive to paradox, inconsistency, and disjuncture. The other was *irenic*, pressing toward coherence and conciliation of divergent cultures into a single view of the world. Ironists tended to see imperial enterprises as revealing the fatuity and danger of any stark opposition between "civilized" Europeans and "savage" or "barbaric" others.[22] On one hand, the bare fact of cultural encounter for them highlighted human diversity, unsettling the easy supposition that their own societies were natural or inevitable.[23] On the other, European atrocities in winning and governing empires laid low the idea of Europeans' moral superiority: if missionaries and colonial governors were looking for savages and barbarians to improve, suggested Montaigne, Diderot, and (sometimes) Bentham, they might begin at home.[24]

By contrast, irenists tended to see cultural encounter as confirming the unity of human experience. Across places and times, human beings pursued the same aims and were answerable to the same moral rules. Differences in societies reflected different positions along a single continuum of development, from savagery to civilization, or different degrees of distance from the cultural and spiritual grace of European Christians. Irenists thus tended to see imperial missions as expressions, even duties, of superiority within a coherent human order, to the point of portraying empire as philanthropic self-sacrifice.[25] Perhaps the most powerful vehicle of this attitude in the high-water era of imperialism was the vision at the center of the historical account here: that of society as arising from and aiming at economic relations of mutual benefit within a larger framework of advancing freedom.

Irony and irenism ran together in early American attitudes, partly because of ambivalence as to whether Americans were colonizers or a colonized people. Americans had formed a settler colony, systematically displacing an indigenous population.[26] During the Revolution their complaints against Great Britain had prominently included the Crown's constraints on their westward expansion.[27] As late as the War of 1812, British victory portended a buffer nation of Native Americans on the new country's northwest flank—in the same territory where American writ was contested in *Johnson*.[28] In their insistence on a white Protestant settler hegemony over the continent, which they opposed to Britain's willingness to govern a multicultural empire of commerce, the Americans were imperialists par excellence.[29]

On the other hand, the American Revolution was a colonists' revolt against the world's leading imperial power, and there was considerable impulse to regard the United States not as an extension of British settler enterprises but as something new in the world. Alexander Hamilton, no fire-breathing radical but very much a nationalist, proposed as much in *Federalist* no. 11, where he aligned America with Europe's once-prone and now resurgent victims.[30] "Unhappily," he wrote, "Europe . . . by force and by fraud, has, in different degrees, extended her dominion over them all. Africa, Asia, and America have successively felt her domination."[31] He continued, "The superiority [Europe] has long maintained, has tempted her to plume herself as the Mistress of the World, and to consider the rest of mankind as created for her benefit. Men admired as profound philosophers have, in direct terms, attributed to her inhabitants a physical superiority; and have gravely asserted that all animals, and with them the human species, degenerate in America—that even dogs cease to bark after having breathed a while in our atmosphere. Facts have too long supported these arrogant pretensions of the European. It belongs to us to vindicate the honor of the human race, and to teach that assuming brother moderation."[32] This remarkable passage aligns the nascent United States with the victims of imperialism and offers the country as a champion of the world's downtrodden. Hamilton also displays some of the ironic sensibility of the great critics of empire, such as Diderot and Montaigne, in his wry evocation of absurd imperial self-confidence. Imperial rulers arrogant enough to believe that American dogs do not bark may be less formidable than they imagine.[33] Seeing through the moral and theoretical poses of power is the consummate achievement of the ironic posture toward empire.

Marshall's approach to the interlinked problems of cultural and legal interpretation occupies an uneasy middle ground between Hamilton's disdain for European imperial arrogance and the emerging political reality of a United States that had become the successor to the European imperial powers.[34] Marshall concluded that the United States was legally the successor to the European colonizers. His language, however, frequently indicates an ironic distaste for imperial presumption, a mockery of the moral self-confidence of imperial apologists. Nonetheless, his reasoning in the end presupposes the irenic view of culture and history that underlay the law of imperialism. Marshall was an ironic irenist, heir to two inconsistent legacies: a political tradition of anti-imperial sentiments and a legal tradition of pro-imperial apologetics, which brings in train a hierarchical view of culture and history. These paradoxes underlie an opinion that is coolly decisive in content, strained and self-questioning in tone.

TWO PUZZLES AND SOME IRONY

Johnson v. M'Intosh has received estimable scholarly treatment and inspired diverse responses. In one view, *Johnson* is an act of acquiescence to power, in which courts and the law of property serve as instruments of colonial expropriation. From this perspective, the case teaches the general lesson that law serves power, and some specific lessons as to the terms on which that service has been provided in the law of property and Native American rights.[35] In a second view, *Johnson* is an uncomfortable—indeed, an untenably fraught—shotgun marriage of law and power, the latter crystallized in colonial expropriation and ethnic cleansing.[36] A third approach treats the case as law, specifically as an application of the customary law of relationships between European colonial governments and Native American tribes in the first two-plus centuries of North American colonization.[37]

Appreciating that *Johnson* is a case in imperial jurisprudence recasts it in a way that partly contradicts each of the competing views. On this interpretation, the portions of Marshall's opinion conventionally regarded as anomalous, embarrassing, or lawless are in fact applications of the logic of essential legal concepts of the time—albeit not principles that Marshall was willing expressly to endorse *as law.* The customary legal principle on which Marshall's opinion rested, that the European sovereign had the exclusive power to sell Native lands, and thus extinguish native property claims, was nested within a higher-order principle of customary international law: a distinction between (at least) two types of sovereigns—full sovereigns whose rights and powers are commensurate with those of European governments and imperfect sovereigns which must yield on certain points to the incursions of full sovereigns. This distinction founded two bodies of international law: one governing relationships among full sovereigns, the other governing those between full and imperfect sovereigns. *Johnson* applies the logic of the second body of law, and many of its otherwise puzzling or ambiguous elements become clear when read in light of that logic.[38]

The interpretation of *Johnson* as an exercise in imperial jurisprudence is not simply an imposition on the case of political thought from the same period. Rather, it emerges from within the case, helping to sort out two doctrinal puzzles and make sense of Justice Marshall's heavy irony toward the presuppositions of his own reasoning.

The first puzzle is Marshall's summary rejection of precedent invoked by the party arguing that Indian land transfers were valid. The litigants invoked the 1757 joint opinion of Great Britain's attorney general and solicitor general, Charles Pratt and Charles Yorke (later Lords Camden and Marsden, respectively), on the legal status of private purchases of land from sovereigns in the Indian sub-continent.[39] The opinion, written to instruct the Privy Council in responding to a petition for guidance filed by the East India Company,[40] read as follows:

> As to the latter part of the prayer of the petition relative to the holding or re-taining Fortresses or Districts already acquired or to be acquired by Treaty, Grant, or Conquest, We beg leave to point out some distinctions upon it. In respect to such Places as have been or shall be acquired by treaty or Grant from the Mogul or any of the Indian Princes or Governments Your Majestys Letters Patent are not necessary, the property of the soil vesting in the Com-pany by Indian Grants subject only to your Majestys right of Sovereignity over the Settlements as English Subjects who carry with them your Majestys Laws wherever they form Colonies and receive your Majestys protection by virtue of your Royal Charters. In respect to such places as have lately been acquired or shall hereafter be acquired by Conquest the property as well as the Dominion vests in your Majesty by virtue of your known Prerogative & consequently the Company can only derive a right to them through your Majestys Grants.[41]

A redacted version of the opinion was in circulation in North America by 1773, without language connecting its reasoning with India and specifically omitting reference to "Moguls" and "Fortresses or Districts."[42] According to Marshall's opinion, the version of the Yorke-Camden opinion submitted by the plaintiffs in *Johnson* was contained in a pamphlet entitled *Plain Facts*, which Marshall de-scribed as "written for the purpose of asserting the Indian title[.]"[43] The version submitted to the Supreme Court appears to have been the redacted version, re-ferring to land "acquired . . . from any of the Indian princes or governments," and omitting reference to "the Mogul."[44]

Marshall set aside the Yorke-Camden opinion based on the specific question to which it was addressed. Observing that *Plain Facts* acknowledged the opin-ion's concern with the East Indies, Marshall flatly stated, "It is, of course, entirely inapplicable to purchases made in America."[45] *Why*, though, should a statement of English law, in part concerned with the universal applicability of that same law (to "Subjects who carry with them your Majesty's Laws wherever they form Colonies") be "of course, entirely inapplicable"? In each case, the question is whether purchases by English private parties from non-European sovereigns are valid without a grant from the Crown. Why is it obvious that the answer to this question, posed about India, can have no bearing on the question when it is posed about North America?

Supporting his assertion that the Yorke-Camden opinion must be irrelevant, Marshall observed that the terms "'princes or governments' are usually applied to the East Indians but not to those of North America. We speak of their sachems, their warriors, their chiefmen, their nations or tribes, not of their 'princes or governments.'"[46] This is a peculiar point because the fact that the Yorke-Camden opinion was addressed to East India was apparently not in dispute.[47] Marshall's observation rather calls attention to differences in the forms of sovereignty in North America and India. "Princes and governments" are terms characteristically applied to European sovereigns as well as those of India: the terms Marshall imputes to Native Americans suggest less institutionally sophisticated forms of sovereignty, defined by holy men ("sachems"), military leaders ("warriors"), "chiefmen," and ethnic or language groups ("nations or tribes").[48]

The second puzzle concerns the distinction between kinds of customary international law. I will suggest that this distinction matches that between perfect and imperfect sovereigns, gets at the same underlying contrasts, and essentially informs Marshall's reasoning in *Johnson*. The best way to approach this issue, however, is through the second puzzle in the opinion: Marshall's reasons for ruling that the customary international law governing relations between conquering and conquered nations did not apply in North America. As Marshall explained it, "That law which regulates and ought to regulate in general, the relations between the conqueror and the conquered"[49] is "a general rule" that humanity, "acting on public opinion, has established."[50] This law forbade inhumane or oppressive treatment of conquered peoples.[51] More specifically, it directed "that the rights of the conquered to property should remain unimpaired; that the new subjects should be governed as equitably as the old, and that confidence in their security should gradually banish the painful sense of being separated from their ancient connexions, and united by force to strangers."[52]

The first thing to note about this "law" or "general rule" is that as a legal principle it appears to stand on all fours with the rule of discovery that controls the result in *Johnson*: both are principles of customary international law.[53] The rule of discovery, too, was "a principle" which the European powers recognized as "necessary, in order to avoid conflicting settlements, and consequent war with each other, to establish[,] . . . which all should acknowledge as the law by which the right of acquisition . . . should be regulated as between themselves."[54] Marshall argued that the rule of discovery was law because the countries of Europe had recognized and abided by it—just as they had the law of conquest.[55]

The greatest ambivalence in Marshall's opinion concerns his refusal to apply the law of conquest to recognize Native American ownership of tribal lands. He wrote that the "restriction" on Native American rights "may be opposed to natural right and to the usages of civilized nations";[56] it was incompatible with "those principles of abstract justice . . . which are admitted to regulate, in a great degree, the rights of civilized nations, whose perfect independence is acknowledged."[57] The "restriction" in effect subordinated the principle that conquerors must respect the property rights of the conquered to the principle of discovery, "that great and broad rule by which its civilized inhabitants now hold this country."[58] Why did the latter principle carry the day? Was it only a matter of the constraint placed on the courts by the rough facts of expropriation and settlement—the legacy of raw power? Or was it more?

Whether these puzzles or something more basic bothered him, Justice Marshall does not write in *Johnson* like a man entirely satisfied with the reasoning he is constrained to apply. His rather heavy irony suggests a suspicion that his decision is rendered in the final act of a historic tragedy, one whose protagonists are as obtuse as they are culpable. His Europeans are the self-satisfied land grabbers of Diderot's and Montaigne's attacks, and their land grabs form the source of governing law for Marshall's opinion. He hints at a similarly grim view of the U.S. law he himself applies: it is unquestionably the positive law of a sovereign that has succeeded the European powers in claiming North America. That sovereign, moreover, generates the law under which Marshall is a justice and his reasoning a judgment; to depart too far from it would be inconsistent with being a judge of the United States: without his sovereign, a judge is only an opinionated man in a black robe. Nonetheless, Marshall relentlessly implies, the law that inevitably guided his opinion is not just.

Thus, describing the Europeans' early views of North America, Marshall reports, "[T]he character and religion of its inhabitants afforded an apology for considering them as a people over whom the superior genius of Europe might claim an ascendancy. The potentates of the old world found no difficulty in convincing themselves that they made ample compensation to the inhabitants of the new, by bestowing on them civilization and Christianity, in exchange for unlimited independence."[59] An "apology" seeks to vindicate or redeem something that needs it; but the word carries a hint of suspicion, starting with the fact that the redemption is so badly needed. Marshall's portrait of the European "potentates'" reasoning is deliberately removed: Marshall tells us not that they reasoned convincingly, not that they discovered true principles, but that, in the dubious status of being judges in their own cases, they "found no difficulty in convincing themselves" of the justice of conquest and expropriation.[60] This is the weakest endorsement Marshall could have given, if it is an endorsement at all.[61]

The same tone appears when Marshall describes the European colonizers' options on realizing (as he asserts they did) that they could neither assimilate Native Americans nor co-exist with them "as a distinct people," as the customary law of conquest would otherwise have required them to do.[62] These two impossibilities put the Europeans "under the necessity either of abandoning the country, and relinquishing their pompous claims to it, or of enforcing those claims by the sword[.]"[63] Marshall has already told us that such claims originated in a self-interested attempt to escape the traditional bounds of customary international law: at this juncture his insertion of the modifier "pompous" reminds the reader that although these claims have the form and force of law, their origins are in self-serving opportunism.

It is no surprise, then, that even as Marshall applied the law, he endorsed it with only the weak suggestion that "it . . . may, perhaps, be supported by reason" despite however much "it may be opposed to natural right"[64] and "however extravagant the pretension" on which it rested.[65] What gives force to a principle with such indecent origins is its status in the U.S. legal system and way of life: it may win rational assent "if it be indispensable to that system under which the country has been settled[.]"[66] In discussing the categorical power of basic social and historical facts, Marshall was careful to counterpose it to the demands of conscience: "Conquest gives a title which the Courts of the conqueror cannot deny, *whatever the private and speculative opinions of individuals may be, respecting the original justice of the claim which has been successfully asserted.*"[67] I do not think it is over-reading to take this passage as a broad hint that the "private and speculative opinions" are Marshall's own.

Yet to reach the opposite ruling, guided by abstract considerations of justice, would have meant ceasing to be an organ of the American legal system, which relied on the legality of European expropriation for both the coherence of its property system and its claim to legitimate sovereignty. If he had called that expropriation illegal, Marshall would have ceased to act as a federal judge of the United States. His irony was thus an expression of independent conscience that was necessarily without legal consequence.

Yet there is irony within the irony. Marshall did not simply assert the ironist's prerogative of maintaining independent judgment in a world full of corruption and compromise.[68] His expressions of ambivalence came along with a capsule history of North America that was not ironic critique but pragmatic justification of European American policy. Marshall placed this history outside both "extravagant" principles of discovery and "speculative" principles of "natural right." Even as he noted that "we do not mean to engage in the defence of those principles which Europeans have applied to Indian title"—only their application—he hazarded that "they may, we think, find some excuse, if not justification, in the character and habits of the people whose rights have been wrested from them."[69] What does that mean, and how is it different from the "pompous claims" and cruel logic which Europe's potentates had no difficulty convincing themselves to accept? Marshall proposed here to move into the realm of what I earlier called "cultural interpretation" and to find some partial resolution there of the paradoxes and ironies that haunted his reasoning.

TWO DOMAINS OF INTERNATIONAL LAW

Each of the passages I have discussed as sources of puzzles in *Johnson* makes critical use of the term *civilized*. It is natural, reading today, to regard that word as an anachronistic gesture of self-congratulation. If it is that, however, in *Johnson* it is also a legally significant term with meaning for resolution of the case. The effect of Marshall's usage is first to distinguish between civilized nations, "whose perfect independence is acknowledged," and others that have achieved neither civilization nor the corresponding status of perfect independence among other sovereigns, and correspondingly to distinguish between two spheres of principle: those that govern relations *among civilized nations* and, by implication, those that govern relations *between civilized and uncivilized nations*. Thus, to say that a principle governs "the rights of civilized nations" or "the usages of civilized nations" does not imply that the same principle governs colonial relations, and thus that deviation from it means moving into power politics. Rather, *civilized* specifies the relations the principle governs and, conversely, those in which it is inapplicable.

This interpretation draws on Edward Keene's recent work in legal history.[70] Describing the governing concepts of international law in the late eighteenth and early nineteenth centuries, Keene contends:

> Within Europe, the leading purpose of international order was to promote peaceful co-existence in a multicultural world through the *toleration* of other political systems, cultures and ways of life. Its basic principle of respecting dynastic rulers' rights to govern their domestic possessions in their own way, which gradually changed into the principle that each nation had a right to self-determination, was rooted in the beliefs that different cultures were equally valuable and should be given space to flourish; and that the best way to ensure peace in the society of states was to encourage its members to eschew violence for religious, cultural, or ideological reasons. Beyond Europe, however, international order was dedicated to a quite different purpose: the promotion of *civilization*. Simply put, Europeans and Americans believed that they knew how other governments should be organized, and actively worked to restructure societies that they regarded as uncivilized so as to encourage economic progress and stamp out the barbarism, corruption, despotism and incompetence that they believed to be characteristic of most indigenous regimes.

Especially in North America, this was also connected with the idea that the whole continent was an uncultivated wilderness, which needed to be civilized through the establishment of properly ordered settlements[.][71]

This formulation combines two issues that were essentially intertwined: the content of the law governing relations among sovereigns and the source and meaning of diversity among nations. In Keene's account, the central difference between the two domains of international law was that "civilized" countries counted as full sovereigns competent to govern all their own affairs (in Marshall's phrase, their "perfect independence is recognized"), while the governments of uncivilized peoples enjoyed imperfect sovereignty. Their sovereignty was conditional on their level of civilization. As Keene puts it, the "independence of indigenous 'semi-sovereign' rulers was constrained by imperial and moral considerations. Their sovereignty was acknowledged, but they were placed under an obligation to obey the paramount [civilized] power in matters of strategic and military concern. *They were also vulnerable to interventions by the imperial power in order to check the dangers of mis-government that, in European eyes, arose from placing political authority in the hands of uncivilized rulers.*"[72]

The legal powers of imperfect sovereigns were thus constrained by their competence to promote a form of civilization specified by a European theory of historical development. Such sovereigns might be judged to lack competence either materially, in the institutional capacity for complex governance, or as a matter of *character*—individual or, more likely in the older accounts, collective or cultural—the wherewithal to make appropriate political judgments.

This view had little explicit jurisprudential authority in the United States at the time of *Johnson v. M'Intosh*. Writing later in the same decade, James Kent asserted the absolute equality of nations and the principle of noninterference as the bases of international law.[73] Kent nonetheless recited and defended the discovery doctrine in his account of *Johnson v. M'Intosh*, contending that in "the necessity of the case . . . [t]he peculiar character and habits of the Indian nations rendered them incapable of sustaining any other relation with the whites than that of dependence and pupilage."[74] He continued, "There was no other way of dealing with them than that of keeping them separate, subordinate, and dependent, with a guardian care thrown around them for their protection. . . . Indian title was subordinate to the absolute, ultimate title of the government of the European colonists."[75] All this, and the characterization of Native Americans as "domestic, dependent nations" relating to the United States as "a ward to his guardian,"[76] was despite Kent's premise that "as far as Indian nations had formed themselves into regular organized governments within reasonable and definite limits necessary for the hunter state, there would seem [to have been] no ground to deny the absolute nature of their territorial and political rights."[77] In other words, American jurists in this period were more wary than their European counterparts about the authorizing power of "civilization." In *Johnson*, the Supreme Court nonetheless carried out the logic of the dual system of international law, even as Marshall avoided explicitly embracing the hierarchical law of perfect and imperfect sovereigns. The effect of this ambivalence—this hostility to the very logic to which American law was simultaneously capitulating— includes the doctrinal puzzles of Marshall's opinion in *Johnson* and the chief justice's manifest reservations about the status of his own reasoning. American courts did not adopt as law the theory governing colonial relations, but its logic deeply shaped their reasoning.

What was that logic? To account for the superior authority of one country based on its level of "civilization," a theory needed three elements. First it had to provide some account of the interests or rights advanced by "civilization," that is, provide a concept of civilization grounded in basic human interests. For instance, this account might specify certain rights whose violation was a per se justification of intervention to the extent necessary to vindicate those rights. This was the primary strategy of the Dominican jurist Francisco de Vitoria in his (mostly critical) survey of possible justifications for Spanish claims to the Americas.[78] In his account of the legitimacy of British imperial rule in India, John Stuart Mill took a more consequentialist view, concentrating on the idea that all persons everywhere have interests in the progressive development of voluntary institutions and freedom-loving personalities, which, when some peoples are trapped in culturally stagnant despotisms, can be advanced only by the intervention and reform of imperial government.[79] I shall be concentrating on this second type of argument because it is the one most pertinent to the episode of legal history I am exploring, and especially to making sense of *Johnson v. M'Intosh.*

Such an account must also diagnose the failure of the imperfect sovereign to secure or promote the interests or rights at stake. This will, of course, be a more complex task when interests of the sort Mill contends for are at stake than in the relatively clear case of a violation of stipulated rights. In such an argument, there must be some account of *how* the imperfect sovereign has failed to promote or secure the interests of the population. Otherwise, specifying the respect in which the sovereign power has shown itself incompetent and may thus be overridden would be difficult or impossible.

Finally, an account of the prerogative of civilized sovereigns should describe how they can vindicate authoritative rights or interests by taking over certain powers from imperfect sovereigns. Without this, the superior sovereign can only identify failures in the imperfect one; the superior sovereign cannot say—or know how to do—what would vindicate the interests the imperfect sovereign has neglected or betrayed.

An account that accommodated all three elements was widely available at the time of *Johnson*. It followed the four-stages portrait of history, associated with the theory of sociability, and treated property regimes as both diagnostic keys and levers for political action. The causal primacy of property regimes, which we saw in Blackstone's account at the beginning of this book, was thus essential to the legal vision that held imperial jurisprudence together.

PROPERTY IN EAST INDIA: THE CONTEXT OF THE YORKE-CAMDEN OPINION

When Marshall so readily set aside the Yorke-Camden opinion, what exactly did it mean to distinguish land purchases from East Indian sovereigns from land purchases from Native Americans? It meant that East Indian governments occupied a different tier in the hierarchy of sovereigns from that of North American peoples, so that in colonial relations East Indian governments retained the power to dispose of property while North American sovereigns lost it. This distinction had essentially to do with the property regimes of the respective imperfect sovereigns and what, by the lights of then-reigning legal imagination, they revealed about those societies' places along the spectrum of progress toward complexity, prosperity, and freedom.

There is a thin but helpful literature on the British view of property law in the Indian colonies. While I trace some of that literature in the notes, I shall concentrate here on an exemplary discussion of the issue by Lord Cornwallis, governor-general of India from 1786 until 1793 (and again briefly in 1805 until his death). Cornwallis's papers on Indian property regimes during his first governorship[80] were among the formative contributions to the British policy of Permanent Settlement, by which India's British overseers sought to turn a feudal tax-based regime inherited from the decrepit Mogul Empire[81] into the foundations of a modern, fee-simple system of property rights.[82] The regime the British found on arrival was one in which "property" rights amounted to a pyramid of tax-collecting powers.[83] The central government annually set an exaction for the *zemindars*, regional and local administrators and landlords, who in turn exacted from farmers (*ryots*) in their jurisdictions enough tribute to satisfy the zemindars' obligation to the government with as much left over as possible. The economic consequences of this arrangement were widely appreciated among British students of Indian affairs. Uncertainty as to the future tax burden (or rent—the systems were one and the terms used interchangeably) created a strong disincentive to improve the land: there was no guarantee of recouping the gains from improvement rather than seeing them consumed by an increased exaction.[84] Agricultural practice remained stagnant out of a kind of sullen self-defense by landlords and farmers, and there was little effort to develop uncleared lands.[85] This failure of dynamic efficiency meant lesser revenues for the East India Company, which had replaced the Moguls at the top of the tax-farming pyramid. It also became a major humanitarian issue after 1770, when famine devastated Bengal.[86] The famine was widely reported in the British and American press, and it was recognized as a symptom of an unstable and confused system of property rights and consequent inefficient land use.[87]

Lord Cornwallis, like most reformers active in Indian affairs, understood the Permanent Settlement as a way of securing the benefits of a modern property system—chiefly dynamic efficiency in the improvement of land. It seemed clear to him that the feckless industry of India and the arbitrary and tyrannical exactions that ran down the tax-farming pyramid were consequences of the legal regime, not of inherent defects in Indians. As he put it, "The habit which the zemindars have fallen into, of subsisting by annual expedients, has originated, not in any constitutional imperfections in the people themselves, but in the fluctuating measures of Government."[88] Developing this theme in a later response to another reformer who had expressed doubt that the zemindars could catch "a spirit of improvement," Cornwallis insisted, "Mr Shore observes that we have experience in what Zemindars are; but the experience of what they are, or have been, under one system, is by no means the proper criterion to determine what they would be under the influence of another, founded upon very different principles. We have no experience of what the Zemindars would be under the system which I recommend to be adopted."[89] He envisioned a day not far away when "a spirit of improvement is suffused throughout the country" by the influence of a new property regime.[90]

Reformers anticipated several types of benefits from the Permanent Settlement. The first was in the motivation and activity of Indians, the "spirit of improvement," which Cornwallis expected to "render our subjects the happiest people in India."[91] The second lay in *raison d'état*, the development of revenue and economic activity to build the power of the sovereign—in this case, a status divided between the East India Company, whose sovereign power was being increasingly absorbed into Parliament, and local governors and institutions. The new "wealth and prosperity" of the Indians, Cornwallis ventured, "will infallibly add to the strength and resources of the State."[92] Third was in political culture. By binding the interests of property holders to the state that secured their ownership, the Permanent Settlement would create patriotic loyalty rather than the shifting allegiances of those who believed they could get a better deal under another ruler.[93] The fourth lay in the structure of government itself. In Cornwallis's view, a state that depended on annual or otherwise regularly revised taxes tended to impose on its subjects arbitrary and shifting demands that were the defining features of despotism. The government that should secure liberty and promote prosperity instead assumed an inconstant and confiscatory attitude toward the population. India's land regime thus trapped not only landholders but also its state in irregular and counterproductive behavior that Europeans regarded as feudal. A modern land regime depended on a modern state; but just as essentially, a state given a modern land regime to administer would become more capable of assuming the regular and rule-governed activity of modern government.[94] This integrated view of economic and political development, with unmistakable roots in the four-stages theory of property-driven history and social order, oriented the work of imperial reformers. In their minds, it authorized them to identify existing property relations as way stations along the path of progress.

In his papers on Indian reform, Cornwallis treated existing Indian property rights just this way. He acknowledged that on his reading of Indian history, "the Zemindars have the best right"[95] to the land and would be due compensation when the British eliminated "a right that was incompatible with public welfare."[96] Nonetheless, he asserted that even if the zemindars had lacked convincing legal "right" to their lands, "I am also convinced that, failing the claim of right of the Zemindars, it would be necessary for the public good to grant a right of property in the soil to them, *or to persons of their descriptions. I think it unnecessary to enter into any discussion of the grounds upon which their right appears to be founded.*"[97] The zemindars were not uniquely entitled rights holders but participants, even placeholders, in a scheme for progress in the productive use of resources and advancement of the Indian state and society into modernity. The British governors of India were constrained—perhaps by the dimension of rule of law concerned with predictability, perhaps by the claim on fairness of extant rights—from certain dramatic disruptions of existing rights, but the ultimate criterion of British power was "the public good" of India, defined not by any present evidence of Indian opinion on the matter but by a table of human interests considered universal and authoritative.

The indigenous Indian government, then, was envisioned as an imperfect sovereign, blocked by its property law and administrative structure from leading its country into civilization. At the same time, however, Indian government also seemed in many respects commensurable with, though inferior to, a European legal order. The indigenous scheme of property rights was intelligible on analogy with the European feudal order, in which tangled, despotic, and inefficient property rights contained the flawed antecedents of a modern property regime.[98] The civilized sovereign's role, therefore, was not to erase and rewrite the legal facts of India's present but to reform the Indian legal order so as to spur the development of the regime's intrinsic potential—a potential anticipated in Europe's own passage out of feudalism.[99]

What insight does this analysis give us into Marshall's dismissal of the Yorke-Camden opinion? It helps show one-half of the contrast on which his distinction rested. East Indian property rights and sovereigns were not equal to those of Europe—their "perfect independence" was not an axiom of international relations—but they were nonetheless similar enough that transactions in rights between those sovereigns and Britons could take place without the intervention of the British Crown. To understand the full significance of this characterization, it is necessary to examine the American side of the contrast. This means returning to *Johnson v. M'Intosh* in light of the law of colonialism and the Indian example of divided sovereignty structured by a conception of progress made operational by a theory of property regimes.

JOHNSON V. M'INTOSH AGAIN

Let us examine the precise terms of Marshall's judgment that colonizing powers cannot be bound to respect the existing property regimes of Native Americans. This is the heart of his dicta, and the part of his discussion most troubling from the point of view of today's anticolonial sensibility and antiracist principle. Marshall, recall, suggested that "those principles which Europeans have applied to Indian title . . . may . . . find some excuse, if not justification, in the character and habits of the people whose rights have been wrested from them."[100] After explaining the customary international law requiring the conqueror to respect and maintain the property rights of the conquered, Marshall continued, "But the tribes of Indians inhabiting this country were fierce savages, whose occupation was war and whose subsistence was drawn chiefly from the forest. To leave them in possession of their country was to leave the country a wilderness; to govern them as a distinct people, was impossible, because they were as brave and high-spirited as they were fierce, and were ready to repel by arms every attempt on their independence."[101]

There are two distinct arguments in this passage. One is that the fierce independence of Native Americans forbade their political integration into an extended multicultural empire in which their form of life would remain unchanged. The second argument fits squarely into the interpretation I have been developing. The fact that Native Americans' "subsistence was drawn chiefly from the forest" placed them in the hunter-gatherer stage of civilization, marked by rights of personal property and collective use rights over those resources that were not in personal hands. In this stage, according to the four-stages theory, no incentive exists for productive improvement of real property, so to leave the Native American property regime in place "was to leave the country a wilderness." As Blackstone had written, without the institution of private property in land, "the world must have continued a forest," with no incentive for individuals to make agricultural improvements. He maintained that only scarcity, following the exhaustion of resources below the level that could maintain a hunter-gather population, had spurred the recourse to property in land and thence to agriculture; "necessity begat property."[102] Without the bite of necessity, the hunter-gatherer condition could persist indefinitely, and the world "continue a forest."[103]

Europeans thus faced a pair of bad choices. They were, according to Marshall, "under the necessity either of abandoning the country, and relinquishing their pompous claims to it, or of enforcing those claims by the sword, and by the adoption of principles adapted to the condition of a people with whom it was impossible to mix, and who could not be governed as a distinct society."[104] The description of Native Americans as "a people with whom it was impossible to mix" refers again to their alleged special fierceness but also goes to the character of their property regime and its place in the timeline of the four-stages theory. Native American possessory customs were incommensurable with English fee-simple property in land, with its individual rights of use, exclusion, and alienation. The two systems could not be maintained concurrently: to follow one was to overrun and negate the other.[105] In consequence, "That law which regulates, and ought to regulate in general, the relations between the conqueror and conquered, was incapable of application to a people under such circumstances."[106] Europeans therefore had to adopt "principles adapted to the condition of a people with whom it was impossible to mix," that is, principles guiding the interaction of two incommensurable property regimes and correspondingly incompatible social orders and systems of government.[107] The principle selected was the rule of discovery, the exclusive right of the sovereign to extinguish Native American possessory rights and assign fee-simple ownership in the land. Although it may be difficult to see the solution as equitable, Marshall noted, "Every rule which can be suggested will be found to be attended with great difficulty."[108] That much would be hard to deny.

Marshall's reasoning in *Johnson* follows the same formula that Lord Cornwallis and John Stuart Mill had applied to British government in India: the indigenous sovereign power is autonomous to the degree it is competent to promote and secure progress. So far as it is incapable of serving that role, another sovereign may step in to vindicate the values of civilization. In both the Indian and the American cases, the main impediment to progress is imagined as being a property system that keeps the society at a "premodern" stage of development: in India, feudalism characterized by personal dependence and arbitrary government; in America, a semi-nomadic hunter-gatherer condition which produces no wealth and from which no institutions of complex government are likely to emerge.

The difference in the European responses—incorporating the colonial power into the local structure as an agent of reform (as well, of course, as exploitation) versus colonizing the country and displacing the local population—seemed to Marshall to reflect a difference in the range of feasible options. Indian property and governance structures struck Cornwallis as sufficiently like their European analogues to be susceptible to incremental reform from within. Native American property and governance seemed to Marshall to be incommensurable with Europe's institutions and so to present the tragic choice he described: expropriate or leave. To leave was to abandon the cause of progress; expropriation, by contrast, made the colonial sovereign the instrument of progress. Marshall's reasoning thus appears to implement the same customary principle that guided the British theory of rule in India in the Permanent Settlement and beyond. The relative authority of perfect and imperfect sovereigns is ordered by the competence of the imperfect sovereign to promote and secure progress. In turn, property regimes both indicate the society's level of progress and are the instruments of further progress: to understand the Native American property regime was to see why it had to be broken and what should replace it. The four-stages vision of property provided the backdrop to a legal imaginary linking Blackstone, the Scottish Enlightenment, British imperialism in India, and Justice Marshall's understanding of the European claim on North America.

Seeing how this legal imaginary guided Marshall's judgment also illuminates the character of his irony. Marshall retained the traditional prerogative of the ironist: an inner sanctum of conscience not violated by the institutional regime of power and principle in which he outwardly moved. In those outward movements, he presented himself as bound twice over: by law, but just as basically by a vision of history in which that law appeared not just as human achievement but as part of a natural course of development. That perceived constraint may have eased Marshall's partial reconciliation of power and conscience, but in the end it also made conscience impotent, which may account for the sharpness and repetition of his complaints.

A LITTLE MORE IRONY?

In the presuppositions of the opinion, as in much of the explicit thought of the period, is a theory of hierarchy among nations and their governments in which the sovereigns of advanced nations may—even must—supplant the power of backward, imperfect sovereigns. Central to the powers of advanced nations in this conception was remaking the property regimes of subordinate peoples in order to spur economic development and produce the stability necessary to nonarbitrary government. Doing less, it seemed to adherents of this perspective, would mean neglecting the duties of progress: leaving India under despotism and North America an undeveloped "wilderness."

What obviously distinguishes *Johnson* as a human matter is the nature of the policy that the ruling blessed: expropriation of an inhabited continent at the cost—even then becoming increasingly clear—of extinguishing a way of life and most of its people.[109] It is ironic that the opinion depended on the same theory that made possible the freedom-promoting view of property that I praised in Adam Smith's thought and traced in early American reformism. The hierarchy of civilizations that Smith and Blackstone posited guided critical choices in Marshall's reasoning. Perhaps more unsettling, the principles that Marshall took from those jurists remain the cornerstones of reasoning about property law. If today's scholars, lawyers, and legislators did not believe that property regimes should be judged by how well they promote economic efficiency and secure ordered political liberty, we would be at a loss to talk about them at all. Marshall's opinion rests substantially on values we still embrace, albeit in different programmatic versions, and to which we lack compelling alternatives.

This unsettling commonality might encourage us to read Marshall's opinion as revealing something about the limits and hazards of a perspective we substantially share. Because legal judgments are complex and sometimes tragic in their results, and complacency about them always supports moral blindness, no set of guiding principles should be permitted to make inevitable what can only be a matter of decision. This recognition is, in fact, a reclamation of the aspect of modern freedom that understands that we not only make our way within our contexts of mutual benefit; from time to time we make those contexts as well. With that in mind, we might manage to be more ironic in our view of both law and history than Marshall was: more skeptical, more self-questioning, less inclined to conclude that we have resolved matters to everyone's satisfaction and best interest. That would be an ironic benefit of a subtle, complex, and elusive opinion whose evasions do not quite manage to wipe the blood from its hands.

5

MEANINGS OF FREE LABOR

The vision of property and social life we have been tracing found its epitome in the principle of free labor: people own their time, talents, and energy, which they may share by contract but can never sell wholesale to another person. The free-labor principle makes uncoerced consent the basis of all economic relations, in contrast to the "despotic dominion" of the master over the slave or indentured servant. In the vision of free-labor society, we do for one another what we choose to do, and only as much and for as long as we choose. Proponents of free labor took the moral spirit beneath the principle to be one of mutual respect: instead of commanding others, people would learn to win their free assent, creating a complex economic order on the bond of chosen and revocable allegiance.

This was something of a utopian vision, an idea of possible justice and freedom beyond any previous experience. Unregulated commerce had seemed to many at the Putney conference to be an invitation to anarchy, every bit as hazardous as political democracy. Now it promised instead to accomplish a perfect reconciliation of two values that had often seemed to stand in tension: social order and individual freedom. Indeed, it had the double face of all utopian projects: the power to inspire reform coupled with the potential to obscure the complex and obdurate reality of social life, replacing facts with ideological wishes in the all-important operations of law. Free-labor thought had both effects, and its successes and failures alike show the power and the hazards of the freedom-oriented reformist vision it carried.

Despite the promise to reconcile freedom and order, there was conflict all along, not just in the distribution of ownership, but in the very definition of the rights to be distributed. From the point of view of property thought, people are both the potential claimants on resources and themselves resources for one another. The time, energy, and skills of others are as indispensable as material resources to a secure and prosperous life, let alone more subtle goals of fulfillment and recognition. Individuals are the unique site of personhood—the capacity to have interests, lay claims, or achieve dignity. At the same time they are susceptible to literal and, in some measure, unavoidable exploitation.

There is no ahistorical, context-free meaning of personhood.[1] Neither is there any timeless and placeless definition of what counts as a resource or what legal consequences follow from that status.[2] Being a person and being a resource are not freestanding abstractions but conditions that reflect the ideas and activities of living people. In defining rights, then, a legal system does not simply respond to facts about the world that precede the formulations of law—although, of course, it also does that.[3] Rather, the law's designation of certain things as resources and certain qualities in people as elements of personhood helps define both concepts and structure the relationships in which our twin natures, as persons and as resources, find their balance. In this chapter, I refer to legal rules restricting the ways in which people may seek to claim others' resource value as the *rules of recruitment.* I call the background conditions of advantage and disadvantage, or bargaining power, the *circumstances of recruitment.* Together these form the *terms of recruitment.*

I pay special attention to how competing solutions have proposed to integrate the three values I see at the heart of property: negative liberty, welfare, and personality. These correspond to three dimensions of freedom, the central value of modern life: freedom from interference in choices, enjoyment of a rich set of acceptable alternatives for choice which wealth helps to make possible, and development of a personality able to identify, pursue, and revise interests and projects. Various proposals to mediate between resource and personhood as aspects of human beings express conceptions of freedom in which these three dimensions occupy different ranks and are imagined to have different relations to one another. This chapter is also, therefore, an exploration by historical example of some prominent approaches to integrating the dimensions of freedom, with attention to the appeal and limitations of each.

Unlike earlier chapters, in which I considered historical examples in themselves even as I developed the book's larger interpretive argument, in this chapter I use historical material to exemplify one of the book's major theoretical problems: the effort to reconcile the positive dimension of freedom, concerning things that one has the real opportunity to do (often determined by the circumstances of recruitment) with the negative dimension of free choice (the centerpiece of some of free labor's rules of recruitment). That problem preoccupied jurists and political economists in the eighteenth and nineteenth centuries, and their efforts to resolve it reveal something about its perennial character and today's alternatives in confronting it.

PERSONHOOD AND PROPERTY IN U.S. HISTORY

The personhood-resource relationship interacted in different but continuous ways in two property regimes: antebellum slavery and the free-labor employment relations of the later nineteenth century. To some extent, I treat both regimes as ideal types. They contained a wide range of legal relations, and judges and legislatures marshaled multifarious common-law and statutory approaches in both settings.[4] Nonetheless, the ideal-type approach helps concentrate attention on the continuity of the personhood-resource problem between two regimes whose advocates tended to understand them as essentially opposed.

Two broad strategies for understanding slavery as a legal and social relationship predominated during the eighteenth and nineteenth centuries. One, the *conciliatory* model, treated the master-slave relationship as part of a spectrum, analogous to other legal bonds arising from agreement or status. The other, the *anomaly* model, understood slavery as essentially different from other relationships and as resisting both conceptual and practical assimilation to the law of labor relations. As a legal question, this problem often took the form of an inquiry into whether traditional common-law categories could accommodate slavery. As a social question, it tended to produce a debate over the character of the economic relations of nonslave and post-feudal "free labor" societies. Was the principle of private consent that organized free-labor relations so distinctive and antithetical to the slave bond that slavery and free labor were anathema, or did the distinct economic systems constitute a spectrum of relations with common features? The conciliatory approach produced ideologically opposite but analytically similar accounts: a right-wing take that defended slavery as a more honest form of exploitation than labor markets and a left-wing take that attacked the free-labor principle of contract as concealing multifarious relations of exploitation.

The anomaly approach produced a different paradox: insistence on the sharp line distinguishing slavery from free labor encouraged the belief that the free-contract principles Adam Smith and others had pioneered completely captured the meaning of economic freedom. Principles that first arose as tools for securing relatively greater freedom in a reformist spirit became, for some, a dogma that foreclosed reflection on their limits. The dogmatic attitude earned free labor a reputation as a complacent ideology, which obscured its experimental and freedom-promoting spirit.

These issues came to life when courts wrestled with the doctrinal consequences of defining one human being as the property of another. Designating someone as property did not erase that person's humanity as a matter of fact; yet the designation prohibited recognition of full legal personhood, even in a time when that category was considerably more differentiated (by gender, for instance) than it now is.[5] Courts determined in what respects slaves were to be treated as property and in what respects as persons. In doing so, they also determined what each of those categories meant.[6]

Courts across several decades and many jurisdictions formulated the problem as one of drawing a line between personhood and property. "In expounding [the] law," Chief Justice Taney wrote while riding circuit in Virginia in 1859, "we must not lose sight of the twofold character which belongs to the slave. He is a person, and also property."[7] "The laws of Georgia . . . recognize the negro as a man, whilst they hold him property," observed that state's supreme court in 1851.[8] The Supreme Court of Mississippi remarked, "In some respects, slaves may be considered as chattels, but in others, they are regarded as men."[9]

The problem of setting this boundary arose when legal dimensions of personhood came into conflict with the legal incidents of property. Justice Taney's pronouncement in *State v. Amy*,[10] for instance, concerned a claim by a slaveholder that imprisonment of his slave for pilfering from a post office constituted a taking under the Fifth Amendment: although she was criminally liable as a legal person, her status as his property made her imprisonment a deprivation of his ownership claim.[11] More frequently the problem arose from violence against slaves: the question was whether the violence crossed lines of immunity slaves held under their legal personhood or instead fell within the owner's power to manage his property.[12] The issue was particularly acute in labor discipline: how far could a master go in coercively extracting a slave's labor? Some judges argued that there was no inherent conflict between personhood and property in human beings, only some avoidable problems arising from masters' overreaching.[13] A model of this approach appears in the dissent in *Commonwealth v. Turner*,[14] argued before the General Court of Virginia in 1827.[15] The majority upheld a master's demurrer to an indictment "for cruelly beating his own slave."[16] They based their acceptance of the demurrer on the existence of a state statute, passed in 1788, that forbade the killing of a slave as of a freeman.[17] As the majority observed, that statute replaced two far more permissive laws, a 1669 statute exculpating any master "for killing his slave under correction for resistance" and a 1723 statute extending the same immunity to a master killing a slave "for any offence whatever."[18] Noting that the common law had not recognized the slave relationship, and thus did not regulate it, the court reasoned that the 1788 statute must represent the extent of slaves' statutory protection from their masters' discipline. Any further constraint would have to come from the common law, but the common law was silent. For courts to enforce common-law restrictions on the master beyond statutory law would be judicial overreach.[19]

In dissent, Judge Brockenbrough argued that the common law contained principles of labor discipline to govern other status relationships that courts could properly extend to reconcile the personhood of slaves with their status as property. "The slave was not only a *thing*, but a *person*," he wrote,[20] "and this well-known distinction would extend its protection to the slave as a person, *except so far as the application of it conflicted with the enjoyment of the slave as a thing.*"[21] Brockenbrough proposed that this formula simply applied to slavery the same standard that the common law imposed on the disciplinary actions of other status superiors against their subordinates, such as parent to child, tutor to pupil, and, above all, master to servant: discipline must fall within "bounds of due moderation."[22] In Brockenbrough's formula, permissible discipline included "every power which was necessary to enable the master to use his property," including sale of the slave and "correct[ion] . . . for disobedience."[23] Severe beatings, however, were as a matter of law unnecessary to labor discipline and thus outside the "bounds of due moderation."[24] Permissible discipline was restricted to what was necessary to manage people in their status as things. When a master overstepped these bounds, the law could regard the slave as a person and offer the protection of the criminal common law. On this reasoning, Brockenbrough satisfied himself that he could "see no incompatibility between this degree of protection [of the slave's legal personhood] and the full enjoyment of the [master's] right of property."[25]

The Tennessee Supreme Court took a similar view in *James v. Carper*, an 1857 trespass action by a master against a man who had rented his slave, then beaten the slave severely upon false allegations that he had stolen money from a white transient in the neighborhood.[26] The defendant argued that the master's inherent right to punish the slave had transferred to him when the master leased the slave, and the trial court accepted this view.[27] The Supreme Court disagreed, declaring that the master's general right of punishment against the slave was among "certain peculiar rights" that attached inherently to the master-slave relationship, "as to the various other domestic relations."[28] The rights of such status-based relationships were not transferable by a contract for services.[29] The renter was thus liable to the master for harm to the slave.

The court nonetheless undertook its own inquiry into the problem of labor discipline and slavery. This inquiry followed the logic of Brockenbrough's proposal that courts could reconcile personhood and property status by limiting punishment to acts necessary for the management of human property. Someone who rented a slave, the court argued, "must of necessity be regarded as possessing the right to inflict reasonable corporal punishment on the slave, for insubordination, disobedience of lawful demands, wanton misconduct, or insolent behavior."[30] Such corporal punishment was not status based in the same sense as the master's inherent power to punish but was bounded by the functional requirements of extracting labor from an unfree human being. The court acknowledged the vagueness of this power and its dependence on the circumstances of any particular act of discipline, noting that "the hirer must always, at his peril, be able to show that there existed reasonable ground for the chastisement, and that it did not, either in the extent or manner of it, exceed the bounds of moderate correction."[31] Moderation was, of course, relative to the task of compelling human beings to conduct themselves as property.

This judicial approach to reconciling slavery with other law-governed relations had much in common with arguments made on the losing side in *Somerset v. Stewart*, the 1773 English case in which Lord Mansfield declared that a slave brought to London from Virginia by his master became free.[32] That case, like the American cases just discussed, was an exercise in common-law interpretation. Positive law in England was silent on slavery, so the question was whether the common law would recognize ownership of a slave imported from a jurisdiction where positive law did establish it. The argument that slavery was compatible with common-law principles proceeded, like Brockenbrough's, by analogy between slavery and other recognized legal relationships. Lawyers for Stewart, the slave owner, stressed the analogy between slavery and servitude, identifying both as law-governed relationships constituted by the relative rights of the parties.[33] They took pains to identify their opponents as anomalists, who imagined the common law as embodying principles of freedom "asserted as a natural right."[34] But in fact, they insisted, "there is no branch of this right, but in some places at all times, and in all places at different times, has been restrained: nor could society otherwise be conceived to exist."[35] By identifying all legal relationships as matters of relative rights, and the idea of an absolute standard of freedom as incompatible with social order, they prepared the way to assimilate slavery as a particularly asymmetric instance of the same logic of relative rights.

Stewart's lawyers made two other kinds of conciliatory arguments. These involved relations between slave and nonslave societies. The first pressed the analogy between servitude and slavery, imagining the plight of a servant's master who, on arriving in England, discovered that his employee would no longer prepare his dinner or drive his coach, the border crossing having annulled their relationship.[36] Countries with trade relations and mobile populations conventionally recognize one another's legally constituted relations even if subjects of one country cannot, among themselves, legally enter into some of the relationships that foreigners may transport across the border.[37] Thus even if a particular type of French servitude contract were technically invalid in England, or the basis of a French marriage would not constitute English matrimony, neither relationship would be dissolved on Dover Beach. The idea that slavery should be similarly recognized appealed both to comity and to the practical reality of an increasingly integrated and mobile Atlantic population whose commerce was inextricable from the slave trade and slave labor.[38]

Stewart's lawyers also argued that to reject slavery would display undue cultural arrogance. Somerset had been enslaved in Africa, and whether as a criminal penalty, a way of enforcing a debt, or a consequence of imprisonment in war, "the law of the land of that country disposed of him as property[.]"[39] That his enslavement could not have arisen under English law was no reason to disregard the law of another country: "We are apt . . . to call those nations . . . whose internal policy we are ignorant of, barbarians. . . . [U]nfortunately, from calling them barbarians, we are apt to think them so, and draw conclusions accordingly."[40] As Stewart's lawyers painted the matter, this was empty self-congratulation, incompatible with the flexible spirit of the common law. As legal relations were relative within legal systems, so they were relative across systems, and the business of the law was to integrate them to the greatest degree possible, not to draw categorical distinctions between valid and invalid classes of relations.

Other courts, while equally committed to the legality of slavery, regarded the conciliatory approach as a pleasant delusion. In their analysis of the slave relationship, the brutality inherent in extracting unfree labor practically annulled any protection of personhood in the slave. In the mercilessly reasoned case of *State v. Mann*,[41] a North Carolinian shot and wounded a slave whom he had rented as she fled after he chastised her for "some small offence."[42] Unlike the court in *James*, Justice Ruffin in *Mann* held that a renter of a slave had exactly the same power of labor discipline as a master.[43] This was so because the master's power was not part of "domestic relations," such as parent-child and master-apprentice ties, but a legally unique relationship governed by the functional requirements of labor discipline. Because those requirements were the same for the renter as for the master, labor discipline had the same bounds in both situations.[44]

Ruffin's rejection of the domestic-relations analogy was critical to his break with the conciliatory approach. On his account, status-based domestic relations had as their purpose the improvement and eventual emancipation of the dependent party, as with children, or an idea of mutual advantage and obligation, as with servants. "With slavery it is far otherwise," Ruffin wrote.[45] "The end is the profit of the master, his security and the public safety."[46] The slave's legal protections, if any, should be defined purely by reference to these ends, with no independent dimension of personhood. For Justice Ruffin the question of the master's authority was entirely one of effective exploitation.

For Ruffin the slave presented a uniquely difficult problem in these terms because he was a conscious agent who, although legally unfree, retained free will. As a slave, denied any share of what he produced, he had no incentive to work except bare survival. He was "doomed . . . to live without knowledge, and without the capacity to make any thing his own, and to toil that another may reap the fruits."[47] The master faced a particular challenge in extracting productive labor from a human being in that position. When laborers have no affirmative incentive to work, because they have no prospect of improving their situation, "obedience is the consequence only of uncontrolled *authority over the body. There is nothing else which can operate to produce the effect. The power of the master must be absolute, to render the submission of the slave perfect.*"[48] The slave's only incentive was avoiding cruel treatment. That cruelty had to be potentially unbounded because anything less would give the slave a sticking point, where he might choose a known measure of suffering over labor with no prospect of reward. Such "discipline" was thus "inherent in the relation of master and slave," not because of the relationship's status quality—the quality in which Brockenbrough had identified "inherent" terms in the relationship—but because of the functional necessities of disciplining unfree labor.[49] The doctrinal result was a massive effacement of any legal personhood in the slave, an effacement justified as the functional requirement of rendering the slave valuable as property.[50]

Ruffin's analysis was specific to the common-law dimension of the issue. The legal stakes of his argument involve the proper role of courts, not the character of slavery as such. Nonetheless, his style of anomalist reasoning found ironic resonance with strands of legal and political opposition to slavery, which were built around the view that such a distinctively brutal and boundless form of interpersonal power violated implicit principles of freedom, reciprocity, or humanitarianism that structured other legal bonds. Thus for the opponents of slavery in *Somerset v. Stewart*, the claim that England enjoyed "air too pure for slaves to breathe it" meant "the laws, the genius and spirit of the constitution . . . forbid the approach of slavery. . . . [O]ur mild and just constitution is ill adapted to the reception of its arbitrary maxims and practices."[51] "Constitution" here signifies the British sense of the word: the governing spirit discernible in the whole body of legal practices and principles that constitute common and positive law. The contrast of a "mild and just" spirit with "arbitrary maxims and practices" proposes a view of that constitution as embodying a version of fairness in private-law relations that the unbounded, "arbitrary" power of a master over a slave contradicts. In England, argued Somerset's lawyer Francis Hargrave, "freedom is the grand object of the law."[52]

The incompatibility was not just conceptual but practical. If the slave relationship could enter England, then forms of discipline that common-law relations disallowed would enter as well, affecting the morals of the country. John Alleyne, also arguing for Somerset, warned that "horrid cruelties . . . perpetrated in America, might, by the allowance of slaves among us, be introduced here."[53] He urged his listeners to envision "a wretch bound for some trivial offence to a tree, torn and agonizing beneath the scourge"—the kinds of punishments that courts approved in *Commonwealth v. Turner* and *State v. Mann*.[54] If such punishments ever became the norm, Alleyne ventured, England might lose its "liberal ingenuous temper," its "feelings of humanity," and the "generous sallies of free minds[.]"[55]

In these common-law slavery cases, personhood and resources entwine in single bodies of law, in single cases, above all in the slaves themselves, who stand in some respects as legal persons and in others as mere resources for the use of their owners. Courts and lawyers struggled with these two aspects of human beings: as persons with responsibilities, aims, and immunities of their own, and as resources whose efficient use required powers of control in those whose property they were. For some, slavery was in every respect an opposite principle to that of free labor: opposed in its underlying theory of property in persons, in the pattern of interpersonal relations it set in train, and in the values it inculcated and those it discouraged. The conciliatory lawyers and judges, by contrast, regarded the contrasting systems of property in human labor as points along a spectrum, which able use of the law could integrate.

FROM LAW TO POLITICAL ECONOMY: THEORIES OF SLAVERY AND FREE LABOR

Slavery and feudalism are often treated separately, in large part because American discussions are shaped by the experience of American slavery, with its basis in racial distinction. Feudalism, as a hierarchical arrangement of social and economic roles *within* an ethnic community, can seem quite a different thing.[56] The thinkers presented here, however, regarded the systems as so similar as to be continuous with each other.[57] These thinkers were opponents of slavery and feudalism and advocates of a commercial alternative based on voluntary contract, the right of exit, and the free sale of labor.[58] In linking slavery and feudalism, they classified both systems by what I call the terms of recruitment—the rules by which one may enlist and govern the activity, in this case the labor, of another. They understood the basic features of recruitment in slave and feudal societies to be command backed by threat. In commercial or free-labor societies, as they understood the contrast, the basic terms were negotiation and consent. These terms, in turn, were thought to produce distinct social relations with consequences for individual character and political culture.

Various thinkers presented these themes in different ways. In a particularly stark account, the economic historian and antislavery theorist Richard Hildreth (he wrote a history of American banking) described relations between slaves and masters as founded purely on the threat of violence. For Hildreth slavery extended a "state of war" into social life: the master extracted labor from the slave on the basis of a direct threat to the slave's life.[59] A subtler explanation came from Adam Smith. Smith recognized the possibility of sympathy and reciprocity between masters and slaves under certain circumstances.[60] Nonetheless, Smith's account of the slave bond had the same core as Hildreth's: the master's prerogative was in principle absolute, requiring only orders, not negotiation. Mortal threat lurked in the background.[61] In this account, then, slave and feudal relations had two defining features. First they were either immediately or ultimately founded on a threat to survival: a villein or slave obeyed the master's will in order to live. Second, even where legal constraint stayed the master's hand from actual violence, the slave's legally protected options were so restricted that the master had no need to appeal to the interests of the slave to induce obedience. Command alone sufficed because the slave had no right to refuse a command or end the relationship.

There is an unavoidable difficulty in approaching this issue through the thought of anti-slavery propagandists. On one hand, Smith's thought and that of his copartisans is a form of social inquiry concerned with how economic and legal regimes shape concrete social interactions among persons, which in turn shape individual psychology and cultural attitudes. On the other, it is polemic, strenuously presenting one side of a hotly contested argument. But examining the thought of partisans is the best way of knowing what those who participated in the debates regarded as the most forceful arguments. Recurrent appeal to certain values (voluntarism and reciprocity over coercion and legally enshrined hierarchy) and empirical claims (that the way people recruit one another affects the psychological and cultural viability of these values) forms a picture of the legal imagination in which the arguers operated.

It was a major part of the argument against slavery that its terms of recruitment psychologically shaped both masters and slaves, training the masters in tyranny and the slaves in abasement.[62] Smith contended that masters' lifelong experience of giving orders that their subordinates could not refuse led slaveholders to prize "domination and tyrannizing" over even wealth.[63] Opponents argued that both slave and feudal regimes produced such personalities.[64] As Hildreth put it, "Habituated to play the tyrant at home, unshackled regent and despotic lord upon his own plantation, where his wish, his slightest whim, is law, the love of domineering possesses all [the master's] heart."[65]

Partisans of free labor argued that this unbounded authority over another human being was the source of what Hildreth described as an ungoverned southern planter personality: given to fierce anger, alcoholism, and spendthrift habits—in short, made chaotic by an experience of social relationships in which nothing checked the expression of appetite and whim.[66] For Hildreth and others, such personalities inhibited the rise of a commercial economy because the ir-regular and domineering southern character was ill-suited to the steady and self-denying habits of accumulation and production that free-labor theorists saw as keys to industry and commerce.[67] Tyrannical personalities were also ill-suited to a conception of democratic society that required a measure of mutual regard among citizens and a willingness to pause, listen, debate, and compromise.[68]

That the argument took this form shows how deeply the antislavery theorists worked within the tradition of political economy that Adam Smith exemplifies, in which preferences, values, and commitments are regarded as endogenous to legal institutions and the economic and social transactions they frame. As we shall see, the antislavery theorists' affirmative view of free-labor society reflected the same debt. It fell to them and, especially, their ideological descendants after abolition to confront the complexity and even contradiction in that vision.

The antislavery and antifeudal position was also a promarket one. Abolition-ists were by and large partisans of free labor, understanding the voluntary labor market as the antithesis of mortal threat.[69] In endorsing commercial society, the critics of slavery endorsed several interlinked values, including the dignity of labor, opportunity and mobility, and the idea of the equality of persons—and, of course, the increase in social wealth that markets were expected to produce.[70]

Readers will recall that Smith and Americans influenced by him, including conservatives such as James Kent, regarded opportunity, mobility, and negotia-tion as training people in self-respect and respect for others. Free labor meant that to recruit another as a resource, one had to appeal to that other's person-hood, addressing the interest and self-conception of the other. For its advocates, commercial society honored rank and power less than the capacity to do one's work well, a source of dignity that could stand open to all in a society of widely shared opportunity. Richard Hildreth wrote the abolitionist tract *Despotism in America* half as praise of the commercial society that slave economies opposed and impeded.

There was an important difference between Smith and many later opponents of slavery, notably Hildreth and the American abolitionist and constitutional theorist Lysander Spooner.[71] Hildreth and Spooner regarded slavery as a violation of natural rights and a poisonous anomaly in the economic order. As we have seen, Hildreth described the master-slave relationship in Lockean terms, as a unique protrusion into civil society of the state of war, an extra-political and nearly lawless relationship of relentless antagonism.[72] Spooner argued that the assertion of the Declaration of Independence that "all men are created equal" expressed a constitutional commitment to individual liberty that should imply the immediate emancipation of all slaves.[73] For figures such as these, slavery was the antithesis of free and legitimate relations. As we shall see, this view had some affinity with the idea that abolition was not only necessary but also sufficient for a free and legitimate order.

Smith's position was somewhat more subtle than these. He yielded nothing to his abolitionist successors in his disdain for slavery: as we have seen, he told his law students that if the great modern achievements of political freedom and growing prosperity increased slavery, it would be morally appropriate to forgo these "blessings."[74] He believed, however, that as a legal and social institution, slavery was susceptible to the same kinds of analysis as any other economic regime. It engaged sympathy and emulation, the appetites for glory and domination, the capacity for moral indifference; so did free labor, and so would any other regime. Smith's argument for free labor was that it set up relatively reciprocal relations that gave a relatively humane turn to each of these qualities. This way of setting out the contrast had a particular advantage: while slavery was just as evil in Smith's account as in any other, the way he presented that evil did not imply that abolishing slavery would end all evils of the same sort. Instead, it presented slavery as a uniquely bad way of addressing a set of problems that would arise under any regime of property in human labor: the terms of recruitment and their consequences in human relations and self-understanding.

Defenders of slavery did not lack for arguments of their own in political economy. George Fitzhugh, a major antebellum apologist for American slavery, argued that no stable economic order could emerge from free-labor principles. The voluntary arrangements of free and equal individuals could not produce a humane economic order, nor could they sustain political liberty. Fitzhugh argued that the premises of free labor mistook the most basic features of human nature and social life and ended up blessing as "freedom" what was in fact a grotesque parody of social relations.

Fitzhugh is best known for his 1856 assault on free labor and defense of slavery, *Cannibals All!* He made the same arguments more systematically and in mildly less theatrical fashion in *Sociology for the South; or, The Failure of Free Society*, which appeared in 1854. The arch-villain of that work is Adam Smith, whom Fitzhugh attacked for allegedly making self-interest the sole valid motive in social life. Smith's "morality . . . of simple and unadulterated selfishness," Fitzhugh wrote, created an economic war of all against all and begot "another war in the bosom of society still more terrible than this[:] capital against labor."[75] Free society was a moral disaster because it threw aside the duties of charity and mutual aid, leaving the sick, the old, the widowed, and other vulnerable people on the brink of starvation. It was a political disaster, a self-consuming system, putting labor and capital in open conflict and producing the sorts of clashes that had shaken Europe in the first half of the nineteenth century, particularly the revolutions of 1848. The only way to overcome these moral failings and avoid the abyss of class war was to acknowledge the unpleasant truth that capital and labor require each other, that people always and necessarily seek to command the productive capacities of others, and that the idea of a "free" economy thus simply masked a new regime of exploitation.

Fitzhugh's core argument was that humans' ineradicable nature as resources sharply constrains any ideal of nonexploitative freedom. "'Property in man,'" he wrote, using the term typically attached to slavery, "is what all are struggling to obtain."[76] Leisure, pleasure, and production depended on securing the bodies, talent, and time of others, and much of social life was simply the effort to do this, structured by whatever rules the law set out. Free labor made all men formally equal as self-owning, voluntary contractors, and "equals must from necessity be rivals, antagonists, competitors, and enemies."[77] By instituting this relationship of indifference and antagonism amid extremely unequal endowments of wealth, free labor created a terrible world: "Capital exercises a more perfect compulsion over free laborers than human masters over slaves; for free laborers must at all times work or starve[.]"[78]

Up to this point, Fitzhugh's argument echoed that of many left-wing critics of laissez-faire economics. His distinctive turn was to endorse slavery as the most honest and humane response to the fallen human estate. Slavery, he contended, acknowledged interdependence and set up a code of reciprocal obligation—slaves labor and the master provides for them, even in illness or old age—that transforms exploitation into a moral and social relationship. Fitzhugh's account of slavery was stereotypical apologetics: he portrayed beneficent masters in harmony with their grateful human property. What distinguished his argument was the contention that slavery was the only economic institution compatible with social order under the conditions of industrial modernity. Between the poles of the inhumane and self-immolating free market and unworkable or authoritarian socialism lay the ancient wisdom of slavery, which Fitzhugh sometimes called the one true and possible socialism.[79]

Although Fitzhugh was idiosyncratic in some respects, he was no intellectual isolate. In their massive study of the ideology of southern slaveholders, *The Mind of the Master Class*, Elizabeth Fox-Genovese and Eugene Genovese argue that before the Civil War a social and political worldview coalesced around the themes set out by Fitzhugh and other antiliberals.[80] In this worldview the trajectory of modern liberty, admirably set in motion by the moderate parliamentarians of the English Civil War and continued in the American Revolution's defense of property rights and national sovereignty, had gone off course during and after the French Revolution.[81] Emancipating politics began as an extension of ordered liberty, above all the rights of private property, but had come to challenge all forms of authority and social order. Seeing in the free-labor society of the North the same currents of social conflict and radical thought that had shaken Europe, southerners defending the slave system came increasingly to regard it as the viable and realistic middle way between tyranny and anarchy: a system of explicit and reciprocal obligation, in which the myth of freedom and equality yielded to differentiated roles, each with its own share of duties, entitlements, and status.

THE PARADOXES OF FREE LABOR AND CONSTRAINT

The master-slave relationship was legally erased by the Thirteenth Amendment, and the Fourteenth Amendment's guarantee of due process became, in the decades after the Civil War, the keystone of jurisprudence concerning the relation between personhood and property that expressed the free-labor idea of personhood, property, and social life.[82] The organizing principle of this new relation was a property rule: energy, time, and talent—in a word, labor—were defined as inherently the property of the person in whose body they resided.[83] They were alienable, but only at retail, not wholesale.[84] Workers could sell their time and energy or the products of their labor; but they could not sell themselves into slavery, in which their labor power belonged outright to another.[85] All labor relations were thus bounded by the right of exit: as the ultimate owners of their labor, workers could take it elsewhere when presented with a better bargain or mired in an intolerable arrangement.[86]

Free labor has received a variety of historical interpretations, with the modern anchor being Eric Foner's classic study *Free Soil, Free Labor, Free Men*.[87] My interpretation in this chapter is largely Foner's. William E. Forbath describes a contrasting version identified with the American republican inheritance and the

mid-nineteenth-century labor movement, which equated free labor with ownership of the means of production or at least a right to enjoy the fruits of one's
labor.[88] Like some other historians interested in lost strands of Progressive aspiration in American politics, Forbath regards the latter tradition as democratic
and cooperative, the former as effectively, if not intentionally, an apology for the
often merciless relations of nineteenth-century capitalism.[89] Foner also notes the
existence of this strain of free-labor thought. While it is real and important, it
does not figure directly in the doctrinal developments that form the core of this
discussion, so I do not elaborate it here.

There has also been considerable work on the origins of free-labor ideas. Forbath, for instance, traces the triumph of the liberal version of free-labor thought
to several strains of political culture in the Gilded Age.[90] One is the rise of industrial capitalism in the North and the resulting presence of a powerful community of interest in employers anxious not to be restricted in their contracts with
employees.[91] Another is the prominence in the bar, particularly the judiciary, of
elite lawyers who had previously been employed by these corporations and were
shaped by experience and association to identify with their interests.[92] A third
is an ideological transformation by which many formerly populist Jacksonians,
who had begun their political careers as enemies of monopolies and politically
favored banks, came to see labor unions and regulation-friendly legislatures as a
new generation of "monopolistic" barriers to the economic liberty of ordinary
people.[93] In this way a populist tradition of economic liberty melded with the
interests of a growing class of large employers.

I do not grapple further with these important debates about the sources and
character of free-labor thought. Instead, I treat free labor as an ideal type, defined
by the property rule of self-ownership and sale at retail only, always bounded
by exit. This presentation captures essential features of free labor as it appeared
in jurisprudence and political economy, but necessarily omits significant varia-
tions. Regarded as an ideal type, free labor marked a basic change in the rules of
recruitment. It lifted the threat to survival or bodily integrity that had been the
backdrop of the slaveowner's prerogative.[94] Although workers might be seriously
constrained in their alternatives, they could not be kept in place by any threatened consequence more severe than denial of their part of the bargain they were
offered.[95]

Free-labor thought thus seemed to dissolve the paradox of slavery jurisprudence: how to regard a human being as both a person and an object of property. The free-labor solution eliminated half the paradox by making personhood
legally incompatible with belonging to another. By the same token, the free-labor
solution assimilated property in oneself to personhood: self-ownership became

a feature of legal personality under the Constitution. The claim of individuals to their own productive capacity was as ultimate and absolute as the master's claim on the slave's body had been in Ruffin's version of the common law.

In the aftermath of the Civil War, partisans of free labor praised it as "the noblest principle on earth" and called freedom of contract "the foundation of civilization," a perfect reconciliation of "free choice and social order."[96] The promise of free labor to solve this problem accounts for much of its nearly millenarian appeal. That vision, however, cloaked the often violent and almost uniformly exploitative terms on which former slaves returned to dependent agricultural labor.[97] Even where it succeeded on its own terms, moreover, the newly regnant principle did not resolve the relation between a human being's nature as a person and status as a resource. Instead the problem shifted, though it remained one of labor discipline. The question now came to be: On what terms can one extract labor from people who own themselves? The old problem was defining the limits of overt coercion between a free master and an unfree slave. The new problem was to set the limits of bargaining among free persons. In seeking to hire another, what might one demand of that person, what might one offer, and what might one threaten?

The point here is not the cynical claim that free labor reproduced the slave relationship in "wage slavery" (although some southern labor contracts, particularly for former slaves, severely restricted the right to quit and otherwise fostered the nearest thing possible to the relationship that the Thirteenth Amendment had abolished). Nor should treating slavery through the same theoretical lens as contractual relations diminish the recognition of slavery as a historically unique wrong. But there is a fundamental problem wherever law regulates control over the productive capacity of others. Although legal change can shape the relationship in practically and morally significant ways, the issue persists.

In the following discussion I explore two strands of free-labor jurisprudence, one rooted in the Civil War amendments to the Constitution, the other in the common law of labor relations. The constitutional strand is particularly associated with *Lochner v. New York*,[98] in which the Supreme Court struck down New York's maximum-hours statute for bakers as a violation of a laissez-faire "right of contract" grounded in the Fourteenth Amendment.[99] That interpretation of the Fourteenth Amendment was derived from a discussion of the constitutional significance of property rights in an earlier case, *Holden v. Hardy*,[100] where the Supreme Court rejected a similar constitutional challenge and upheld a Utah maximum-hours law for miners. In *Holden*, Justice Brown began his analysis of the Fourteenth Amendment with the observation that the Amendment's phrase "due process of law" traditionally included the principle that property, "or right to property, shall [not] be taken for the benefit of another, or for the benefit of the state, without compensation."[101] He then proposed a corollary of that principle: if the Due Process Clause protects existing property rights, it must also protect the right to acquire property. A prohibition on this right "would also be obnoxious to the same provision,"[102] for it would permanently exclude those who presently lack property from all the benefits of ownership. In a third step, Justice Brown derived the right to contract from the right to acquire property: "[A]s property can only be legally acquired, as between living persons, by contract, a general prohibition against entering into contracts with respect to property, or having as their object the acquisition of property, would be equally invalid."[103] The right to contract was therefore derived, at two stages' remove, from the Due Process Clause's protection of property rights.

Two essential ideas marked this reasoning. The first was that the right to property, including ownership of one's own labor, was not mainly a right to static enjoyment of what one already had. Rather, property rights were instruments for participation in a world of free exchange and self-improvement. Merely to protect existing property claims without setting in motion the churn of contractual exchange would obliterate the social purposes of property: mobility and opportunity.[104] The second idea was that the property governed by this rationale included the labor power of individuals. Legal personhood was marked by the power to acquire and transfer property, including labor itself, a power which courts rendered as the right of contract. In this way freedom of contract became the keystone right in the free-labor theory of self-ownership: it was, in effect, the power to transfer the property one intrinsically held in oneself. This derivation demonstrates the debt of free-labor jurisprudence to the social imaginary in which modern property ideas have their origin: a vision of mobility and circulation in a sociability-based economic order of mutual benefit. The property rights that Justice Brown envisioned were constitutive of that order, and their constitutional dimension was protection of the characteristic social relations of that order, free contract for labor.

The contract right, though, was qualified by two considerations. One was protection of the health and welfare of certain classes of workers. This judicial concern arose from the idea that people were in certain respects state resources, and the demands of private industry must not degrade them past being able to reproduce and fight wars, two functions the justices imagined a state as entitled to require of its citizens. Thus in *Holden*, the Court held that even though a miner might consent to work until his health broke, "The state still retains an interest in his welfare, however reckless he may be. . . . [W]hen the individual health, safety, and welfare are sacrificed or neglected, the state must suffer."[105] Dissenting in

Lochner, Justice Harlan defended New York's statute on the grounds that long hours of work "may endanger the health and shorten the lives of the workmen, thereby diminishing their physical and mental capacity to serve the state."[106] In *Muller v. Oregon*,[107] upholding a maximum-hours law for female employees, Justice Brewer wrote that "as healthy mothers are essential to vigorous offspring, the physical well-being of a woman becomes an object of public interest and care in order to preserve the strength and vigor of the race"—that is, women must be healthy enough to bear children.[108] Oregon's maximum-hours law was thus "not imposed solely for [women's] benefit, but also largely for the benefit of all."[109] These claims expressed an important element of thought about the relation between self-ownership and the claims of others on the resource of one's body.

The second consideration returns to the core of this chapter: the negotiation between personhood and property in the limits of permissible labor discipline. Free labor notionally solved this question by way of self-ownership: the terms of labor were always products of free agreement, never coerced in the manner of slave relations. The difficulty was that parties reached agreement in light of the extent and intensity of their need and the other options open to them. Depending on these factors, the decision "freely" to accept a set of terms could be either a choice among meaningful alternatives or an empty choice between a single tolerable option and privation. The slaveowner's offer to the slave was something worse than a Hobson's choice; it was a Hobbes's choice: obey or be punished. Free labor repudiated this arrangement, but it left open the possibility of a Hobson's choice: a choice that was no choice at all because made among meaningless alternatives. The new problem was how to determine when, if ever, exigent circumstances so constrained the "free" laborer's decision that the contract was not a product of genuine choice but instead equivalent to coercion—the very thing free labor forbade.

In the pro-regulatory opinion of *Holden v. Hardy*, Justice Brown laid out the problem that unequal bargaining power posed for free labor: "[T]he proprietors of these establishments [mines and smelting works] and their [employees] do not stand upon an equality, and . . . their interests are, to a certain extent, conflicting. The former naturally desire to obtain as much labor as possible from their employ[e]es, while the latter are often induced by the fear of discharge to conform to regulations which their judgment, fairly exercised, would pronounce to be detrimental to their health or strength. In other words, the proprietors lay down the rules and the laborers are practically constrained to obey them. In such cases self-interest is often an unsafe guide, and the legislature may properly interpose its authority."[110] The essential threat open to the employer was Brown's "discharge." Firing was enshrined in the logic of free labor, the corollary of the power to quit. The practical question was how hard a bargain the employer could drive. When a worker with a bleak set of options would take a bad offer rather than be fired, the free-labor vision of autonomy within interdependence could become a hollow ideal.

The Supreme Court's justices argued most aggressively that hard circumstances could annul free choice in a decision apt to strike the modern eye as most unpalatable for other reasons: a sex-based defense of a maximum-hours law for women in *Muller v. Oregon*.[111] Justice Brewer noted that the women of Oregon had been granted "equal contractual and personal rights with men," and thus in economic life "they stand on the same plane as the other sex."[112] This formal equal liberty, however, did not mean that the logic of free-labor jurisprudence applied alike to men and women. On the assumption that women were less physically able than men, and thus at a competitive disadvantage in the labor market, the Court found that "from the viewpoint of the effort to maintain an independent position in life, [women are] not upon an equality."[113] Rather, formal liberty took its substance—choice among meaningful alternatives—only "where some legislation to protect her" was provided "to secure a real equality of right."[114] The distinction between formal equality and "a real equality of right" bespoke the line courts sought to draw between the circumstances in which labor agreements expressed free choice and those in which they reflected choice among such straitened alternatives that "real equality" gave way to unjust exploitation.

Particularly strong judicial commitment to the employer's power to extract concessions with the threat of firing came not in *Lochner*-era substantive due process but in a contemporaneous line of common-law Massachusetts Supreme Court decisions. Those cases addressed employees' injuries in hazardous workplaces where they had remained, after objecting to a manifest risk, only because they decided that the certainty of firing was worse than the probability of being hurt. The circumstances these cases address constitute the troubled border between the positive and negative dimensions of freedom—between free labor's rules of recruitment and the circumstances in which bargaining takes place.

Massachusetts applied a common-law version of free-labor principles, holding that when employees accepted a hard bargain they ratified all its consequences, however unpalatable their alternatives might be. Oliver Wendell Holmes, then chief justice of the Massachusetts high court, gave the classic statement of this doctrine in *Lamson v. American Ax & Tool*,[115] just five years before his dissent in *Lochner*. The plaintiff in *Lamson* was an employee whose position as a hatchet painter became dangerous when his employer purchased badly designed new racks that tended to let the hatchets drop on Lamson's head.[116] Lamson had earlier complained about the Damoclean axes, but "was answered, in substance, that he would have to use the [new] racks or leave."[117] A hatchet did indeed fall, injuring Lamson. Holmes found that Lamson had assumed the risk of his employment by declining to exercise his free-labor right to quit. As Holmes put it, "He perfectly understood what was likely to happen. . . . He complained, and was notified that he could go if he would not face the chance. He stayed, and took the risk."[118] It was critical to Holmes that Lamson identified and accepted the hard choice he was up against: "He [assumed the risk] none the less that the fear of losing his place was one of his motives."[119] The choice between being fired and remaining in what the sketchy facts of the case suggest was an unreasonably dangerous workplace was free and self-authorizing, and the worker who took the option of staying accepted the consequences.

The starkest expression of the logic governing these cases came in *Leary v. Boston & A. R. Co.*[120] A laborer was ordered to ride a locomotive as a fireman, a considerably more dangerous duty than his ordinary job.[121] He sought damages from his employer when he was injured, and the railroad refused to compensate him. The court acknowledged that the plaintiff had accepted the dangerous additional duty in the face of a threat of firing but held that it was precisely in this choice that he assumed the risk of his employment.[122] Much as Justice Ruffin had done in the merciless reasoning of *State v. Mann,* the court recognized the aspect of threat and coercion in the employer's presentation of alternatives but found them legally in-bounds: "To morally coerce a servant to an employment the risks of which he does not wish to encounter, by threatening otherwise to deprive him of an employment he can readily and safely perform, may sometimes be harsh."[123] Such coercion was, however, the practical power created by the reciprocal rights of free-labor relations: the employee's right to sell labor or take it elsewhere and the employer's right to hire and fire at will. That these decisions might be taken in hard corners—in conditions of need and with few or no viable alternatives—made them no less free according to the courts of Massachusetts, which found for these purposes that free employees stood, in the words of the Supreme Court, "upon an equality" with their employer.

The jurisprudence of free labor, then, highlights the difficulty inherent in identifying just one dimension of freedom with the multifarious value of freedom itself. Treating as "free" and self-authorizing choices taken under severe constraint narrowed economic liberty to a dogmatic formula. The formula was appealing because it seemed to resolve a basic dilemma between freedom and exploitation. In practice, however, the free-labor formula reproduced the same dilemma while diminishing the conceptual vocabulary for identifying and addressing it. Applying a strong version of the principle seemed a kind of blindness to real circumstances, but the principle itself did little to make those circumstances conceptually tractable.

The sharpest charge that bargaining conditions made a mockery of the freedom of free labor came from Robert Lee Hale, the Legal Realist and institutional economist. Hale described what I have called the circumstances of recruitment this way: "The law confers on each person a wholly unique set of liberties with regard to the use of material goods and imposes on each person a unique set of restrictions with regard thereto. The privileges, rights, and duties of each person differ from those of every other person."[124] Hale's concentration on the *uniqueness* of each person's rights and duties under property law emphasizes not the abstract categories of the law—the forms of ownership, for instance, which define the various rights over things that people may hold[125]—but the concrete social world in which each person is the owner of certain resources and not of others. Recruitment takes place against this distributive background, in which each person's starting point is unlike every other person's.

Building on this account of bargaining, Hale described economic life as a system of mutual coercion among all participants. Like Adam Smith, whose theory he set out to invert, he began from the power of exclusion.[126] Unlike Smith, Hale concentrated on the threat to exercise that power against other individuals who need one's resources. This description amounted to a rhetorical reversal of the conventional account of market relations as a voluntary exchange for mutual advantage, which highlights the inducement to become better off by consummating an exchange.[127] To that inducement, Hale contended, there corresponds the threat of nonconsummation, of sticking at exclusion and denying the other the benefit of one's resources. The point of Hale's shift of focus is not that owners want to exclude others from their resources but that they want to exact the most favorable terms of access from others who need those resources for their own aims, which the threat of exclusion enables them to do.[128]

On this account, the allocation of resources essentially shapes the threats one party may make against another: if both are relatively well-endowed, the cost of being excluded from each other's resources (the opportunity cost of declining a proffered bargain) will not be difficult to absorb. If, however, one party needs the resources at issue, while the other is well-enough off to be fairly indifferent to the outcome of the bargain, then the poorer party will be subject to a significant threat.[129] As a theoretical matter, Hale saw coercion as mutual, even in situations of great inequality. The propertyless worker exercises coercion over the factory owner in declining to work. That is simply a weaker bit of coercion than the factory owner exercises in refusing to hire a worker who demands a wage increase.[130]

In Hale's account, "coercion" represented not a judgment about the balance of power in a specific transaction but the elementary term in a general analysis of economic life as a system of coordination based on the balance of threat.

Hale's account of property relations as reciprocal coercion was at once a theoretical innovation and a rhetorical choice meant to shift the meaning of "voluntary" exchange.[131] The jurisprudence he attacked was built on formal voluntarism and characterized as free nearly any transaction undertaken without threat of violence, blackmail, or other overt coercion.[132] In the strict version of that view, which we have seen in action earlier in this chapter, the fact that a bargainer had to choose between one highly disadvantageous option and several truly dreadful alternatives would not make the resulting transaction less free, so long as it was not exacted under threat of overt coercion, such as harm to body or property.[133] Hale's description shifted attention to the range of viable alternatives each party confronted and the costs and benefits associated with each alternative. He showed the difficulty of blessing as neatly voluntary a labor contract that resulted from pitting the worker's small coercive power (the threat of withholding labor) against the great coercive power of the employer (the threat of withholding employment).[134]

Hale's description of economic life as a system of mutual coercion revealed a great deal, but it also obscured the importance of the rules of recruitment. Hale took market society's rules of recruitment as given and argued that they were not enough to secure a compelling version of economic freedom. Ironically, then, even as he redescribed markets as systems of unequal power, Hale inadvertently naturalized, and thus put outside the express terms of his analysis, the basic terms of market relations, in which overt coercion was out of bounds.

Yet to do this slights the distinct contribution of market rules to freedom. It is no minor fact that under the laissez-faire law that Hale attacked, recruitment could not include overt coercion. That prohibition was not ideological legerdemain; it was the moral core of a legal regime that arose in direct repudiation of slavery and feudalism. In this register, free-labor thought inspired an idea of democratic community. In contrast to the white-supremacist vision of citizenship that Chief Justice Taney had expressed in *Dred Scott*[135] and the "mud-sill" theory that social life depended on a degraded class of workers who did the demeaning work, free labor contended for a different conception of personal dignity and social membership. The heart of the idea was that honest labor under conditions of equal opportunity meant a fair chance for all and was also dignifying in itself. No one was condemned by birth to inferior status. Rather, everyone had a fair chance at becoming a person of substance, and an inherent claim on dignity.

Indifference to the moral appeal of free-labor thought is an ironic similarity between Hale's critical account of market society and that of George Fitzhugh, the apologist for slavery. Both described human beings as locked in a perennial struggle to capture one another's labor by whatever coercive or quasi-coercive means their legal order offered. For both, a laissez-faire labor market was no more or less than a legal channel for this ubiquitous ambition. The claim that such a market was a special embodiment of human freedom and individual dignity was preposterous apologetics in their eyes.

Taking Hale seriously while also going beyond Hale would mean allowing for what was false or incomplete in the free-labor promise to reconcile our character as resources with our character as persons, without losing sight of what in it was true. That would lead naturally to a question that is as much aspirational as critical: What would be necessary to make the ideal of reconciliation more nearly true? Addressing these questions means returning to the freedom-promoting tradition of reform and trying to integrate the negative dimension of freedom, exemplified in free-labor thought, and the "positive freedom" issue of what choices are actually available, emphasized by those critics who saw the social reality of free labor as undermining its promise of individual choice.

In this discussion we have tracked a problem through two very different legal contexts: the master-slave relationship and the relationship, whether constitutional or at common law, of free laborers and their employers. Both regimes were premised on interrelated legal definitions of personhood and property. In each case a regime of property in human bodies, energy, and talents defines both resources and personhood, and shapes the relationship between these two aspects of human beings.

The basic operation of property law, regardless of its details, rests on the functional need to assign relative rights over scarce and valued resources. Without such resources, little that people wish to do is possible. Without enforceable rights in resources, cooperation stalls or breaks down, insecurity grows, and freedom shrinks in all its dimensions. Property, then, addresses our material dependence on a world in which we are also socially interdependent with other human beings who are at once our competitors and our collaborators.

Picking apart the dimensions of freedom and the questions they address is the necessary preparation for integrating them. The integration, partial though it inevitably is, happens in particular institutional arrangements, addressed to specific resources and human relationships. That was what Adam Smith attempted for the early-modern economy of small-scale industry and growing commerce. No neat answer arose in recasting the problem for the new circumstances of the nineteenth and early twentieth centuries. We now turn to the prospects of these questions in the twenty-first.

Part Three

RECLAMATIONS

The last chapter concentrated on the paradoxes and failures of free labor while insisting on the power of its core ideal: reconciling the multiple dimensions of freedom in a noncoercive economy. That ideal may not be realizable in any simple way, but this does not mean it has no value. It can serve as what Kant called a regulative principle, which we cannot expect to realize in full but which nonetheless can guide our choices toward ever-closer approximations to it. We might also describe it as a utopian vision immanent in our tradition of market-making property, which, like any utopia properly understood, is not a blueprint but a way of setting out certain aspirations so that we do not lose track of them as we make our immediate and unavoidably constrained choices.

The problem is how to make mutually reinforcing a set of values that are each basic to the modern vision of freedom and to our tradition of understanding what market-making property is supposed to achieve, but that often contradict one another. These are the freedom from interference in choice that is often called negative liberty, the enjoyment of a reasonable set of attractive alternatives that some have called positive liberty, and the capacity to perceive, pursue, and revise one's own interests and projects that is the psychological precondition of exercising the other two. More abstractly, the problem is to reconcile the features of human beings that the two master metaphors of modern property thought embody. The first of these is the inherent self-sovereignty of the natural-rights tradition, with its recognition of the infinite value of the individual—in the image of the Leveller Thomas Rainborough at Putney, each naturally free in body and mind, with a life to live as much as any other. The second is the interdependence of the tradition of sociability: the fact that we need one another, are mostly powerless without one another, and are always, as Fitzhugh and

Hale insisted from opposite political perspectives, at risk of being seized upon for one another's use. The great ambition of property thought, and the institution of property, has been to build a political economy on the reconciliation of these two enduring conditions.

Allowing that there is no simple way to achieve this aim, but also that it is not purely futile, the question is how to pursue it fruitfully. Here is one way of thinking of the features of a property system that succeeds in partial integration. Such a system will, as the previous chapter set out, structure interdependence by setting the terms on which people recruit one another to their projects. The great aim of free labor was to exclude the threat of force from recruitment, a transformation whose advocates understood it as inaugurating an economic system ordered by consent. The recruitment appeal would be to interest alone, as judged by the free mind of each consenting individual. The first great complaint against that libertarian picture has always been that formal consent does not imply substantive freedom because we choose our alliances in painfully unequal circumstances. The second great complaint, the Romantic one, has been that the calculus of interest is too flat to capture the range of human value: it quashes imagination and creativity and dulls experience. In both lines of criticism the reality of life under free-labor principles is understood as betraying the announced aim of ordering interdependence by the freedom and infinite worth of the individual.

An economic order that can better reconcile the three dimensions of freedom will pursue three values: reciprocity, responsibility, and self-realization. First, recruitment will take place on terms of relative reciprocity, that is, the range of alternatives and resulting bargaining power that each participant faces will be as equal as is compatible with wealth-producing incentives and personal responsibility. These are broad terms, which have been elaborately explored by theorists of distributive justice. The point here is simply that those who design, interpret, and reform any property system should strive to give the terms robust meaning within the workings of that system. The examples in the following chapters give somewhat more sense of what they might mean concretely.

To secure responsibility, the role of arbitrary fortune in producing inequality (which implies nonreciprocity) should be as small as possible. An economic order that takes personal freedom seriously should not permit it to be structurally constrained by factors that do not arise from choice. This point motivated the insistence on equal freedom throughout the free-labor tradition, and thinkers such as Bruce Ackerman and Ronald Dworkin have given considerable attention to its meaning in a complex economy. Again, the aim here is to view it as an ambition that is intrinsic to the best understanding of our property inheritance and to set out some examples of how it might be taken seriously.

An economic order should also move recruitment appeals along a spectrum from survival toward what one might call flourishing or self-realization (again, to the extent compatible with wealth production and responsibility). Our interdependence has three aspects: we need one another to survive, to prosper, and to realize ourselves. An archetypical recruitment appeal exists for each. For survival, "Join me, and I will let you live," the terms of slavery and, at least at their inception, feudal systems. For prosperity, "Join me and your interest will be better served than otherwise," the characteristic appeal on free-labor terms. For self-realization, "Join me, and you will become more yourself than you could otherwise be." While these interact and have vague borders—an appeal to interest may have starvation as its alternative, or flourishing as the interest at stake—they refer to distinct aspects of our need for one another and ways we bargain from it.

6

———————•◆•———————

CHOOSING FUTURES

How do we choose our own future? How should we? Recall that the legal imagination this book is tracking is bifocal. On one hand, it concentrates on the social and economic relations that take place in a familiar legal framework. On the other, it includes the power to remake our world by redefining and reallocating rights. Such transformations brought about our familiar world, and making them remains a defining, if hazardous, power.

How to discipline that power, to use it well and deliberately? This is the problem of how to assess the futures we might have, beginning from what we know to be and extending that knowledge to cast light on what might be. In choosing future property regimes, and the economic orders they create, what we believe about our present order—what it does, what is valuable in it, what its failings are—is critically important. The first question, then, is how to understand our own property rights and markets as we extend them prospectively into the future.

Welfarists often locate the value of property in its power to set markets in motion. Clear claims on resources are a cornerstone of a system of efficiency-enhancing transactions. Without clear property rights, uncertainty would erode static efficiency (because it would be difficult to ascertain who owned what) and dynamic efficiency (because the benefit of improvements and innovations might end up in someone else's pocket). These two welfarist virtues of property rights are also the core virtues of markets: they get goods to those who want and can afford them, and they encourage improvements that increase wealth over time. We might, then, think of property rights as somehow derived from the idea of a market, handmaidens of a lordly concept.

The difficulty is that conceptually and practically, markets do not come first:

property comes first, and it makes markets not just in the sense that it facilitates them but in the stronger sense that it gives them their shape. Amartya Sen points out that there is "an extraordinary aspect of the market mechanism that is often overlooked," that "the specification of the market mechanism is an essentially *incomplete* specification of a social arrangement. Even with the purest, perfectly competitive market mechanisms, we are not in a position to understand precisely what will happen until we know something more about the rest of the social arrangements, in particular the distribution of endowments and resource ownership."[1] Decisions *among* markets, rather than for or against, are frequently where the action is. This amounts to saying that the power of market analysis to tell us what to do with property law is limited by a paradox: a market is incomplete without the specifications *that property law provides*. As emphasized in the last several chapters, defining and allocating property rights has been a heavily disputed enterprise, one that is closely connected with the rise of distinctive ideas of social order and freedom.

Choices among markets are choices among futures, and thus also choices of the conditions in which future decisions will take place. While such choices can benefit from rigor in specifying certain relevant considerations, they are inevitably exercises of social imagination and persuasion. Indeed, these capacities are themselves aspects of freedom. We apply our capacities for imagination, persuasion, and qualitative judgment to economic life by reforming our institutions, as Adam Smith urged his contemporaries to do, and we exercise those capacities within the economic frameworks we create, imagining different futures and trying to persuade one another of their value even as we go about our everyday affairs.

The freedom-promoting tradition in property is not consigned to the past, and the paradoxes and compromising entanglements that have dogged it are not insuperable. The idea that property and the markets it sets in motion are institutions for integrating distinct but complementary dimensions of freedom is still a valuable one for defining and allocating claims on resources. While it should not supplant the now-dominant approaches, this qualitative and integrating approach is a useful complement to them. Indeed, the limitations of those approaches are in some respects products of their commitment to some aspects of the multifarious value of freedom, with resulting indifference to the other aspects.

THE CURIOUS MODESTY OF WELFARE ECONOMICS

The problem of how to define and allocate property rights is, from the point of view of economics, a question of *social choice* or *welfare economics*. Social choice means, in effect, an effort to bring the individual problem of how to make choices up to the level of collective decisions: how to use resources and how to define and allocate rights in them. In welfare economics, we try to get a grip on these problems by evaluating the well-being, or welfare, of the individuals who make up a society, then assessing how well off they would be as a result of one social decision or another.

Let's pick up this theme a little more than a half-century ago, when the thirty-year-old economist Kenneth Arrow, a product of New York City's elite public high schools and universities, published a work that became the turning point in twentieth-century social-choice theory. Arrow's argument in *Social Choice and Individual Values* (1951) was technical, but its conclusion is relatively straightforward. Let us suppose that we are looking for a social-choice formula, a guide to social decisions that will translate the preferences of all the individuals in society into policy judgments on behalf of the whole. It turns out that no such formula is possible, at least if we also insist that any formula must meet certain modest and reasonable conditions.[2] Hence the argument has come to be called "Arrow's impossibility theorem."[3]

For those who are not professional economists, Arrow's famous proof is less interesting for what it proves as a technical matter than for what it shows about the terms of debate on economics and social decisions. Arrow wrote in the aftermath of World War II, when democracy had narrowly bested one challenge from European totalitarianism and was beginning to confront another from Soviet communism. It was also a time of fierce debate over the relative merits of economic planning and the free market, with positions ranging from the libertarian views of the Austrian economist Friedrich Hayek to various hybrids of democratic politics and socialist economics. Arrow pointed out that his proof need not hold if everyone in society had the same preferences—but, he might as well have added, in that case why would the question even arise? The whole problem of social choice is that people's values are diverse. Taking that diversity seriously, Arrow's finding implied, had to mean giving up on the ambition to create a rational master rule for social decisions, a technique for reconciling all values without recourse to the fractiousness of politics. His hyper-rational proof was a subtle reproach to the social and political ambitions of rationalism. We would have to make our choices without the reassurance that they were justified by some complete and final theory, which Arrow showed could be only a pleasing illusion.[4]

An illusion, that is, according to Arrow's rather strict specifications. The other interesting thing about Arrow's argument is what information it includes and what it keeps out. Within Arrow's scheme there is no way to ask which social decision will improve human well-being overall. The information about individual preferences that Arrow's formulas tried and failed to translate into social choices took this form: given any pair of alternatives, which would an individual prefer? The one an individual would choose was defined as bringing that person more utility, meaning simply a greater satisfaction of the person's preferences. The reasonable assumption behind this definition was that people choose alternatives that bring more rather than less satisfaction. This is the standard of Pareto efficiency, which compares pairs of alternatives by asking whether one option is preferred by at least one individual while no one else prefers the alternative: in that case, the more preferred alternative is "Pareto efficient." This formula admits no more information than the pairwise comparison of preferences. It registers no information about the level of well-being, the "welfare" that any person has in any alternative.[5]

To make this point more concrete, imagine two individuals confronting a choice between a pair of social arrangements, called Aruba and Baghdad. Aruba is a middle-class society with high employment, universal health care, and peaceful diversity. Baghdad is poor and wartorn, with a life expectancy at birth twenty years below that of Aruba. By Arrow's rules, our social-choice formula cannot "know" any of this. It can only take into account for each person whether that individual would rather live in Aruba or Baghdad. It would be possible to jigger the situation to get various kinds of results from this set-up, but the main point is that there is no way to take into account what would seem most natural to consider: whether people overall are better off in one alternative than in the other. *Overall* could mean many things, of course: the greatest level of aggregate well-being, the greatest average well-being, or some other formula. But any such formula is impossible here, because to know which arrangement was "best overall," it would first be necessary to say how well any given person was doing. That information is excluded. We can only consider rank-order preferences.

This exclusion may seem perverse. Sen, among others, has argued that the right response is to let in more information about how people are doing, so that we can imagine an approach to social decision that incorporates more of the considerations relevant to comparing social arrangements.[6] Before going on to some ways of doing just that, it is worth pausing to consider ways that the exclusions are not simply perverse but methodological expressions of a concern for individual freedom. Throughout the nineteenth century and into the early decades of the twentieth, welfare economists in Britain and the United States assumed that they could assess social decisions based on exactly what Arrow's model excludes: commonsense considerations of well-being. Confronted with two versions of a national budget for infrastructure, they might have pointed out that creating hygienic sewers in London would reduce the risk of cholera for hundreds of thousands of people, while replacing existing bridges in Wessex would only make travel slightly faster and safer for a few tens of thousands. To make these judgments in practice they took into account fairly uncontroversial human interests: health, physical security, and general-purpose capabilities such as literacy.[7]

In the 1930s this way of doing welfare economics came under attack, notably by the prominent British economist Lionel Robbins.[8] Robbins was influenced by logical positivism,[9] a theory of knowledge whose proponents argued that all knowledge, and indeed all meaningful statements, must be based on observable facts. (Some logical positivists made an exception for mathematics, but that is not important here.) When someone says, "A bomb has just exploded on the highway to the airport," we know exactly what the speaker means and how to find out whether it is true. But when the same person says, "Security is more important than freedom," it simply means that the speaker prefers security to freedom. How can we find out whether "more important" is true or false? The "more important" part is meaningless except as an aggressive misstatement of "I prefer security to freedom." We can have no knowledge about which is more important because there is nothing to know. Robbins argued that claims about people's well-being, happiness, or utility—however you cared to put it—were either subjective assertions of personal preferences or unverifiable speculation about what happened in other people's heads—Is this person happier than that one?[10] Either way, there was no finding an answer that would count as knowledge. Welfare economists were asserting what *they* thought was important and what *they* imagined others were experiencing and passing it off as science. By contrast, Robbins thought that economists *could* observe that individuals presented with a choice generally prefer one alternative to another, and that by keeping track of these preferences and assuming that what people prefer is what makes them "better off" or gives them "utility," economists could assemble scientific knowledge.[11] The approach Robbins endorsed had been recommended decades earlier by prominent continental economists, notably Wilfredo Pareto, father of the Pareto criterion,[12] but Robbins's arguments decisively introduced these information exclusions into Anglo-American welfare economics. What Arrow's social-choice inquiry excluded is what Robbins classified as unscientific.[13]

Robbins and his allies were not just being persnickety about what could count as knowledge. Robbins's examples emphasized that human experience is deeply diverse, sometimes intractably so. Are new boots really more important than opera tickets? You may think so, and so may the economist at the Ministry of Economics, but does that make it so for me? What if opera moves my soul, while boots only keep my feet warm? Robbins asked, If an Indian Brahmin (this was the closing era of British imperial rule in India) asserts that because of his refinement he can experience ten times as much satisfaction as an Untouchable, how will you persuade him that he is wrong (or, as a logical positivist might have put it, "wrong")?[14] From one hostile point of view, Robbins and the logical positivists turned people into preference-generating robots, mindlessly creating rank orders among the alternatives they encountered. From the opposite point of view, however, the traditional welfare economists were the ones who made people automatons, leveling their individual experiences so that everyone became a vessel for homogenous utility. Robbins might have said that he made economics more modest by reining in its pretensions before they breached (or claimed to breach) the soul, and that the abstention he proposed left our specificity, our uniqueness, unviolated. He might also have said that this change was especially important because the welfare economists' agenda sometimes had political power behind it: policies such as social spending and prohibitions on "welfare-reducing" behavior were the natural and intended results of judgments about the well-being of the country.

Robbins's methodological change, then, expressed respect for individuality on two fronts: that people have different values and priorities from one another, and that we care about being free to reach our own conclusions and choices, not having them dictated by a supposed science of well-being. These premises are at the core of liberalism, the tradition of social and political philosophy that begins from individual freedom. John Stuart Mill, one of the greatest exponents of that tradition, had them in mind when he wrote, "[T]here is no parity between the feeling of a person for his own opinion, and the feeling of another who is offended at his holding it."[15] My judgments about my life are not just data for a social well-being machine: they are special because they are mine, just as yours are special because they are yours.

UTILITARIANISM AND INDIVIDUALITY

Ironically, the material-welfare approach which Robbins rejected had also begun from a recognition of individuality. The approach to welfare economics that Robbins confronted, with its effort to assess the overall well-being of the society by starting from the objective well-being of individuals, had not fallen far from the tree of Jeremy Bentham's utilitarianism. Bentham was a tireless reformer in an age of revolution, an enemy of superstition, obscurantism, and all kinds of social and political privilege. "It is the greatest happiness of the greatest number that is the measure of right and wrong" he wrote in 1776, the year of Smith's *Wealth of Nations* and the American Declaration of Independence.[16] At the heart of Bentham's thought lay the additional principle that the happiness and unhappiness, the pleasure and pain, of each individual mattered exactly as much as that of every other individual, whether an Oxford don or a beggar, or whether one enjoyed reciting Ovid in the original or liked to drink beer and play darts. Bentham believed this truth was what reason revealed; the rich and powerful had concealed it by concocting obscure theories of law and politics that preserved their own privileges while keeping the lower orders from a fair share of life's satisfactions.[17] He called himself a partisan of "Reformation, and that Liberty which is Reformation's harbinger," particularly free judgment, the power to inspect an inherited institution and find it deficient by the lights of your own reason. As the logical positivists would later do, but in much more vivid language, he accused his opponents of concealing their illegitimate value judgments in

> a perpetual vein of nonsense, flowing from a perpetual abuse of words, — words having a variety of meanings, where words with single meanings were equally at hand—the same words used in a variety of meanings in the same page,— words used in meanings not their own, where proper words were equally at hand,—words and propositions of the most unbounded signification, turned loose without any of those exceptions or modifications which are so necessary on every occasion to reduce their import within the compass, not only of right reason, but even of the design in hand, of whatever nature it may be;—the same inaccuracy, the same inattention in the penning of this cluster of truths on which the fate of nations was to hang, as if it had been an oriental tale, or an allegory for a magazine:—stale epigrams, instead of necessary distinctions,— figurative expressions preferred to simple ones,—sentimental conceits, as trite as they are unmeaning, preferred to apt and precise expressions,—frippery ornament preferred to the majestic simplicity of good sound sense,—and the acts of the senate loaded and disfigured by the tinsel of the playhouse[.][18]

With that attitude toward rhetoric, it is no wonder that beer and darts seemed at least as good as poetry, from the point of view of human emancipation. Bentham tried to put social decisions on a sound basis, one that recognized that everyone's happiness and unhappiness is equally important. Much as Robbins would more than a century later, Bentham tried to reclaim for the reason and judgment of individual men and women choices that he believed had been overtaken by dogma. Ironically, it was a version of Bentham's own antidogmatic formula, the equal happiness of the living, that Robbins later felt compelled to reject as dogma, setting up the difficulties for social judgment that Kenneth Arrow would explore.

Seen in this light, the rise of the uninformative Pareto principle as a touchstone for welfare economics resembles the vicissitudes of laissez-faire and anti-liberal views of property regimes recounted in Chapter5. Like those swings of the ideological pendulum, this version of welfare economics represents a failure to integrate the competing dimensions of freedom—a failure that, ironically, arose in part from taking one dimension of freedom very seriously and seeking to protect it from intrusion in the name of other dimensions—in this case, to protect the autonomy and individuality of negative liberty from the well-being concerns of welfarism.

Another lesson of Arrow's theorem is that the ambition to provide an authoritative formula for assessing institutional alternatives can be self-defeating. Ironically, the ambition is incompatible with the values that motivate it in the first place. The aim of social-choice theory is to guide collective decisions in ways that give equal consideration to the interests of all while recognizing the individuality of each. The utopian ideal of these motivations would be to reconcile, without remainder, the competing aspects of individual freedom and turn them into a formula for justification of state action in terms of individual values. That ideal, however, is impossible, and efforts to achieve it end up highlighting its impossibility.

Indeed, to come back to Bentham, the most insightful commentators on his thought have not seen it as a total theory, though Bentham himself often aspired to that. Instead, it is foremost a critical device for pointing out where law fails to treat the interests of different individuals alike, usually by preserving forms of privilege that implicitly value some over others. Bentham's utilitarianism is also a statement of the *kinds* of things that government decisions should take into account. Pointing to the critical function of the theory, F. C. Montague, an editor of Bentham's work, wrote in the middle of the nineteenth century, "The truth is that such a principle as the principle of utility is valuable not as a creative, but as a critical principle. It is valuable as a test, not as a germ. Its true potency is negative, a potency to lay bare injustice, to unravel sophistry, to cancel verbiage. . . . Is a law really and not merely apparently partial? Is it an instrument for aggrandizing a class of citizens without any reference to the common weal? If so, it will not bear to be tried by a standard which requires the legislator to seek the happiness of the greatest number of each individual equally with every other individual. . . . But for purposes of creation any single axiom, even the axiom of utility, is utterly inadequate."[19] Montague also pointed out the theory's second role, as a statement of orientation for public policy, with equal panache and greater brevity: "Bentham's concern was with the huge states of the modern world, in which the number of the citizens makes it impossible for the legislator to discriminate fairly between the sensibilities of individuals."[20] That scale of decision making required criteria addressed to the generic conditions of human life, the broad sweep of well-being that concerned the material-welfare theorists who followed Bentham.

VARIETIES OF WELFARE ANALYSIS: FROM STATIC TO DYNAMIC, FROM DOLLARS TO FREEDOMS

Partly because it is so uninformative, the Pareto criterion that shaped Kenneth Arrow's analysis has not been at the center of the welfare economics practiced by legal scholars. Instead they have used varieties of cost-benefit analysis, a method that generates cash equivalents of the harms and benefits from any policy choice. This method effectively ignores the problems with interpersonal comparisons of well-being that Robbins insisted on. Cost-benefit analysis aims to provide a master ranking of alternatives according to an objective criterion or, more modestly, to set out in some roughly consistent and intelligible way the relative pluses and minuses of various alternatives.[21] More modestly still, it may serve in the critical register that Montague diagnosed in Bentham: as a way of pointing out irrationalities in policies that do not even achieve their stated aims when other approaches can do so more efficiently.[22]

Typically, in this method goods are "priced" in one of two ways.[23] First is willingness to pay, which tracks prices in actual markets. For instance, the premium paid employees in high-risk positions might serve as a basis for pricing a human life and thus attaching a number to the benefits column of a policy forecast to save a certain number of statistical lives. The second method is contingent valuation, asking people what they would pay to enjoy or preserve a good. I do not wish here to assess the challenges directed at cost-benefit analysis: that the willingness to pay overvalues the preferences of those with high incomes; that contingent valuation does not produce consistent or even coherent valuations; that the standard accounting technique of discounting future money is distorting and inappropriate when applied to values such as human life; that fixing all kinds of values in a single metric obscures their distinctiveness; or that the technique cannot adequately account for low probability but catastrophic possibilities such as global ecological disaster.[24] My aim here is different: to find a way to expand and diversify the information base of evaluation by integrating competing dimensions of freedom.

Although this approach harkens back to Adam Smith, its contemporary touchstone is the freedom-based welfare economics of Amartya Sen. Sen's starting point is that we value institutions because, and as far as, they promote freedom. That is only a bare beginning to the inquiry because as Sen rightly insists, "Freedom is an irreducibly plural concept. While we can attempt to combine the different aspects and sub-aspects in some integrated formulation, the most important task is to be clear about the different facets of freedom—how and why they differ, and in what way they have their respective relevance."[25]

Sen responds to Arrow's impossibility theorem by arguing for admitting more kinds of information into social evaluations. He proposes to begin where Arrow ended, by giving up the conceit that there could be an all-embracing theory of social choice and instead aiming for a less (theoretically) ambitious but more (practically) inclusive account of what matters to us in evaluating social arrangements.[26] The ultimate ambition of such a project must be integration: to incorporate in a meaningful way both the humanitarian, egalitarian concern for welfare that motivated Bentham's interpretation of equal freedom and the individualist libertarianism that prompted Robbins's skeptical response, as well as the third dimension of freedom, the development of a personality able to make good the potential of the other aspects.

Sen proposes that both "negative" protections and "positive" entitlements should be understood in terms of what they enable persons to do, that is, the "capabilities" or "functionings" they make possible in a person's life.[27] The right not to be arbitrarily imprisoned, the right to a subsistence, and the right to participate in one's political community enable people to do certain things: make and pursue life plans, form intimate and civic attachments, cultivate their talents. They are aspects of a form of life, an arrangement of institutions, rules, and practices that together produce or facilitate the capabilities of their members. To be more rather than less free is to enjoy greater capabilities.[28]

Sen adopts a basic distinction between two aspects of freedom, which he calls the process and opportunity dimensions.[29] The process aspect consists of not being interfered with by others in making decisions and reasonably pursuing the projects one has chosen.[30] For instance, ground rules that establish that joint activity will be coordinated by voluntary contracts, negotiated on the basis of private claims to property, and bounded by each party's freedom of exit protect process freedom in economic life. The process aspect of freedom secures one of the most important capabilities, the deliberation and self-scrutiny that ground our choices. This is also the heart of the libertarian dimension of freedom. As Sen puts it: "A person is not only an entity that can enjoy one's own consumption, experience and appreciate one's welfare, and have one's goals, but also an entity that can examine one's values and objectives and choose in the light of those values and objectives. . . . We can ask what we want to do and how, and in that context also examine what we should want and how."[31] The capacity to reason in this way is one of our most significant capabilities, which the process aspect of freedom secures.

Sen calls the second dimension in his account of freedom the opportunity aspect.[32] Freedom from interference—process freedom—means little to a person faced with "a choice over three alternative achievements that are seen as 'bad,' 'terrible,' and 'disastrous,'" even though from the perspective solely of process freedom, this person will enjoy "exactly as much freedom as [if she or he had] a choice over . . . three alternative achievements which are seen as 'good,' 'terrific,' and 'wonderful.'"[33] The opportunity aspect of freedom enables people to act physically, operate socially, and pursue those projects that they value—the capabilities that, like process freedom, lead us to call someone "free." Opportunity freedom encompasses both the range of choices open to individuals and the value of the alternatives to them in light of their unique interests and commitments.

The level of resources needed to achieve a given capability may vary greatly from society to society. Thus the "same" level of wealth may result in very different choice sets. For instance, appearing in public without shame may in one setting require only a single length of cloth, appropriately wrapped and tucked; in another setting (say, a contemporary Western workplace or school), a person may need to change clothes every day of the week. To buy and sell goods in one setting a person may need only sandals to walk to the marketplace; in an exurban American setting, most people need a car. Thus, to identify a person's set of viable choices, it is necessary to know not just what resources are available but also what those resources are good for in each setting.

The third dimension of freedom is internal: it consists of self-regard and aspiration, an idea of oneself as an agent with purposes, plans, and interests. As Sen puts it, describing this aspect by reference to its negation: "The most blatant forms of inequalities and exploitations survive in the world through making allies out of the deprived and the exploited. The underdog learns to bear the burden so well that he or she overlooks the burden itself. Discontent is replaced by acceptance, hopeless rebellion by conformist quiet, and . . . suffering and anger by cheerful endurance."[34]

Limitations on this aspect of freedom include delusion, inhibition, neurosis, or other impediments to perceiving, acknowledging, or acting on one's preferences or commitments. Interpersonal interference or structural constraint can foster internal barriers to freedom that grimly complement external barriers. This constraint on freedom is distinct from the objective fact of interpersonal domination or structural constraint. A view of oneself as unable to formulate and act on interests and commitments can inhibit free action all by itself.

An institution might be freedom-promoting with respect to each dimension of freedom. It might protect libertarian free choice in its rules of recruitment. It might provide each person with a large enough set of viable choices to ensure a minimum of opportunity freedom. And it might aim to unsettle the expectation and experience of domination and deprivation, helping people to gain insight into the present bounds and ultimate potential of their freedom.

The several dimensions of freedom that figure in Sen's account are also those that figure prominently in the leading ways of assessing property institutions: libertarian, welfarist, and personhood approaches. Sen's analysis, like Adam Smith's long before it, treats each of these as a dimension of freedom that property regimes should seek to integrate with the others. Both the libertarian and personhood dimensions underscore the importance of change in preferences, values, and commitments. The choice that libertarian freedom protects draws power from the fact that we do not form our attachments willy-nilly but by processes that we can revisit and revise. These changes can take guidance from the core personhood values of increased self-understanding and psychic strength. Both kinds of change, in turn, will flourish within institutions that promote favorable conditions—protective of libertarian forms of choice and friendly to the substantive forms of autonomy that uphold personhood. In this respect, a choice of institutions is also the choice of a path along which future choices will take shape.

The act of choosing among institutions itself expresses an aspect of freedom, not personal but collective: the political power to remake the context of our joint activity, which the Realist approach to property insists on so adamantly. Arrow's impossibility theorem underscores that this sort of political choice is indeed a choice, an exercise of collective agency to form the context of our next iteration of judgments about value, both personal and collective. Thus, even as personal choices interact with the institutions in which they find shape and expression, those institutions also take shape through political choices.

These dynamic aspects of institutional design are the most distinctive contribution of the freedom-promoting approach to the standard cost-benefit versions of welfare economics. They come at acknowledged cost to formal precision: by admitting multiple qualitatively distinct dimensions of value, this approach thwarts the accountant's ambition of generating a single number at the end of the inquiry. This is a considerable concession; but if the relevant values really are plural, and there is a principled structure to their plurality, then the less precise calculus may more accurately represent the values at stake. In evaluating the future that an institutional choice is expected to bring about, it may be important to consider not just its effect on value metrics that will stay constant over time, such as economic productivity, but also those that by their nature will change: people's preferences, values, and commitments. Individuals and societies re-make themselves under conditions only partly of their own choosing; but the conditions are partly theirs to choose, and that choice is an essential component of the process of remaking.

TWO WAYS TO LOOK AT MICROFINANCE

This argument may be best approached by example. Consider microfinance, the provision of small-scale loans to the poor, often at subsidized rates (and never at the predatory rates of traditional usurers). The loans are frequently combined with community-organizing projects that also serve as repayment instruments: in the classic model, a group of borrowers agree to stand surety for one another's loans and meet regularly to discuss their finances. Pioneering microfinance projects in India and Bangladesh arose out of research identifying exclusion from credit networks as a major constraint on women's financial capabilities, and much microfinance has involved lending mainly or solely to women.[35] Some microfinance programs build in nonfinancial education programs, such as training in maternal health and child care, and experiments are now under way in training participants in measures that reduce the spread of HIV/AIDS. The financial benefits to participants have been impressive enough that microfinance has become perhaps the world's most visible development initiative. The Gates Foundation has promised to devote a major part of its multibillion-dollar anti-poverty effort to expanding microfinance.[36] Some have even expressed doubt that such a successful model needs subsidy from the nonprofit sector: for-profit microfinance efforts are also under way, particularly in Latin America, and under consideration as global initiatives.[37]

The appeal of the microfinance model is straightforward. Economic agency requires resources. Achieving economic change in one's life, moreover, requires excess resources: capital to invest in small enterprise, education, land, or whatever else. The world's poor, often living near the edge of survival, tend to lack exactly that: many live in a hand-to-mouth cycle in which saving and investing are not serious possibilities. Those less fortunate fall into debt and may end up as someone else's capital, dragged by contract into debt slavery. Even in wealthy countries, most important economic change involves credit. Mortgages, education loans, and credit for business startups are the stepping stones of a modern life, and access to them is a basic expectation of social membership in the United States. It may thus seem perverse to ask the world's poor to do much without credit. Conversely, providing credit might seem to promise a big increase in economic agency.

The first few decades of microfinance have accomplished that, at least in many cases. Enthusiasm for the model comes from the success of the pioneering programs, especially Bangladesh's Grameen Bank and the Bangladesh Rural Advancement Committee (BRAC). The World Bank economist Shahidur Khandker concluded in 2005 that for every hundred taka (the Bangladeshi currency) that these two programs (and a third) lent to women, annual household expenditure increased by twenty taka.[38] That amounted to a 20 percent return on the investment represented by the loans. Khandker also found poverty rates declining more rapidly among program participants than among nonparticipants and larger numbers of participant households climbing above the poverty threshold with each year of participation.[39] Participants in the earliest major Indian program, the Self-Employed Women's Association, had an income that was 56 percent higher than that of nonparticipants.[40] While many smaller-scale studies had also shown benefits to borrowers, these were the most systematic inquiries, comparing participants to nonparticipants both within and outside communities served by the programs. The sources of economic achievements are extremely complex, of course, and it is nearly impossible to "control for" the fact that ambitious women who are trying to improve their lot will be most likely to take advantage of microfinance. But the data are strong enough to put microfinance at the center of economic development agendas.

An underlying question is concealed in the deserved enthusiasm for microfinance. How does it work? Is it static, enabling borrowers to do things they would already have wanted to do? Or is it dynamic, intervening in economic and social life at a critical point that affects many relationships and decisions, setting in motion a process by which participants reconsider what they want, what they can expect, and even what they are worth? This is not a question about whether microfinance's benefits are essentially those of the market, which they surely are. Instead, it is a question about whether to understand "the market" as an impersonal and universal set of principles or a web of social interactions in which people make and revise choices, values, and commitments.

A model of the static understanding is the Peruvian economist Hernando de Soto's argument for giving squatters legal title to the land they occupy, thus converting it to legally cognizable property. Like microfinance, titling is a capital-provision program, so from a strict economic perspective, the two do roughly the same work. As de Soto describes it, capital links people into an economic network of buyers, sellers, investors, and producers that is potentially global. It gives those who hold it something to offer, and so something to lose, in transactions.[41] It is, in other words, the price of admission for moving from the informal world of small-scale exchange of goods into the formal, universal world of abstract value, where purchasing power makes desire effective at any distance. In the context of micro-finance, entrance into that world means that a charitable donation in Chicago turns into a subsidized loan in Bangladesh, which in turn is used to purchase the sewing machines for a clothing contractor's piecework operation, whose garments turn up with a brand label (maybe a sweatshop-free label) in Hamburg. The woman who undertakes the piecework operation can do so only because she has entered the network of exchange that capital facilitates, leaving behind (at least in part) the close horizons of a local economy in which she earns to survive. The premise of this analysis—what makes it static—is that she must always have wanted to engage in these new investments and transactions, and that the tool of capital enables her to do so for the first time, providing new powers directed to familiar wants.

In many cases there is a lot to this. Microfinance began in grassroots recognition that ordinary people's economic ambition was being frustrated by their inability to acquire even small loans at affordable rates. Similarly, much of the power of de Soto's work comes from his extensive on-the-ground study of squatter communities in Peru, which shows the (legally) landless struggling to engage in market transactions but hampered by their lack of title, and therefore of capital. The question is not whether this static analysis is a true story but whether it is the whole story, and if not, how important is the part it leaves out.

What it might leave out is how capital loans to poor women interact with what the borrowers want and believe is possible. Microfinance programs are linked not just with borrowers' turning a little wealth into a little more but also with women's "empowerment," a much broader and more dynamic outcome. (I put *empowerment* in quotation marks only to indicate that researchers use it in various ways, each with the aim of specifying how borrowers' lives change.) In a mid-1990s study of participants in Grameen Bank and BRAC microfinance programs, researchers compared the participants to nonparticipating residents of the same communities and to residents of communities not served by the microfinance programs. They measured empowerment by eight indicators: *mobility*, whether women had ever visited various places, such as markets, hospitals, movie theaters, and locations outside their villages, with special note of whether they had traveled alone; *economic security*, whether respondents owned a home, productive land, or savings, and whether they used any of these as investments; *small and large purchases* (two categories), whether women could buy various

items, from cooking oil to saris, for themselves without their husbands' permission; *involvement in major decisions* for the family, such as whether to lease or
buy land, and whether women's money was used in these expenditures; *freedom
from family domination*, such as having possessions taken against their will, being
prevented from visiting their hometowns, or being forbidden to work outside the
home; *political and legal awareness* of women's rights and the names of politicians; and *participation* in political campaigns or demonstrations.[42] Responses
suggested that participation in both BRAC and the Grameen Bank affected core
areas of economic empowerment: economic security, the capacity to make small
and large purchases autonomously, and legal and political awareness. Moreover,
BRAC participants were significantly more mobile than nonparticipants, while
Grameen Bank members were significantly more involved in major family decisions than nonmembers.[43] Participants in both programs were also much more
likely to make important contributions to the family's income.[44] The study also
suggested that women who made important contributions to family income were
much more likely than noncontributors to be empowered in all dimensions except family domination and legal and political awareness. This finding suggested
that women's increasing economic importance gave them bargaining power in
family financial decisions and that this was key to their empowerment: it also
suggested that certain traditions of patriarchy persisted, particularly in family
domination.

Continuing research found these empowerment trends pressing into areas
farther and farther removed from the core of economic activity. Women who
participated in Grameen Bank and BRAC credit programs were significantly less
likely to be subjected to domestic violence than nonparticipants.[45] Interestingly,
whether the participants made major contributions to family income did not make
much difference in their vulnerability to violence. In fact, the economic factors
bearing on violence were complicated.[46] In some cases, husbands resented their
wives' new independence and took out their frustration in beatings.[47] In others,
they simply expropriated their wives' loans for themselves, diminishing other dimensions of economic empowerment but encouraging future loans by not beating their wives.[48] The researchers found some evidence that retaliatory beatings
declined with time, suggesting that the men accommodated themselves to the
women's new roles, and that this was particularly the case where women established themselves as large contributors to family income, cementing changes
in their family role.[49] They also suggested that weekly meetings with other loan
participants could make a major difference in women's lives by creating support
networks and making their lives more publicly visible. Intangible changes in the
women's self-perception that arose from the programs could inspire resistance to

domestic violence, perhaps reinforced in cases where men came to accept the women's changing social and economic roles.[50]

Participation in Bangladesh's microfinance programs also appears to increase women's rates of contraceptive use significantly: the rates increased with time in the programs. This suggests that the economic and social changes that microfinance helped set in motion redounded to extremely intimate choices. Breaking down the findings across the aspects of "empowerment" suggested, however, that the relations between microfinance and contraception decisions were complex. Only three dimensions of empowerment were tied to increased contraceptive use: mobility, economic security and family contribution, and freedom from domination within the family. Of these, freedom from domination was the one dimension that microfinance had not improved during the earlier studies, while mobility had increased unevenly. Economic power seems to matter to contraception decisions, then, but it does not matter more than subtler influences and more intimate experience: travel and diverse social encounters, which expand women's sense of the possibilities in their own lives, and resistance to traditional, intimate forms of coercion which may sometimes seem so obvious and legitimate as not to be felt as coercive at all. Mobility and nondomination capture these latter factors, which do not follow automatically from controlling more capital. The interplay of self-conception, economic wherewithal, and choices, intimate and otherwise, is complicated and multifarious, and passes through the economic, family, and other social bonds that the program participants inhabit.[51] The value human beings place on one another is both economic and moral. So is the value they place on themselves. Economic and moral considerations interact, as do self-conception and institutional context.

To further understand the interactions of economic structures, intimate relations, and agency, consider a related issue. One of the more striking and troubling symptoms of the differential value human beings place on one another is the sex asymmetry among children and young adults in East and South Asia. Better known as the problem of missing women, the phenomenon now comprises some 100 million young men and boys in excess of the corresponding female populations in India, Pakistan, China, Taiwan, and neighboring countries.[52] Although scholars offer competing accounts of the causes behind the asymmetry, no one seriously disputes that one major cause is that sons are culturally more valued than daughters in the countries where the asymmetry has developed.[53] This bias inspires both sex-selective abortion to eliminate female fetuses and greater spending on medical care and nutrition for boys than for girls.[54] In consequence, fewer girls than boys are born, and fewer of those survive to adulthood. My interest here is not in this demographic problem per se, but in taking sex differentials in survival as a statistical expression of the differing value placed on girls and boys. By aggregating the results of hundreds of millions of family decisions, these numbers reveal who counts in the marginal decisions of families that are often on the edge of privation. They also suggest when and how the valuation changes.

Standard indicators of development, such as male literacy, average income, urbanization, and access to medical care, do not reduce the sex asymmetry; on the contrary, they sometimes correspond to growing sex gaps.[55] These facts are unsurprising, given that families prefer sons over daughters. Development enables people to accomplish their will more effectively than they otherwise could. Wealth and medical care make sex-selective abortions accessible and affordable. Literacy brings access to information, including information about these procedures. Apart from such direct means of choosing sons, increased household wealth may increase overall childhood survival rates, yet also increase the survival gap if a disproportionate share of the increase goes to investments in the health of boys.

Another unsettling potential of economic development is the paradox of emulation. Where elite norms are sexist, poorer families may adopt these values as their wealth and mobility increase. The sociologist Naila Kabeer, who has studied women's experience of development in detail, attributes some of the growing spread in Indian sex ratios to "sanskritization," meaning that "upward mobility and increased prosperity have led to the emulation of the practices of the northern propertied castes who have traditionally reported the most severe forms of gender discrimination."[56] In other words, new ambitions and ways of imagining one's own life do not always support gender egalitarianism. All parts of "progress" do not necessarily move together. Wealth can sometimes produce a freedom-promoting interaction between people and context, opening choices and equipping people to reflect on new alternatives. It can also strengthen dominant groups, reinforcing or propagating limiting self-conceptions.

The dominant tendency of growing wealth seems to be toward greater freedom. The analytics of economic life that I have been developing, the findings on women's empowerment and specific programs such as microfinance, and large-scale correlations between national income and human development or political freedom all reinforce this impression. Nonetheless, the causal relations are complicated and multifarious, and a virtuous cycle of freedom is not an automatic result.

To make the analysis finer grained, it helps to ask whether the preference for sons is common to all family members or enforced by husbands, and if the latter, under what conditions women can enforce contrary preferences. Addressing this issue, Amartya Sen describes families as sites of "cooperative conflict,"[57] meaning that the various members of a family hold partly overlapping and partly conflict-ing interests and values that taken together will determine how the family uses its resources.[58] Any family will settle on priorities and decision-making procedures, usually informal, for making its decisions. These arrangements may be relatively egalitarian or unequal.[59] A family is thus, among other things, a unit that relies on negotiation among interdependent individuals.[60] What happens when economic change adjusts the balance of interdependence?

There is provocative evidence that when women's bargaining power increases, survival rates for girls rise relative to those for boys. That is, the family's decisions become more sex-egalitarian as women increasingly enforce egalitarian or pro-female preferences. More precisely, two variables correspond to reduced sex in-equality in childhood survival rates: women's literacy and women's participation in the workforce.[61] These are indicators of development in general, but they are also, specifically, indicators of how much *women* have participated in the bene-fits of development.

These data suggest that certain kinds of women's development, despite oper-ating mostly in the public setting of the market, strengthen women's bargain-ing position in the household. These changes help rework the terms of coopera-tion among family members. How might this work? One picture would portray women as having a constantly sex-neutral or profemale concern for their chil-dren, which wealth and options enable them to enforce. In this model, control of material resources, above all bringing wages into the household, would be the most significant change. Literacy would be chiefly instrumental to employment. Women might spend their own wages to care for their daughters, threaten to withhold money if a husband demands a sex-selective abortion, or use the pos-sibility of economic self-reliance to threaten to leave in disputes over household decisions.[62]

One might also take a more dynamic view of the relation between women's control over resources and their preferences, values, and commitments. Perhaps the economic status of women influences their self-regard and estimation of their daughters' prospective lives so that they do not simply enforce preexisting preferences as their bargaining power grows but develop increasingly egalitar-ian values as their experiences and capabilities change.[63] Where women work outside the home, the result may be new everyday interactions, experiences of competence and recognition, and expectations about the regard others should show them, all redounding to the sense of agency and ideas of how life might be lived.[64] Literacy, too, broadens awareness of the kinds of lives one might hope to lead.

Kabeer has argued that an integrated account, considering economic power alongside interpersonal experience and self-conception, is the best way to explain the changes that come with women's employment. Along with income-based bargaining power, she attributes change to the social networks that emerge in factories, where women encounter one another as capable equals; the experience of freedom and autonomy that comes with the mobility of working away from home; and the self-reinforcing cycle of thinking of oneself as an agent with interests and standing.[65] This last kind of change may depend on the raw fact that income brings potential bargaining power, but it also depends on the ignition effect of a woman's willingness to assert herself and make that potential real. In this approach, there is no separating the self-understanding of the people involved from the economic circumstances in which they find themselves, and each will shape the other over time.

The sex disparity I have described arises when female children are regarded as less morally valuable than males and family decisions enforce that valuation. Increases in the family's resources and capabilities do not diminish the disparity. What does make a difference is women's ability to assert economic power in family decisions. In a striking historical continuity, the critical institution in this change, the labor market, is the same that figured so centrally in the free-labor account of how changes in the rules of recruitment could make interdependence and freedom mutually reinforcing. At least in the family's internal negotiations, the early-modern liberal vision of free labor seems to come true today.

None of this is meant to overlook the extent of suffering and injustice in both the labor markets and households of developing countries, nor to portray participation in an often merciless private economy as a simple experience of emancipation. That would recapitulate the too-simple optimism of free-labor ideologues, who brought a once-emancipating idea of formal equality and voluntarism into the service of justifying harsh and effectively unequal economic relationships. Nonetheless, the power of controlling a resource in oneself is real and considerable, and it can foster an increasingly egalitarian idea of personhood—of how and why people matter.

7

SOCIAL VISION FOR THE NEXT ECONOMY

Today's property regimes developed as part of a social vision, an integrated conception of freedom and progress founded in a picture of common life in which institutions arose from economic relations of mutual benefit. At its inception this was a reformist vision, even a radical one, whose adherents imagined its institutional features interacting dynamically with the preferences, values, and commitments of those who professed it, above all through the way the institutions shaped everyday activity.

In many cases, appreciating this history has mainly interpretive benefits: it illuminates past developments in the law of property and political economy and helps make sense of divisions among theories of property today. For some problems, however, it can also provide practical guidance. These are cases where allocating claims on resources involves new and basic decisions about how we will live—choices among futures. This chapter is a sketch, by way of three examples, of how we might approach such questions as occasions for social vision. The examples are income supports, global climate change, and intellectual property law. The implications of these questions are deep and pervasive enough that in resolving them we will inevitably change ourselves. Social vision, now as in early-modern property debates, is an attempt to understand the multifarious aspects of that change in a way that helps us be as clear as possible about what future we wish for.

RESPONSIBILITY WITH LESS ARBITRARINESS

The first example addresses the uncomfortable fact that individuals' economic fates depend as much on sweeping technological and other structural changes as on their own skills, energy, and choices. The American factory worker and computer scientist in 1980 were headed in opposite economic directions for reasons they could not control and, often, could not have foreseen. The forces that elevated the programmer and disinherited the line worker are also the drivers of creative destruction, with its gifts of innovation and growing wealth. By embracing creative destruction, we decide (though we seldom admit it) to make economic sacrifices of those who become obsolete. A changing world greatly diminishes the range of their choices and thus the richness of their freedom in a way that bears scant relation to any responsibility implied by their own choices.[1]

Anticipating such disruption can push personal choices toward excessive caution. Some who might have trained as researchers in a high-risk, high-reward field of science such as genetic engineering or nanotechnology end up instead in civil engineering or law school because the downside risk of specialized training is too great, and while there are second acts in American economic life, they are uncertain and often a long time in coming. The social cost of these self-protective choices is partly a loss to innovation, which depends on risk taking.[2] The personal cost is in the range of viable alternatives from which individuals choose and also in self-realization, the exploration and refinement of identity that bold choices can produce: people with a sense of vocation give it up or never discern it. The rationale for all this mercilessness is, of course, to enable creative destruction and enforce economic discipline on unproductive personal choices, such as those of bad poets and boring documentary-film producers, whose sense of vocation others feel neither the wish nor the duty to subsidize. These are welfarist considerations par excellence, bearing directly on the wealth, and hence the range of choices, that future generations will enjoy. Yet the loss to freedom is also real: in the arbitrary disruption of life plans, narrowed alternatives for choice, and diminished self-realization.

Is it possible to have more freedom now without sacrificing the future? The economist Robert Shiller has proposed an approach that might help. It would protect people from some of the downside risk of daring choices without encouraging wasteful careers and idle noncareers. The idea is that before beginning training in a field, people could buy a novel form of income insurance.[3] Instead of guaranteeing a set level of income, it would ensure that if the field of employment—nanotechnology or intellectual-property law, for example—performed worse than expected, everyone in that field (and covered by the insurance) would receive a subsidy, regardless of how well each individual did. By contrast, if the field did better than expected, meaning that a person trained in it should have ample opportunity to make a good living, participants would receive no support, even if they did poorly or left the field altogether. How fields were expected to do would be a function of market pricing, as in more familiar kinds of insurance. (Because many trainees have little money, it might be appropriate to finance insurance along the lines of student loans.) This would amount to setting up voluntary risk spreading across sectors of the economy, making it possible to share the benefits of creative destruction while limiting its costs. Because the policies would be market driven rather than simply redistributive, and because individuals could not game the system by opting out of productive careers, this scheme would also be compatible with market efficiency and its welfarist benefits. From the point of view of individual choice, it would be a way to create both more security and more freedom to choose a career, and to stop sacrificing the futures of the unlucky to overall economic dynamism.

The conviction that individuals do, and should, bear responsibility for the shape of their own lives limited only by energy and initiative is a halfway splendid idea. The splendid half is the idea of responsibility itself: that people can choose and make their choices effective. The belief that we have the power to shape our lives may also help us respect one another. But this idea has a cruel corollary, as we have seen in the discussion of free labor and its limits: your failure is regarded as your own, even in the face of crushing constraint. The belief in responsibility turns out to be at once optimistic and merciless, respectful and cruel.[4]

The paradox underlies the value of an economic order that fosters the greatest possible individual achievement while protecting people as much as possible from market forces beyond their control. Such an arrangement is the only way to make libertarian and welfarist impulses mutually reinforcing and make responsibility a real premise of economic life rather than the hollow hope that Robert Hale denounced. Where these values are mutually reinforcing, the chance for self-realization will be greater, too. The greatest opportunity for success and the least exposure to arbitrary failure must be the formula for a political economy that can be called freedom promoting.

CLIMATE CHANGE AND MODERN POLITICAL ECONOMY

The issue of how to design and achieve a regime for allocating claims on the earth's atmosphere can benefit from an understanding of the economy as a dynamic engagement with values, in which each choice of organizing principles creates the setting in which future values will emerge to guide later choices. Approached one way, taking our present economy as a fixed set of principles, the problem can seem nearly insoluble. Approached with a broader view, the issue looks less hopeless.

Begin with the pessimistic take. Climate change might have been designed to confound modern political economy. Take the first principle of economic life: the idea, made cliché in Adam Smith's metaphor of the invisible hand, that when individuals pursue their respective self-interest, their choices will combine to create maximum social welfare.[5] This idea depends, of course, on the premise that people take on—internalize, in the economists' language—the benefits and harms that flow from their decisions. Otherwise, externalities kick in: benefits and harms that do not redound to those who create them.[6] These may lead people to do too few beneficial things, because they do not themselves get the full benefit, or—what is important here—to do too many harmful things, because the damage falls on others.

Climate change threatens to be the externality that ate the world. Within a year of emission, carbon dioxide is uniformly distributed throughout the global atmosphere. The person who uses energy derived from fossil fuels gets the full benefit of that power while evenly dividing the atmospheric harm with (at the time of writing) somewhat more than 6.6 billion people.[7] That is a ratio of benefit to harm guaranteed to create overindulgence. (Imagine being able to enjoy a certain elevation, giddiness, and self-confidence with every drink you took, while distributing hangovers, weight gain, chemical dependence, and impaired driving across the entire human population. For a while we'd all be pretty giddy, excepting the Mormons, and distilleries would do a booming business; but eventually everybody else's drinking would leave each of us wretchedly sick.) When the aggregate result of externality-driven overuse is potentially catastrophic climate change, the principle of maximizing social welfare through self-interested individual decisions has hit a tragic juncture, in which externalized harms overwhelm internalized benefits.

The invisible-hand premise of economic life has a complementary political premise: when individual pursuit of self-interest runs off the rails, political decisions can correct the problem by rearranging property rights or otherwise regulating activity.[8] Paradigm cases of such political intervention include bans on self-interested activity that offends core moral sensibilities, such as inducing others to enter contracts of enslavement or to sell their organs,[9] and correcting externalities, as pollution-control laws do. Correcting greenhouse-gas externalities is, technically speaking, relatively straightforward. Either a tax on emissions of carbon dioxide and its heat-forcing equivalents or a cap-and-trade system could impose on emitters a monetary expression of the harm their emissions cause.[10] This would reduce short-run demand and, more important, spur investment in alternative energy sources and more efficient energy use.[11]

The difficulty is that political and legal decisions have their own scales of space and time, which are not those of climate change. Spatially, most political decisions occur at the scale of the nation-state and its subdivisions. A truly global problem reproduces for any jurisdiction the same problem of externalities that confounds individual choices: a national public must absorb the full cost of any measure to address climate change but will receive only a fraction of the globally distributed benefit—a benefit, moreover, that may be overwhelmed by others' growing emissions.[12] From the point of view of a politician proposing measures to address climate change, the proposal can resemble a massive foreign-aid project: a U.S. policy, for instance, would distribute 95 percent of its benefit to foreigners on a per capita basis.[13] National-level action is likely to be both politically unattractive and environmentally ineffective for these reasons. The scale of a political fix may have to be that of the problem: all the earth.

The difficulty is even worse for international action. The anticipated effects of climate change are diverse. Thus by some prominent estimates, the United States would have been a massive net loser from adopting the Kyoto Protocol because the costs of implementation would have been much greater than the cost of unmitigated climate change.[14] Some other countries, notably Russia, might be net *gainers* from climate change, at least for many decades.[15] Because every major country must participate to create a comprehensive regulatory scheme, such diverse interests present a serious barrier to an effective international regime.[16] It should be possible in principle to redistribute the benefits of climate-change mitigation by buying off reluctant countries, as Europe did to induce Russia to join the Kyoto accord.[17] But this approach presents serious difficulties, such as strategic misrepresentation of anticipated national interest as countries jockey to be bought off; the problem of holdouts, even when countries do not misrepresent themselves; disputes about the appropriate international distributions of benefits and burdens; and political reluctance to subsidize the mitigation efforts of foreigners.[18]

The problem of temporal scale is even more basic. Each year's greenhouse-gas emissions commit the global atmosphere to decades of atmospheric change, and the sum of these changes may emerge over an even longer time as natural and anthropogenic influences interact.[19] This means that the benefits of mitigating climate change will accrue to future generations while the living bear the costs. Domestic political decision making, particularly in democracies, is tied to electoral cycles ranging ordinarily from two years (the U.S. House of Representatives) to seven (the maximum period between British parliamentary elections). Within any political cycle, it is highly likely that the costs of a serious mitigation effort will outweigh the benefits. Moreover, the benefits are unavoidably uncertain because so many elusive and perhaps unanswerable questions attach to climate forecasting.[20] Indeed, the benefits are never knowable because they are calculated in harms that did not occur, relative to unavoidably speculative alternative scenarios. A politician seeking constituent support for climate-change policy must make the case for present sacrifices in the interest of future generations. Those beneficiaries are strangers to the generation that bears the cost, and their benefits are matters of guesswork, both now and in the future.

It might seem, then, that climate change is the Achilles' heel of modern political economy, a problem whose spatial and temporal scale produces overwhelming externalities and confounds political responses. The scholarly literature has suggested as much;[21] more popular commentators describe the issue as if it called into question the basic premises of our political and economic life.[22]

So a way of understanding economic and political decisions that envisages people as rational in a microeconomic way—that is, as maximizing their own self-interest—leads to a set piece of pessimism. Of course, it is *conceivable* that people could be motivated to address climate change if they were highly altruistic, selflessly concerned about both living foreigners and future generations; but generally speaking, they are not.[23] If anything, conventional rates of discounting for the value of future lives probably overstate the willingness of the living to make concrete sacrifices now for the well-being of future generations.[24] Conventional rational behavior by individuals with conventional values looks like a recipe for shared disaster.

A similarly pessimistic picture emerges if we begin from a different and complementary view of decision making: the psychological portrait of individuals' persistent and patterned deviation from microeconomic rationality. Ranged together under labels such as "cognitive bias" and "behavioral economics," these deviations constitute ways in which individuals differentially assess alternatives that, viewed according to some canon of rationality, are not different in any way that supports that distinction. For instance, in assessing the importance of a phenomenon—say, the magnitude of risk associated with it or the urgency of doing something about it—people overestimate greatly the importance of phenomena that are *salient*, that is, readily available to the mind.[25] Salience is frequently a cultural fact, often occasioned by a highly visible event. For instance, terrorism acquired great salience in the wake of September 11, 2001, with the result that Americans not only ranked it very high among threats and problems facing the country but estimated their personal risk of suffering a terrorist incident at a little over 8 percent—a vast overstatement, which would have more than 25 million Americans a year directly affected by terrorism.[26] Historically, environmental legislation has often been prompted by salience-producing incidents, such as the burning of the Cuyahoga River, which contributed to the Clean Water Act, and the discovery of toxins at Love Canal, which inspired Superfund legislation.[27]

So far, such events have been elusive for climate change, perhaps because the relevant causal links are subtle and open to dispute. Hurricane Katrina was horrific—enough so to make salient the impression that the Bush administration was incompetent and callously indifferent to governance—but linking it to the Intergovernmental Panel on Climate Change's general forecast of more severe storms could easily seem like special pleading.[28] The same goes for droughts and hot summers: is any particular season evidence of the general phenomenon of climate change? Purely speculative images, such as the immersion of coastal areas in the computer simulation in *An Inconvenient Truth*, seem to be received as science fiction, or guesswork, not salient fact.[29] It may be that the mind's appetite for salience demands specificity and causal definiteness of a kind that a global and causally complicated set of changes does not provide. If so, that would be a considerable barrier to political action on the issue.

Consider another cognitive bias: people value, and seek to help or avenge, individual victims of wrongs.[30] As the number of victims multiplies, the value observers place on each individual victim falls.[31] Asked to contribute to a humanitarian cause, respondents give much more to help a single victim whose face they are shown than to alleviate a general problem—say, a drought or political oppression—that produces such victims.[32] In fact, when shown the victim's face *and* given the general description of the problem, they give *less* than when confronted with the face alone.[33] Knowledge plus sympathy is less motivationally powerful than sympathy uneducated.[34] This is an especially precise rendition of Stalin's grim quip that while one death is a tragedy, a million deaths are a statistic.[35] Global climate change may be, in Stalin's sense, the ultimate statistic: too diffuse and encompassing to concentrate moral attention in the way an individual face can do.[36]

Recent developments in public opinion regarding climate change are consistent with this pattern. A growing share of poll respondents affirms that climate change is a real, human-caused problem and that something should be done to address it.[37] When, however, respondents are invited in an open-ended fashion to name the most important challenges facing the country or the issues most important to them, or when they are asked to rank a list of issues in importance, climate change makes a weak showing.[38] An issue with this profile may not develop the kind of committed constituency that will reward politicians for pursuing it.

Microeconomics, then, suggests that few people will consider the benefits (to others) of dealing with global climate change worth the costs (to them). The appeal of microeconomic accounts of rationality is their supposed psychological realism: those who hold them are meant to be free of illusion about what motivates people.[39] This view has the weight of former treasury secretary and Harvard

University president Lawrence Summers's much-invoked dictum that no one in human history has ever washed a rented car.[40] A similar appeal attaches to accounts of cognitive bias: this, and not some more ideally moral or rational model, describes the messed-up human predicament.

The problem is that neither model can account for some of the most important events in political history. For instance, the 1838 act of Parliament that abolished slavery throughout the British Empire has confounded generations of scholars attempting to explain it as an expression of economic self-interest, whether of the empire in relation to competitors or of interest groups within the empire.[41] David Brion Davis, the foremost living scholar of slavery, has concluded that British abolition amounted to self-administered "econocide," a devastating blow to the imperial economy, and that Britons well understood this.[42] To take another example, while the microeconomic theory of rationality predicts that public officials will always seek to maximize the resources and power of their branch of government, a recent comprehensive study of U.S. executive-branch practice shows that it is not so: for many decades, presidents and their representatives did not assert certain technically viable claims of constitutional prerogative against the legislative branch.[43] They were certainly capable of imagining and making those arguments; but they did not do so.

Switching from microeconomic rationality to cognitive-bias theories of political psychology, we again find critical and relevant events that confound the conventional account. Here the problem is one of question begging. What determines the meaning of a salient event? Take the burning of the Cuyahoga. The conflagration that preceded the Clean Water Act was not the first time the river had burned: earlier events had not inspired a perception of environmental crisis.[44] Moreover, viewed as if by an anthropologist from another culture, a burning river is not necessarily a symptom of environmental crisis, rather than an entertaining side benefit of an industrial economy—like Teflon and the space program, but more fun to watch. For this to be the meaning of the burning river, a whole series of earlier exercises in persuasion had to occur, including John Muir's Romantic evocation of unspoiled American nature as a redemptive counterpoint to industrial society and Rachel Carson's image of a world poisoned by human misjudgment.[45] These drew in turn on long traditions of moral rhetoric and imagery, notably literary Romanticism for Muir and the apocalyptic tradition for Carson.[46] There is no such thing as a natural neurological fact called salience, which leads the brain to fire signals of moral distress upon certain highly visible events: the moral valence of salient events, and perhaps even their salience itself, is a cultural fact formed by traditions of argument.[47] This is even true in some degree of such deep patterns as the moral-psychological importance of individuals and their faces. We learn to regard the faces and lives of those different from us as signifying less human value than those like our own, or we learn the opposite.[48]

Of course, the kinds of motives that led Parliament to abolish slavery and American presidents to refrain from indefinite claims of executive power can be perfectly well modeled as self-interest: as a formal matter, one can have an interest in seeing one's values realized. Here, however, the model is no use in making sense of politics unless it involves some premises about what people's goals are, and these are generally modeled as money and bureaucratic power. Even as basic a concept as externalities depends on what counts as a harm and what a benefit, that is, what the relevant actor values. Those with perfectly altruistic preferences would not regard a selfless decision to give up fossil fuels as producing a positive externality: instead, they would see themselves as receiving the full benefit of the choice by the very act of benefiting others. An externality is not a natural fact unless people's preferences are natural facts. The earlier, standard analysis of the role of externalities in climate-change politics smuggled in the reasonable premise that most people pursue standard economic self-interest most of the time. The lesson of the historical counterexamples is that this is not always the whole story, and the rest of the story—the additional motives that drive superficially counterintuitive decisions or fill in the cultural meanings of salience—are historically and culturally particular. To understand past decisions and the prospects of future ones, therefore, it is important to understand these motives and appreciate how they arise and change.

At least three kinds of moral motives are relevant here—and there are certainly others, such as sympathy, which this discussion does not take up. One is righteousness, the desire to be on the side of justice.[49] This works on the level of identity and is expressed through such declarations as "I am not a racist," "I wouldn't work for Blackwater," or "I stand up for the unborn." Such considerations figure all the time in choices of career, political contributions (it is impossible to explain hundreds of thousands of small-denomination contributions in simple public-choice terms as individual attempts to purchase desired policy outcomes), participation in charity and civic life, and so forth. One of Davis's conclusions about British abolitionism is simply that millions of Britons had come to believe that slavery was profoundly wrong, and they wanted no part of it.[50] Their desire to be right overwhelmed material self-interest.

A second moral motive is protecting dignity—the qualities, generally close to the core of one's identity, that command respect. Experimental economics shows that people will give up considerable cash rewards to punish others who have tried to "short" them or otherwise failed to show them respect.[51] Davis's interpretation of British abolitionism places dignity near the heart of the relevant motives. He argues that a new register of personal dignity among the working and middle classes of Britain, the ideal of free labor, drove their abhorrence of slavery.[52] The free-labor ideal held that laborers, artisans, or smallholders had special dignity arising from self-ownership and autonomy.[53] What made free labor "free" was always defined in part by the counterpoint of slavery.[54] New social classes drove the empire to "econocide" because the imperial slave economy was anathema to their identities and sense of dignity. To return briefly to the other historical example, presidential power and the self-restraint of many executives: the historian Gordon S. Wood concludes that a vision of republican dignity, in which an honorable man sought power not for its own sake but for the public good, was the source of early precedents for executive restraint.[55] Presidents did not behave as certain conventional models of rationality predict not because it would not have occurred to them to do so but because grabbing as much power as they could would have been a self-inflicted insult.

A third relevant moral motive is reciprocity. When people decide whether to participate in a scheme of cooperation, ranging from a small-numbers game to a society-wide practice such as voting or paying taxes, they are much more likely to cooperate if they believe others are doing so as well.[56] Studies suggest that for most people reciprocal cooperation is a basic form of satisfaction, connected with positive social reinforcement and interpersonal recognition.[57] Those who try to cooperate and discover others refusing to, by contrast, feel slighted; they feel like suckers, and they stop cooperating themselves.[58] The ideal of free labor was also an ideal of reciprocity, a vision of social order as governed by the voluntary agreements and reciprocal negotiation of autonomous yet interdependent individuals.

With all this in mind, we can return to climate change with sharper vision. What follows from this discussion? First, we should understand the politics of climate change—in presidential contests and other political forums but also in the broader cultural debate—as an attempt to work out how the issue relates to some of our basic moral motives. One question is whether we will develop a moral vision of global ecology that will power value-based decisions by people whose identity involves doing the right thing by the planet. We know this is not just airy talk—not necessarily, anyway—because it has been a precondition of our politics concerning other environmental issues, such as water pollution and open-lands conservation. There are already signs of such a thing in states', regions', and municipalities' adoption of climate-change measures.[59] Seen in the light of conventional self-interest, these decisions are paradigms of futility, almost caricatures of the problems of scale that I outlined earlier—as if Salt Lake

City could affect the global climate![60] Seen as an aspect of working out moral motives whose content is partly a product of intertwined political and economic life, they are both efforts to be on the right side of a global crisis and attempts to persuade others to do the right thing in relation to climate change. They are intended to "scale up" not just as policy models in the laboratory of democracy but as imperatives for a responsible polity. Policies can themselves be efforts at persuasion, and these seem to fall into that category.

Economic activity can also be an effort at moral persuasion and training moral attitudes. For the advocates of free labor, slave societies reproduced themselves by training their members to identify with hierarchy and subordination, while free economic relations taught people to approach one another with respect and forbearance. By comparison, every aspect of the current economy reflects and reinforces the expectation that greenhouse-gas emissions are costless, from non-dense housing and transport patterns to energy-inefficient architecture. Local climate policies and individual decisions such as buying carbon offsets are efforts to create the opposite expectation, to model an economy that would be relentlessly oriented toward taking account of the harms of emissions. Adopting national legislation that puts a price on such emissions, either by tax or by cap and trade, would affect static judgments about the relative costs and benefits of consumption and investment decisions; but it would also dynamically affect attitudes about what is a morally appropriate economy. Such attitudes percolate up from smaller-scale economic and regulatory initiatives to affect the prospect of ever passing such legislation. This, then, leads to a third point: economic and political decisions will be mutually reinforcing in the developing debate about climate change.

Finally, there is an unavoidable argument about what counts as reciprocity in climate policy. The failure of the Kyoto Protocol in the United States had a lot to do with a conception of fairness: that for the United States to take on mitigation costs while major developing-country emitters do not would make American taxpayers suckers in a nonreciprocal global scheme.[61] A different sense of fairness is at work in some developing countries, such as India, where the conventional view is that rich countries contributed most of the current anthropogenic atmospheric carbon, and it would make suckers of developing countries for them to take on the costs of mitigating a problem whose benefits have flowed mostly to generations of rich Europeans and Americans.[62] Any global climate accord will have to overcome conventional forms of the collective-action problem; but it will also have to contend with this difference in ideas of what would count as a scheme of reciprocity. Success on this front will depend not just on mediating among existing ideas of reciprocity but on revising those ideas going forward.

(This need not mean, by the way, that there will have to be global consensus on values, or that values rather than material interests will be the main drivers of an agreement, just that the terms of any agreement will both depend on and affect how people in relevant countries understand fairness and reciprocity in climate change.)

Addressing climate change will involve moral and social vision, a conception of economic life as inherently incorporating qualitative engagement with values. These same issues are prominently at stake in debates about property rights in digital activity, another area where today's decisions amount to a choice of futures.

FREEDOM IN A DIGITAL AGE

Legal scholarship's most explicit engagement with the political economy of freedom is in the debates over the future of intellectual property. A new generation of intellectual property reformers argues that this field of law should promote democratic debate in an increasingly visual culture and empower individuals to influence the technological and social structures that they inhabit. Recognizing the common cause between these new scholars and activists and the freedom-promoting tradition in property would help participants in this and other areas of reform to understand themselves as not disparate tinkerers and malcontents but a movement.

The debate over intellectual property as a problem of freedom has gained visibility from the appearance of Yochai Benkler's important work on the political economy of peer production, Lawrence Lessig's *Free Culture*, and James Boyle's *The Public Domain*.[63] This body of freedom-oriented intellectual property scholars has been branded the "copy left" by the *New York Times Magazine*, ever a reliable observer and creator of cultural currents.[64]

Several distinct conceptions of freedom inform intellectual property debates.[65] Lessig's treatment of copyright law in *Free Culture* chiefly addresses the cultural and political stakes of "semiotic democracy,"[66] or, in the formulation I prefer, free speech for a visual age. The rise of sophisticated and inexpensive digital technology enables individuals to "rip, mix, and burn" visual elements of the common culture for satirical, editorial, or expressive purposes. The same technologies, however, also facilitate monitoring by copyright owners to block newly possible expressive uses. Conjoined with expanded copyright protection, these developments mean that people are prohibited from exercising substantial capabilities they would otherwise enjoy, so their expressive and political freedom may be significantly restricted.

The capability to join in the hurly-burly of visual culture is all the more important because of the continuing movement of American popular and political culture from verbal to visual expression. One has only to read Abraham Lincoln's career-making address on slavery and the Constitution at New York City's Cooper Union—a text that reads today like an uncommonly articulate law review article but which elevated Lincoln to stardom in the young Republican Party—to understand how much has changed.[67] Such a speech would today be a heroic if not an impossible feat, while the manipulation of spectacle—witness President George W. Bush's then-popular but ill-fated arrival on an aircraft carrier under the banner proclaiming "Mission Accomplished,"[68] Michael Dukakis's devastating ride in a tank,[69] or Bush's facial expressions during the first presidential debate of the 2004 general election[70]—is the common currency of politics. This trend holds despite the impressive eloquence that Barack Obama has recently brought to national politics.

This change affects the political stakes of intellectual property. In an age of visual politics, the ability to use clips of presidential television appearances, musical soundtracks, ad logos or advertising slogans, and other rip-and-mix materials for political and cultural commentary is as essential as free access to the dictionary was for pamphleteers in the eighteenth century. Review the widely watched satirical video of George W. Bush and Tony Blair as mutually enamored young lovers[71] or Jon Stewart's collage forming an acrimonious debate between George W. Bush the isolationist of 2000 and Bush the Wilsonian expansionist of 2004,[72] and consider what it would mean for the satirists to lack access to these materials. What if King George had owned the words *tyranny* and *liberty,* and the American colonists had been obliged to do their pamphleteering without these and other essential terms?

Maybe a more apt counterfactual is to consider what might have happened had the American colonists and their descendants been able to control subsequent uses of the phrases that defined their vision of liberty. The language and imagery of the Declaration of Independence became a template for public announcements that one subordinate group or another would no longer accept subjection. Many of these uses both extended the announced principles of the original document and attacked the hierarchical worldview that many of its signatories held. The Declaration figured in the public language of anticolonial risings for well over a century, into the period when the United States had moved from settler colony to quasi-imperial power.[73] It was the model for the Declaration of Sentiments issued by a pioneering gathering of feminists at Seneca Falls, New York, in 1848.[74] One of the signatories of that document was the former slave Frederick Douglass, an abolitionist orator and writer, who with fellow activ-

ists Lysander Spooner and Gerrit Smith created a school of constitutional interpretation that put the promise of the charter of rebellion, "all men are created
equal," at the heart of the much more restrained 1789 charter of governance.[75]

Ripping and mixing changes the structure of cultural production from one in
which a few companies produce spectacles that everyone else consumes to one
in which many decentralized creators vie with one another for the attention of
many disparate audiences. The result is not a Habermasian Enlightenment salon,
nor an idealized town meeting of deliberative democracy.[76] It is, however, less
hierarchical and centralized than the present arrangement.

It may also be less likely to train its audience in passivity, as each viewer is
also a potential creator and commentator. That is a democratic advance in the
tradition of free speech, even if it has less to do with systematic presentation and
assessment of reasons than with the opportunity of ordinary citizens to portray
the emperor unclothed. The model wielder of this liberty is the skeptical and
creative citizen who refuses to have his or her cultural field defined by CNN,
CBS, and FOX News. The appropriative artist is, in archetypal spirit, what the
poacher once was: a populist hero defying the prerogatives of enclosure. Free
speech, one is reminded, has a pair of complementary functions: it contributes
to the structural integrity of democracy by permitting the open vetting of issues
and personalities and it makes possible the existence of a certain kind of citizen—iconoclastic, self-confident, willing to play David to the nearest Goliath.
The interest of "semiotic democracy" spans both dimensions: democratic func-
tioning and democratic personality.

Lessig draws a telling contrast between free culture, in James Boyle's sense of
"[f]ree access to innovation and expression,"[77] and permission culture, an intellectual property regime in which rippers and mixers would need owners' permission to use cultural materials.[78] The thrust of the idea is that one should not have
to ask permission to use a part of one's own culture or propose new meanings to
others who share that culture.

The image of free culture is both an exercise of social imagination and an
account of the legal conditions that make such exercise possible. It describes two
possible worlds, one of cultural constraint, the other of increasing openness and
egalitarian innovation. The freer world is an ideal, a destination. It is also a world
in which other such ideals are easier to produce and more readily shared, where
the imagination has more to draw on and more to respond to than in a permission culture. In a (very important) static way, free culture means that people can
imagine, reflect on, and choose their projects and attachments without having to
anticipate, adjust to, and finally win over the veto of another. In a dynamic way,
it means even more for how people generate shared meanings. These meanings

make up the repertoire of principles, life paths, and sources of dignity and plea-sure that everyone draws on in forming choices and attachments. Like the rela-tion between static and dynamic efficiency in the analysis of private property's purely economic benefits, unconstrained individual choice at any moment con-tributes to a system of innovation in which the next iteration of choice confronts a richer set of alternatives than the last.

APPEALS TO FLOURISHING IN THE PRODUCTION
OF CULTURE AND KNOWLEDGE

Recall that Adam Smith described market society as occupying a middle ground in its choice of social organizing principle. In it, people recruit one an-other to their projects mostly by appeal to economic interest, the appetite for prosperity. This appeal is in contrast to force on the one hand and love — Smith's term — on the other. *Love* in this sense is more than an intimate sentiment. It means recruiting one another by appealing to feelings of identity and purpose. For sound reasons of overall economic benefit, however, these kinds of appeals take the second chair (and occasionally the third) in our version of market so-ciety.

Benkler argues that changes in the capital structure of cultural production cre-ate new opportunities to organize some economic activity by appeals to love, or self-realization, rather than prosperity.[79] The backdrop to this thesis is a picture of the modern economy that has much in common with Robert Shiller's. Because industrial production requires concentrated capital, exemplified by the factory, political decision makers have chosen to govern modern economies by rules that promote maximum productivity under conditions of capital concentration: allo-cation of resources by markets and management of productive relations through hierarchically organized firms.[80] Those rules have the incidental effect of inhibit-ing individual initiative in production and creativity, both because individuals often lack access to enough capital to produce industrial-era goods and because they tend to work in hierarchically organized firms.[81] The burden of Benkler's argument is that, even assuming that these industrial-era arrangements were the best for their time, new technologies make productivity compatible with greater individual initiative. It might be practicable for people to enjoy a broader range of choices of productive activity, including work they feel called to do for reasons of self-realization.

Benkler concentrates on several technological phenomena. One is the prolif-eration of productive capital on a scale suited to individual ownership, in pack-ages that routinely include substantially more capacity than the owner typically uses.[82] The paradigm is the personal computer.[83] Benkler argues that freely sharing this excess capacity is often a cheaper way to put it to use than selling it. Moreover, such sharing may result in uses that are just as socially productive as the uses that market transfers would produce. Benkler cites schemes in which computer users turn over their excess capacity for large-scale computational, mapping, and other tasks that are more cheaply performed by many networked units than by a single mega-unit—particularly where the networked capacity is donated.[84]

From the example of networked computers, Benkler moves by a clever (but mostly implicit) analogy to suggest that people, like their laptops, frequently hold excess productive capacity relative to what the market induces them to sell: people have free time and unused talent. The same technology that puts excess computing capacity to use also permits people to combine their talents and energy in new ways.[85] Participants provide their respective knowledge and effort to a digital stone soup and correct and improve one another's contributions. Benkler's favorite examples are free open-source software, which powers much of the world's information processing; Wikipedia, the collaborative online encyclopedia; and Slashdot, a collaborative news-and-commentary compendium for technophiles.[86] These are significant technological and cultural products, generated by the voluntary and decentralized coordination of talents and energies. Although Benkler does not explicitly identify the motivation that leads people to this work, it is not much of a stretch to suppose that some part of it falls along the axis of flourishing: self-realization and even play.[87]

By making collaborative production possible, network technology turns many who might have been solitary hobbyists into participants in social production. Voluntary, decentralized production gets a boost from the digital technology that has radically reduced the cost of producing and distributing cultural goods. Videos, music, and books (where rendered electronically) are now relatively easy to create and costless at the margin to reproduce—facts that threaten obsolescence for the industrial-model gatekeepers of culture.[88] This development promises to return some cultural production to the craftsman ideal that long attracted both left-wing and right-wing critics of industrial market production: independent creation by people who control their own productive capital and thus can operate outside hierarchical firms (if not outside market imperatives).[89] Record companies, publishing houses, and the film industry have all played roles analogous to that of factories in industrial production: those who wanted to live by creating had to go through them. Now that may cease to be true, at least for some creators. The chance to engage in voluntary, decentralized production outside markets altogether may be an even more radical possibility.

Benkler is interested in increasing the range of choice among forms of productive activity. Benkler contends that modern industrial societies have restricted themselves to hierarchical, spatially centralized forms of production—the model being the capitalist factory—because the technologies of the industrial age made this the most productive mode of organization. New technologies, however, may allow high levels of productivity alongside voluntary and decentralized production.[90]

How best to understand these possibilities in terms of freedom? What aspirations might people achieve under an optimal peer-production scheme that would not be possible in hierarchical production? Here are a few candidates.

First is the capability to work out of inclination as much as out of necessity. Achieving this would mean blurring the distinction between work and leisure. Where that distinction is firm, we trade our time and energy in work for a sum of satisfactions in leisure. The more we find our satisfactions within our main expenditure of time and energy, the less stark the distinction. The difference then diminishes between the "work" activity in which we are not "fully ourselves" because we do it to purchase "our own" time and the activity in which we recognize ourselves as fully present and satisfied.

The second aspiration made achievable by peer production is the capability to be generous without being self-sacrificing. Ever since Aristotle identified the rich man's capacity for magnanimity as a justification of economic inequality, the idea has stuck that social arrangements are better, other things being equal, if they enable people to express generosity. This is not because Aristotle's defense of inequality was entirely satisfactory (that version of generosity relies on another's deprivation, after all) but because of the recognition that generosity is a good virtue to be able to exercise.[91] Participants in peer-production projects such as Slashdot[92] are magnanimous: they meet a need by the voluntary expenditure of their time and skill. They win in return both the subjective moral satisfaction and the social esteem that accompany the magnanimous spending of skill and resources.

One might object that participating in production under a standard firm model has the same benefits: making a living by contributing to the production of something that by the definitions of market analysis satisfies an existing demand—that is, a (perceived and effective) need. The response is phenomenological: you can't be magnanimous in work you have chosen out of necessity. The psychology of magnanimity depends directly on the voluntary character of the activity.

The third capability made possible by peer production is a democratic one: participation in the experimental, incremental reorganization of basic collective activity—in this case, economic production. Because our institutional structures profoundly affect the viable alternatives from which we choose in shaping our lives, the capability to engage with and reform institutions is as important as any more immediate capability. The more legal rules open up experiments with peer production, the greater this experimental capability becomes; the more those rules foreclose experimentation, the more the same capability is diminished.

For another aspiration consider Benkler's analysis of peer production in connection with the theoretical issue of how property regimes mediate interdependence. I have already noted the paradox of the labor market: it brings process freedom with relative indifference to opportunity freedom. There is a basic and probably willful confusion in Adam Smith's characterization of market relations as free and reciprocal. The offer of a shilling is *not* an exercise in persuasion,[93] though it *is* an appeal to interest, and the very fact of the appeal carries the concession that was so important to the early defenders of markets: that people must be recruited by winning their assent, not by wresting it bodily from them. As Hale recognized, however, in offering a shilling one proposes to win the other's assent by appealing to a wish to avoid deprivation—at the limit, absolute deprivation. Moreover the appeal to need is not really an interpersonal one: with prices set by market aggregation, workers know what their labor is worth and how much they must earn to satisfy needs and wants; all bargaining proceeds in the matrix of market pricing, so that a recruitment appeal to one individual's need is in a real sense just an instance of a general calculus of need. The participants are from this perspective fungible features of the system.

How might this change when an economy takes on some of the qualities Benkler identifies: diffusion of productive capital; an increase in the economic value of unique rather than fungible human capital, such as creativity, aesthetic or ethical judgment, or broad and synthetic knowledge; and increasing opportunities to participate in nonmarket production motivated by desire for the esteem of peers, consonance with one's own values, or self-expression? The critical difference will be in the type of recruitment appeal most likely to be effective. Consider, for instance, how entrepreneurs in a peer-production scheme will appeal to contributors whose music, essays, videos, or other products they wish to solicit. How can an individual entrepreneur stand out from other would-be impresarios of the peer-production world? The entrepreneur cannot do it by simple capital accumulation because the mode of production is premised on widely distributed productive capital; where a factory owner controls a major piece of capital whose concentration is necessary to industrial production, that advantage is not available here.[94] In addition, whatever appeal the entrepreneur makes will have to take account of competition from others with similarly low capital-based barriers to entry. Finally, in recruiting nonfungible, creative resources, entrepreneurs may have to consider a dynamic relationship between the manner of the recruit-ment and the quality of the product: more dramatically than in the case of repli-cable physical tasks, the quality of creative products reflects the state of mind of the creator. A grudgingly composed sonnet, symphony, or screed, absent certain perverse forms of genius (both O. Henry and Douglas Adams were reportedly locked in hotel rooms to induce them to finish their best work), will probably reflect the resentment of the creator more vividly than a grudgingly completed oil change or sheetrocking job. Indeed, as an orchestrator of human talent, the kind of person I am describing here may be less an entrepreneur, as traditionally understood, than an impresario.

Under such circumstances, the impresario must appeal to the self-understandings of the recruited participants, offering the proposed activity as a source of meaning in their lives. This type of appeal is familiar from advertising and branding—that is, appeals to people as consumers rather than producers.[95] It is standard in those areas to appeal to people's ideas of who they are or would like to be: progressive and environmentally conscious shoppers at Whole Foods supermarkets, discriminating and upscale diners at Babbo, Chez Panisse, or Per Se, sleek and athletic wearers of the Nike Swoosh, elevated and intimidating drivers of Hummers, and so forth.[96] In the recruitment of people as producers it is a commonplace that the pleasantness of the work, which may include short or flexible hours or some more basic compatibility with the tastes of a prospec-tive worker, is part of the compensation. The effect of the change imagined here would be to increase the importance of this aspect of recruitment, even making it central to the recruitment appeal. This would mean tilting recruitment away from the need-prosperity axis and in the direction of the flourishing axis, whose chief appeal is this: join me, and you will be more yourself than you would other-wise be.

Finally, let us return to the idea that opened this chapter: the tradition of thinking of property's frontiers as opportunities for social imagination. Does this add anything to the concrete analyses and proposals that scholars and reformers have already developed and that have been drawn in this chapter into a single, loosely bound portrait of reform prospects?

It does in at least three ways. First, recognition that these exercises of social vision fall into a tradition of reform answers a perception of idiosyncrasy, a cer-tain peninsular aspect that may seem to attach to the critical scholars and re-formers of the intellectual property world. "Copyright?" asks the skeptic incredu-lously. "You mean you're the guys who think Negativland and 2 Live Crew are bulwarks of freedom?" Shiller's proposed reforms too easily seem to resemble the wonkish and marginal innovations of public policy mavens, admirable as far as they go, but boring insofar as they are effective, naive insofar as they are interesting. Microfinance has captured the imagination of those who care about poverty reduction, but it has mostly enjoyed the gauzy charisma of good works. Each proposal reveals some of its power when regarded as part of a tradition of freedom-promoting political economy and legal reform.

Second, self-aware exercise of social imagination is a powerful check on the tendency in any reform program to grow fixated by its instruments and become dogmatic where one should be flexible and pragmatic. Microfinance, for instance, can be understood as either an automatic source of "the magic of markets" or as a context-dependent, flexible institutional expression of the "magic" of human innovation and collaboration, which claim various versions of market-making institutions among their tools. The same tendency to make tools into dogmas contributed to the tragic ossification of free-labor thought in the nineteenth century, when principles designed to create new, emancipating social arrangements became formulas for rejecting reform and shutting down innovation—producing, not coincidentally, an unproductive opposition between process-freedom economic conservatism and managerial economic progressivism. The tradition of social imagination bent toward freedom-oriented political economy has always pictured property rights as instruments for the promotion of capabilities, reciprocity, and resistance to domination.

Third, recognition of that tradition means recognition of a common cause. Traditions and movements rest partly on self-interpretations that enable people to think of themselves as joined across space and time. Membership in a movement or tradition is thus not a simple fact but rather the product of activity interpreted, which in turn inspires further activity in the same spirit.[97] Proponents of the public domain, architects of complex risk-management policies, and microfinance entrepreneurs are not disparate public policy eccentrics. They are participants in a broad but genuine tradition. It might not be too much to say that they are part of a movement, if they could but see themselves that way.

This tradition draws attention to the importance of reciprocity as an essential variable of economic systems. Both the liberal free-labor position and the critical strand of thinking that attacked it sought to promote reciprocity: the first by replacing prerogative with consent, the second by seeking to enrich the set of choices that people confront in offering or withholding their consent. Moreover, as Smith first emphasized (first, that is, in the economic analysis of law), reciprocity plays a special role in the endogenous relation of values and preferences to property regimes. By guiding recruitment appeals from coercion toward interest and flourishing and giving each bargainer a relatively wider set of values to consider in making choices, reciprocity sets in motion an open-ended engagement with values that inform both personal identity and social and political commitments.

The tradition of reform that a freedom-promoting approach to property inherits follows a single arc: the incremental replacement of nonreciprocal forms of dependence with reciprocal forms, which are more hospitable to freedom in all its dimensions. In each episode, successful reform requires three elements. One is material conditions that make change possible—for instance, by increasing the overall social surplus that is up for grabs (as the rise of industrial production did) or changing the capital structure of production in ways that affect bargaining positions (as digital technology has done). The second is recognition of the possibility of change: the insight that some dimension of nonreciprocal dependence is now an artifact of human arrangements, not necessity, and a proposal as to why a different arrangement would be better. The free-labor agenda in law and political economy expressed one such recognition, and the proposal to build voluntary, distributed production around digital technology is another. The third element in each episode is a program of institutional action that can concretely change the terms of recruitment. Such programs range from the Thirteenth Amendment to minimum-wage laws to guarantees of access to cultural material for purposes of low-capital creative activity. An increase in all of freedom's dimensions will most likely never be either a pure artifact of political will or a sheer bequest of changed material conditions but always the product of moral and institutional imagination exercised at the juncture of novel technological potential and deliberate political choice.

Sometimes impossibility really is impossibility. At other times, it is potential that has not yet become real. A short list of things thought impossible by the best minds of previous centuries includes some of the axioms of present life: racial and sexual equality, orderly democracy, and economies based on individual choice and self-interest. These were the wild-eyed utopian dreams of other times, up against widely shared assumptions about human nature and institutional limits. Two of those onetime utopian dreams, markets and democracy, are now sources of our own sense of limitation, our reasons for suspecting that climate change may be insurmountable. One, our dominant vision of property as a matter of exclusive rights applied to all valuable resources, may stand in the way of fully realizing the potential of a digital age. At the same time these inheritances can inform today's decisions as we experiment with our institutions and revise our preferences, values, and commitments.

Both climate change and the digital age demand as much technical expertise, and as broad a range of it, as any problems in history. Natural science, engineering, and conventional economics are all indispensable. Nonetheless, the problems are more than technical. Technical solutions will interact with developing ideas about what is right, fair, and dignified. Success will mean moving outward the limits of the possible. That, too, is part of our property inheritance.

AFTERWORD

This book addresses the place of property in the modern legal imagination—that is, how property rights have been thought to secure a society of voluntary coordination, mutual benefit, and flourishing personality. I have found it useful to describe the interlinked, sometimes competing ideals instinct in this vision of society as aspects of freedom with which ownership has been identified: libertarian, welfarist, and personhood-oriented. I have explored relations among these ideals, and between the ideals and the major criticisms of property rights, as expressing some of the tensions that inhere in this social vision. Throughout the book I have tacked between drawing out these tensions, as in Chapters 2 and 4, and urging the partial integration of the ideals as the best way to make good on them and answer the criticisms, as in Chapters 5 and 6 and the Introduction.

How do I imagine that these arguments will affect readers? The arguments of the book are interpretive and, to use a term sometimes associated with Wittgenstein's later work, therapeutic. They concern how we have come to pose normative questions as we do: how we have learned to conceive of our favored values and how we imagine that institutions such as property rights promote or impede those values. They all return to the core idea that divisions in property thought are also divisions in the aspirations of collective life. Among these fragmented views, purity is more likely to be a vice than a virtue. Recognizing the overlap and conflict among competing positions encourages navigating carefully among them rather than cleaving zealously to only one.

Even at their most successful, these arguments will have different effects on different readers. Libertarians might acknowledge that the negative liberties they defend are not crystalline axioms that automatically reconcile freedom and order. Instead, they are instruments impressively but imperfectly formed to promote a social order of dignity and reciprocity. Libertarians convinced of this version of negative rights might rethink certain stances that would follow from a simpler version of the view, such as supporting organ sales, markets in babies, and laissez-faire prostitution, or opposing such mandatory features of contracts as the minimum wage. Even if they retained their beliefs, they might accept that whether to extend libertarian principles to those areas would depend on whether the extension promoted dignity and reciprocity because those aims would seem constitutive of the successful operation of negative liberty.

This is not to say that libertarians will become social democrats: quite the contrary. In fact, libertarians might conclude from this book that the prudential, skeptical part of their tradition, founded on aversion to ambitious uses of state power, emerges better-founded than ever. They might take Robert Hale's realist version of freedom as a warning sign posted over a road best not taken: the dissolution of formal rights into a welfarist, functional account of capabilities and relative power—if everything is freedom, libertarians would conclude, then nothing is freedom, and hence the potency of libertarianism's crystalline principles. Libertarians might also find in Lord Cornwallis's headlong Indian reforms, or even Justice Marshall's complacency in *Johnson v. M'Intosh*, cautions to all would-be welfare-maximizing engineers and support for those who respect prior claims and insist on bargaining from them. But libertarians might also accept from these examples, and in light of their own origins in radical reform, that the danger is in not in reformist social vision itself but rather in exercising power over the relatively powerless and voiceless.

A welfarist who reads this book sympathetically might come to appreciate, with the libertarian, that personal freedom is an essential part of well-being—in its capabilities dimension, to be sure, but also in the dimension that libertarians emphasize, that of irreducibly individual deliberation and choice. Welfarists with this view might also accept that well-being is much diminished for those whose autonomy is psychologically restricted, regardless of their material circumstances—such as, by some accounts, twentieth-century housewives whose labor-saving devices made much less difference in their lives than the waves of new agency that emanated from the feminist revolution. In both respects, welfarists would gain a new appreciation of Jeremy Bentham's substantially libertarian view of property and commitment to the freedom of the mind—essential conditions of his view of welfare.

There is hardly such a thing as a pure personality theorist—the category encompasses a set of motives and arguments rather than a camp—so it is best not to be too schematic here. Instead, let us consider what the critical stances on property, some of them motivated by personality concerns, might take from this book. Romantic critics of property rights might be reached by the deep commitment to personality that figures in the early-modern integrated view of Adam Smith. Such critics, accustomed to understanding libertarians and welfarists alike as partisans of an impoverished vision of the self, might understand both the libertarian and the welfarist programs instead as guided by many of the same goals as guide their own. They might, moreover, find welfarists and libertarians more congenial inasmuch as they accepted those goals as ongoing elements of their own programs. Republican critics concerned with deliberation over values in a democratic polity might also find libertarians and welfarists less hostile so far as members of those camps aim to contribute to a social order in which citizens form the qualities of reflectiveness and self-assurance that make political participation a good idea—central commitments in sophisticated welfarism and libertarianism alike.

Consider also the realist insistence that political choices and political power lie behind the property regime of any large and complex society (if not always those of smaller and tighter-knit communities). The realist criticism also tends to a yet more radical position: denying any clear distinction between public and private exercises of power and treating power instead as a continuum, if not (as it sometimes seems in Hale's work) a brooding ubiquity. The best melioration I can offer such critics is that a commitment to property rights, even to property rights as a special legal category, need imply no naturalizing impulse or obtuseness about the state's role in defining and enforcing rights. Smith, the great "libertarian" integrator with his rich view of free society and personality, was a legal reformer who sought to redefine rights via politics. So, much more emphatically, was Bentham, the great "welfarist" with the commitment to personal liberty and free personality. The naturalizing tendency may reflect an understandable and misguided effort to give a version of social order firmer foundations than any should seek, but it is only contingently connected with property rights, and shaking it off entirely would represent a kind of restoration of an older and more integrated approach to property theory.

The critics do not stand on this book's imagined stage merely to be instructed. The Romantic understanding of personality as a deep, complex, and variegated thing is indispensable to appreciating the full meaning of today's debates in intellectual property, particularly the pathos of "free culture" and the potential of distributed creativity. The realist perspective should always serve to open the imagination, pointing to the extraordinary potential of state power to remake legal arrangements and bring our practice nearer to our vision. Moreover, as I have insisted in this book, seeing the social world as a product of collective choices and political agency is itself an essential aspect of modern freedom and

the visions of order that it informs. While often remote from the everyday operation of property regimes, this insight powered the reforms that helped create
those regimes and also shadows their ordinary activity with the specter of contingency and openness to change. None of this, naturally, resolves the deep tension
between the sovereignty of the state and the voluntary relations of individuals as
modes of achieving social order; indeed, this is the constitutive tension of modern social and political thought, and it runs through property theory as through
much else.

I have argued that adherents of the major approaches to property might be
moved by a picture of history, one joined to an interpretation of the present
anchored in that history. Why? Here, too, the answers are diverse but intercon-
nected. Societies are built on stories and unspoken presuppositions that detail
why and how their practices are legitimate, beneficial, or natural: these lend
shape to the practices of everyday life and help define the purposes and limits of
power. Such repertoires also have critical, even insurrectionary potential: they
make it possible to argue intelligibly that what one's own society does is illegitimate, harmful, or even unnatural. These repertoires, which make up what I have
called the social and legal imagination, tend to have a temporal dimension: they
say not just how we are, but how we came to be as we are. In this respect, we
make sense of the social world through more or less self-aware participation in
traditions. Such traditions are inevitably selective in the elements they choose
and contingent in how they relate these to one another. We inhabit an inchoate
and partly obscured tradition: a view of property, and political economy more
broadly, as aimed at an integrating approach to freedom. Bringing that to the
foreground, making it explicit, is a matter partly of recovery, partly of interpretation, and partly—as with any living tradition—of creation.

To what end? The history of ideas and forms of imagination can seem instructive in several ways to us in the present. The answer is multifarious because the
reality is also that way. By showing the coherence and persistence of a freedom-
promoting ambition of reform, it may clarify and encourage commitment to that
ambition. Of course, it might go the other way instead. By showing the diversity
of ways that people have tried to square the circle of plural values, it might also
inspire some combination of libertarian skepticism about reform and the deeper
prerogative of the skeptic, wariness and ironic reserve in the face of human ambition. Or by showing the emergence, eclipse, and transformation of ways of
thinking of ourselves, it may convince us of the contingency of at least some of
our present habits and lead us to ask what changes we might want to make, and
how we might begin making them.

Notes

INTRODUCTION

1. 2 William Blackstone, Commentaries on the Laws of England *2 (1765–69). This and all other citations to Blackstone's Commentaries refer to the canonical pagination for this work, conventionally indicated by * pages.
2. Id. at *1–2.
3. Id. at *2.
4. Id.
5. Id.
6. Id. at *9.
7. Id.
8. Id. at *8.
9. Id. at *4.
10. Id. at *7.
11. Id.
12. Id. at *2.
13. Id.
14. Id. at *8.
15. Margaret Jane Radin, Contested Commodities: The Trouble with Trade in Sex, Children, Body Parts, and Other Things 53–101 (1996); Carol M. Rose, Privatization: The Road to Democracy? 50 St. Louis U. L. J. 691, 718–20 (2006).
16. Carol M. Rose, Canons of Property Talk; or, Blackstone's Anxiety, 108 Yale L. J. 601, 606 (1998).
17. Id.
18. Id. at 607.
19. 2 Blackstone, Commentaries at *8.
20. Rose, Canons at 622.

CHAPTER 1. PROPERTY AND THE
LEGAL IMAGINATION

1. Charles Taylor, A Secular Age 177 (2007).
2. See id. at 25–89.
3. The exemplary statements of this view are the writings of Robert Filmer and Joseph de Maistre. In Chapter 5 we shall encounter an American descendant of those figures, the pro-slavery apologist George Fitzhugh.
4. See Richard Tuck, The Rights of War and Peace: Political Thought and the International Order from Grotius to Kant 78–108 (on Grotius and the political stakes of his jurisprudence), 140–81 (on Locke and Samuel Pufendorf) (1999).
5. See id. at 140–81; Istvan Hont, Jealousy of Trade: International Competition and the Nation-State in Historical Perspective 159–84 (2005).
6. See Taylor, Secular Age at 176–85.
7. Id. at 181.
8. Id. at 184.
9. Id. at 173.
10. Id. at 172.
11. Id.
12. Johnson v. M'Intosh, 21 U.S. 543 (1823). These issues figure prominently in Chapters 3 and 4.
13. Valuable recent scholarship on Smith's thought and milieu is well captured in Emma Rothschild, Economic Sentiments: Adam Smith, Condorcet, and the Enlightenment (2001). Much of the important early English-language work on the rediscovery of Smith's complex and subtle thought is captured in Wealth and Virtue: The Shaping of Political Economy in the Scottish Enlightenment (Istvan Hont and Michael Ignatieff, eds., 1983). For a general introduction, see The Cambridge Companion to the Scottish Enlightenment (Alexander Broadie, ed., 2003).
14. Smith brings out these themes with particularly force in Smith, The Theory of Moral Sentiments (TMS) 53–90 (2000) (1759). In this portion of the book, Smith outlines his account of "the passions," the basic psychological motives that he takes to be general among human beings. He identifies sympathy, the desire for one's thoughts and feelings to be in harmony with those of others, and emulation, a specific attraction to harmony with the powerful, wealthy, eminent, and graceful, as among the basic principles of social interactions, including economic life.
15. This argument is developed in the section of TMS just cited and in Adam Smith, Lectures on Jurisprudence (LJ) 172–90 (R. L. Meek, D. D. Raphael, and P. G. Stein, eds., 1982) (1762–63). It also receives helpful exposition in Rothschild, Economic Sentiments. Smith wrote, for instance: "Nature, when she formed man for society, endowed him with an original desire to please, and an original aversion to offend his brethren. She taught him to feel pleasure in their favorable, and pain in their unfavorable regard. She rendered their approbation most flattering and most agreeable to him for its own sake; and their disapprobation most mortifying and most offensive" (TMS at 70). On the power of emulation to shape social relations and values, he wrote: "The

man of rank and distinction is observed by all the world. Everybody is eager to look at him, and to conceive, at least by sympathy, that joy and exultation with which his circumstances naturally inspire him" (id. at 51). Such high-ranking figures strike observers as fit to be seen, "[t]o be observed, to be attended to, to be taken notice of with sympathy, complacency, and approbation," while the "poor man goes out and comes in unheeded, and when in the midst of a crowd, is in the same obscurity as if shut up in his own hovel" (id.).

16. Smith, TMS at 70.
17. The contrast with feudal society is chiefly developed in Smith, TMS at 53–90, and that with slave society in Smith, LJ at 172–90.
18. Smith, TMS at 87.
19. Id.
20. Id. at 88.
21. Smith, LJ at 186.
22. Id. at 181.
23. Id. at 186.
24. Id. at 184.
25. Id. at 185.
26. Id.
27. Id. at 352.
28. This characterization of what is distinctive in property rights has recently experienced a revival in contemporary scholarship, notably in the work of Thomas Merrill and Henry Smith. See Henry E. Smith, Property and Property Rules, 79 N. Y. U. L. Rev. 1719 (2004); Thomas W. Merrill and Henry E. Smith, What Happened to Property in Law and Economics? 111 Yale L. J. 357 (2001); Merrill and Smith, Optimal Standardization in the Law of Property: The Numerus Clausus Principle, 110 Yale L. J. 1 (2000). Merrill and Smith have also given a recent exploration of the moral attractiveness of this form independent of its welfare-producing features. See Merrill and Smith, The Morality of Property, 48 Wm. & Mary L. Rev. 1849 (2007).
29. For an insightful and illuminating treatment of this issue in early American property law, see Claire Priest, Creating an American Property Law: Alienability and Its Limits in American History, 120 Harv. L. Rev. 385 (2006). Priest appreciates the interconnections among alienability, risk, and social mobility, and their unity in the social vision of commercial republicanism.
30. See Smith, Property and Property Rules.
31. See, e.g., Robert Nozick, Anarchy, State, and Utopia (1974); John Rawls, A Theory of Justice (1971).
32. For discussions of an approach founded in tradition, see Alasdair MacIntyre, After Virtue: A Study in Moral Theory (1984); MacIntyre, Three Rival Versions of Moral Enquiry: Encyclopedia, Genealogy, and Tradition (1990). Charles Taylor, Sources of the Self (1984) and A Secular Age (2007) are less partisan examples of the same approach, which is defended in its methodological premises in Taylor, 1 Philosophical Papers: Human Agency and Language 45–76 (1985) (setting out Taylor's account of human beings as "Self-interpreting animals") and Taylor, 2 Philosophical Papers:

Philosophy and the Human Sciences 15–57 (1985) (setting out the relevance of contextual interpretation to any understanding of human action). My approach in this
book is much closer to Taylor's in having no brief for a neo-Aristotelian account of the
virtues; rather it is founded on the premise that contextual interpretation is essential
to social inquiry. For an earlier study of American property thought in this vein, see
Gregory S. Alexander, Commodity and Propriety: Competing Visions of Property in
American Legal Thought, 1776–1970 (1997). Also in this vein, with somewhat more
commitment to a neo-Aristotelian view, is Eduardo M. Peñalver, Property as Entrance,
91 U. Va. L. Rev. 1889 (2005); Peñalver, Land Virtues (unpublished manuscript, on file
with author).

33. These two concerns structure most of Chapters 1 and 2 and in some measure Chapter 3.

34. This is much of the concern of Chapters 4 and 5.

35. This is the project of Chapters 6 and 7.

36. See Isaiah Berlin, Two Concepts of Liberty, in The Proper Study of Mankind: An
Anthology of Essays 191, 193 (Henry Hardy, ed., 1997).

37. See Richard Pipes, Property and Freedom 282 (1999) (arguing that property is a necessary prerequisite for political liberty); James W. Ely, The Guardian of Every Other
Right: A Constitutional History of Property Rights 26 (1998) (describing how "the
protection of property ownership was an integral part of the American effort to fashion
constitutional limits on governmental authority"); James M. Buchanan, Property as
a Guarantor of Liberty 59 (1993); James V. DeLong, Property Matters 46–49 (1997);
Richard A. Epstein, Takings: Private Property and the Eminent Domain (1985) (arguing in favor of an absolutist conception of property rights); Milton Friedman, Capitalism and Freedom 7–21 (1962).

38. See Richard A. Posner, Economic Analysis of Law (6th ed., 2003); Thomas W. Merrill and Henry E. Smith, Optimal Standardization in the Law of Property; Robert C.
Ellickson, Property in Land, 102 Yale L. J. 1315, 1320–21 (1993). Welfarism is so influential as to be a default mode in normative discussions of property law, but these are
three of the outstanding, indeed iconic, figures in the field. An enormous amount of
descriptive work is closely related in assuming that economic efficiency is the purpose of private property regimes. For an illuminating summary of this approach, see
Thomas W. Merrill, The Demsetz Thesis and the Evolution of Property Rights, 31
J. Legal Stud. 421 (2002). For one of the most supple recent applications of this approach, see Henry E. Smith, Exclusion Versus Governance: Two Strategies for Delin-
eating Property Rights, 31 J. Legal Stud. 453 (2002).

39. See Margaret Jane Radin, Property and Personhood, 34 Stan. L. Rev. 957 (1982). A
novel and extremely illuminating application of this approach to the domain of intellectual property is the "autonomy" branch of Yochai Benkler's account of the values
that an information-driven political economy can serve. See Yochai Benkler, Freedom in the Commons: Towards a Political Economy of Information, 52 Duke L. J.
1245, 1247–48, 1254 (2003) (describing how new technology presents an opportunity
to make personal autonomy and economic productivity mutually reinforcing). This
argument is also recognizable in Jeremy Waldron, The Right to Private Property 301–2

(1988) ("It is necessary for the free man not only to be independent of others, but actively to assert himself as a free and independent will and to be recognized as such by others.").

40. See Radin, Property and Personhood.

41. See Peñalver, Property as Entrance.

42. For an excellent summary of this line of argument, see Barbara Fried, The Progressive Assault on Laissez-Faire: Robert Hale and the First Law and Economics Movement 29–107 (1998). For canonical original statements, see Robert L. Hale, Freedom Through Law: Public Control of Private Governing Power 3–34, 385–99 (1952) (diagnosing property rights as establishing economic relationships of reciprocal threat and exploring modes of legal mitigation and equalization of threat); Joseph W. Singer, The Reliance Interest in Property, 40 Stan. L. Rev. 611, 650–51 (1988) ("As Hale tried to teach us, every transaction takes place against a background of property rights. And the definition, allocation, and enforcement of those entitlements represent social decisions about the distribution of power and welfare. No transaction is undertaken outside this sphere of publicly delegated power; the public sphere defines and allocates the entitlements that are exchanged in the private sphere. At the core of any private action is an allocation of power determined by the state."). The original canonical statement of this view is Morris R. Cohen, Property and Sovereignty, 13 Cornell L. Q. 8 (1927).

43. See Hale, Freedom Through Law.

44. Particularly instructive here is Fried, Progressive Assault on Laissez-Faire at 71–107 (setting out the realist criticism of "the empty idea of property rights").

45. See Joel M. Ngugi, Re-Examining the Role of Private Property in Market Democracies: Problematic Ideological Issues Raised by Land Registration, 25 Mich. J. Int'l L. 467, 499–500 (2004) (arguing that Kenyan land-titling programs were driven by opportunistic elites who used the government's reform to create a landed gentry at the expense of farmers); James Boyle, The New Enclosure Movement and the Construction of the Public Domain, 66 L. & Contemp. Probs. 33 (2003) (analogizing current developments in intellectual property rights to the movement to enclose common property in England); Khiara M. Bridges, Note, On the Commodification of the Black Female Body: The Critical Implications of the Alienability of Fetal Tissue, 102 Colum. L. Rev. 123, 158–61 (2002) (arguing that black women, because of economic necessity and internalized oppression, will be uniquely vulnerable to the dehumanization of a market for fetal tissue); Emily Marden, The Neem Tree Patent: International Conflict over the Commodification of Life, 22 B. C. Int'l & Comp. L. Rev. 279, 292–93 (1999) (discussing the benefits Western pharmaceutical companies derive from patents on plants discovered in India, where commodification of such living things runs counter to long-held traditions). In some ways the origin of this line of argument is Pierre Proudhon, What Is Property? An Inquiry into the Principle of Right and of Government 14 (Donald R. Kelley & Bonnie G. Smith, trans., 1994) (declaring, "property is theft").

46. See Margaret Jane Radin, Contested Commodities: The Trouble with Trade in Sex, Children, Body Parts, and Other Things 54–60, 83–88 (1996). Radin has elsewhere

expressed the idea as follows: "We want the legal system to make a commitment to an ideal of noncommodification of love, family, and other commitments close to ourselves. . . . [S]ome people think that if we start talking about children as things we own, and about one as being fungible with the other, and we expect them to maximize our pleasure in life, we might start actually trading them one day" (Radin, Conceiving a Code for Creation: The Legal Debate Surrounding Human Cloning, 53 Hastings L. J. 1123, 1126 [2002]). See also Lee Taft, Apology Subverted: The Commodification of Apology, 109 Yale L. J. 1135, 1146–47 (2000) (arguing that the use of apologies as bargaining chips in settlement negotiation drains a "moral process" of meaning by making it a "market trade"); Jennifer Fitzgerald, Geneticizing Disability: The Human Genome Project and the Commodification of the Self, 14 Issues L. & Med. 147, 151–52 (1998) (arguing that regarding the self as a bundle of alienable resources stunts the ability to discern noneconomic value in persons); David E. Jefferies, The Body as Commodity: The Use of Markets to Cure the Organ Deficit, 5 Ind. J. Global Legal Stud. 621, 655 (1998) (considering the argument that a market in organs will reduce altruism); Norman W. Spaulding, Commodification and Its Discontents: Environmentalism and the Promise of Market Incentives, 16 Stan. Envir. L. J. 293, 311–13 (1997) (considering the psychological experiences of "commodity fetishism" and "alienation" as consequences of commodification). See also generally Note, The Price of Everything, the Value of Nothing: Reframing the Commodification Debate, 117 Harv. L. Rev. 689 (2003) (surveying arguments concerned with the devaluation of commodified goods and relationships, and proposing that it arises less from the designation of the goods as commodities than from the character of the consequent transactions, in which the fungibility of values is assumed).

47. See Gregory S. Alexander, Commodity and Propriety 1–4 (1997); Peñalver, Land Virtues; Michael J. Sandel, Democracy's Discontent: America in Search of a Public Philosophy (1996); Sandel, Justice and the Limits of Liberalism (1982); Jennifer Nedelsky, Private Property and the Limits of American Constitutionalism: The Madisonian Framework and Its Legacy (1990).

48. See Amartya K. Sen, Rationality and Freedom 581–695 (2002) (reprinting Sen's 1991 Kenneth J. Arrow Lectures and setting this argument with both conceptual lucidity and technical detail).

49. See the discussion of commercial republicanism in Priest, Creating an American Property Law.

CHAPTER 2. NEW VISIONS OF ORDER

1. Extract from the Debates at Putney, 102, 119 (statement of Thomas Rainborough), in The English Levellers (Andrew Sharp, ed., 1998).

2. Hugo Grotius had already composed a theoretical jurisprudence combining natural sociability and natural rights into a new account of society, but the arguments at Putney suggest that such a vision was only beginning to work its way into the legal imagination, even of radicals. For discussion of Grotius on these issues, see Richard

Tuck, Philosophy and Government, 1572–1651, 154–201 (1993) (locating Grotius's methodological innovation within the jurisprudential and political currents of his time, as well as the events of his own life); Tuck, Natural Rights Theories: Their Origins and Development 58–81 (1979) (emphasizing the radicalism of Grotius's methodological reliance on individual rights and their voluntary, conditional surrender to a sovereign).

3. Locke uses the language of political authority to define inherent self-sovereignty: a person in the pre-political condition is "absolute lord of his own person and possessions," commander of an "empire" in himself, and not yet "subject . . . to the dominion and control of any other power" (John Locke, Two Treatises of Government, 2.9.123 [Peter Laslett, ed., 1960] [1690]). His account of how political order was constructed voluntarily from these natural-rights building blocks continued in paragraphs 131–49.

4. Putney Extract at 110 (statement of Oliver Cromwell).

5. Id. at 108 (statement of Henry Ireton).

6. Norah Carlin, The Causes of the English Civil War 147 (1999). As Carlin stresses, this overarching ideology did not imply consensus on the content of constitutional values. On the contrary, the agreement about the character and source of authority contained substantial differences in emphasis and interpretation, which emerged in the rapid efflorescence of English political ideas after 1642, and it accounts, for instance, for the marriage of natural-rights and ancient-constitutional arguments in the Leveller case at Putney. See id. at 147–54.

7. J. G. A. Pocock, The Ancient Constitution and the Feudal Law 31 (1957). An illuminating discussion of these issues is at 30–55.

8. For an exemplary contemporary discussion of these events, see Michel de Montaigne, Of Cannibals, in Essays 150–59 (Donald M. Frame, trans., 1976). For historical discussions of the significance of the events, see Anthony Pagden, Lords of All the Worlds: Ideologies of Empire in Spain, Britain and France c. 1500–c. 1850 (1995); Tzvetan Todorov, The Conquest of America: The Question of the Other (Richard Howard, trans., 1984).

9. See Tuck, Philosophy and Government at 31–64 (describing the rise of new modes of social and political thought within the disruptions of European politics).

10. See id. at 39–64.

11. See the materials on Grotius in Tuck, Philosophy and Government; Tuck, Natural Rights Theories.

12. Bacon, Aphorism 28, Book 1, Novum Organum (1620).

13. Bacon, Introduction to Novum Organum.

14. See Charles Taylor, A Secular Age 25–89 (2007) (setting out a traditional view and its premises).

15. See Carlin, The Causes of the English Civil War 1–12 (1999) (briefly surveying the history of the historiographic quarrel) and passim (elaborating); R. C. Richardson, The Debate on the English Revolution Revisited 1–9 (1988) (briefly surveying) and passim (examining the history of histories on the topic from the seventeenth century forward).

16. For a partisan but vivid and informed discussion of this literature, see Christopher Hill, The World Turned Upside Down: Radical Ideas During the English Revolution (1972).
17. See Putney Extract at 102 (Statement of Ireton).
18. Id. at 110 (statement of Cromwell).
19. Id.
20. See Carlin, Causes of the English Civil War at 155.
21. Id.
22. Putney Extract at 104 (statement of Ireton).
23. Id. at 117.
24. Id. at 108.
25. Id. at 104.
26. Id. at 106 (statement of Rainborough).
27. Id. at 105.
28. Id. at 103.
29. For a discussion of this issue, see Eduardo M. Peñalver & Sonia K. Katyal, Property Outlaws, 155 U. Penn. L. Rev. 1095, 1153–54 (2007) (discussing the necessity excuse for theft in relation to Aquinas).
30. Putney Extract at 114 (statement of Ireton).
31. Id. at 109.
32. See Tuck, Philosophy and Government at 241–53 (discussing the Levellers' conception of electoral democracy and its relation to their idea of legitimacy).
33. Putney Extract at 110 (statement of Cromwell).
34. Id. at 108–9 (statement of Ireton).
35. Id. at 108.
36. Id. (emphasis added).
37. Adam Smith, An Inquiry into the Nature and Causes of the Wealth of Nations 25 (R. H. Campbell, A. S. Skinner, & W. B. Todd, eds., 1976) (1776) (drawing attention to this aspect of human nature). Smith's view of humanity was deeply informed by the ideas of sociability discussed in this book, while Ireton's were not.
38. Putney Extract at 103 (statement of Ireton).
39. Id. at 109.
40. Montesquieu identified the birthplace of commerce as "among men who are constrained to hide in marshes, on islands, on the shoals, and even among dangerous reefs. . . . [F]ugitives found security there. They had to live: they drew their livelihood from the whole universe. Commerce, sometimes destroyed by conquerors, sometimes hampered by monarchs, wanders across the earth, flees from where it is oppressed, and remains where it is left to breathe: it reigns today where one used to see only deserted places, seas, and rocks; there where it used to reign are only deserted places." See Jedediah Purdy, Being America: Liberty, Commerce, and Violence in an American World 40 (2003).
41. Putney Extract at 108 (statement of Ireton).
42. For a thorough discussion of the engagement of the early sociability theorists with the compromised Aristotelian legacy and the stark alternative represented by Thomas

Hobbes's unsociable theory of natural rights, see Istvan Hont, Jealousy of Trade: International Competition and the Nation-State in Historical Perspective 159–84 (2005).

43. See id.

44. See Thomas Hobbes, Leviathan (Richard Tuck, ed., 1992) (1651). For a discussion of Hobbes in the context of the English Civil War, see Tuck, Philosophy and Government at 312–45. For a discussion of Hobbes's bearing on the development of sociability theory, see Hont, Jealousy of Trade at 159–84.

45. See Hobbes, Leviathan at 88 (declaring of mankind in the state of nature: "men have no pleasure [but on the contrary a great deal of grief] in keeping company, where there is no power to over-awe them" because they are driven to compete and seek to dominate one another by "competition" for "gain," "diffidence" in the interest of "safety," and "glory" in pursuit of "reputation").

46. See id. at 88–90. Competition for gain is, for Hobbes, one of the three great sources of the conflict that identifies human existence without a sovereign as a state of war.

47. Orderly commerce appeared to Hobbes to be impossible in such circumstances. There could be, he wrote, "no place for Industry; because the fruit thereof is uncertain: and consequently no Culture of the Earth; no Navigation, nor use of the commodities that may be imported by Sea; no commodious Building," a series of negations and absences leading up to the pronouncement of "continuall feare, and danger of violent death; And the life of man, solitary, poore, nasty, brutish, and short" (id. at 89). Without the establishment of sovereignty, there could be "no Propriety, no Dominion, no Mine and Thine distinct; but onely that to be every mans, that he can get, and for so long, as he can keep it" (id. at 90).

48. See Hont, Jealousy of Trade at 39–40 ("Smith described three kinds of society: the society of fear, the society of love or friendship, and, in the middle, commercial society. . . . Smith's third type of society was modeled on Pufendorf's secondary natural sociability. It rested on the need for material self-preservation and on utilitarian reciprocity as its modus operandi").

49. See Albert O. Hirschman, The Passions and the Interests: Political Arguments for Capitalism Before Its Triumph (1981).

50. See Hont, Jealousy of Trade at 45–46 (explaining how mutual need produced a kind of society in Aristotle's view but of a sort that fell short of political society and was centered institutionally on the extended household rather than in larger webs of commerce).

51. See id. at 173 (describing Pufendorf as establishing, or restoring, "the concept of [economic] society as an organizational form independent of the civitas" and thus giving social order "a separate foundation in men's sociability rather than in state power founded upon contract").

52. See id.

53. Id. at 364.

54. Id. at 179.

55. Hont discusses the relation of the four-stages theory to the account of sociability in Jealousy of Trade at 100–102, 364–67.

56. 2 William Blackstone, Commentaries on the Laws of England *3 (1765–69).

57. Id. at *6.

58. Id.

59. Adam Smith, Lectures on Jurisprudence 459–60 (R. L. Meek et al., eds., 1978) (1762–63).

60. This theme is at the center of Chapter 4, on the social and legal imagination attending Chief Justice Marshall's opinion in *Johnson v. M'Intosh*.

61. Even this contrast is unstable because, as Hont points out, Pufendorf was more committed than Grotius to an individualistic view of the person in the state of nature but rigorous in his commitment to sociability as a distinct and interest-based source of social order, while Grotius, although he adopted a mechanism of natural rights and sovereignty as the basis of his jurisprudence, imagined an innate human taste for social life that brought him somewhat nearer to the civic strand of Aristotelianism than Pufendorf. See Hont, Jealousy of Trade at 160–64.

62. See Taylor, Secular Age at 165–70 (setting out the economic vision of society and identifying it intellectually with Grotius and Locke).

63. See James Tully, An Approach to Political Philosophy: Locke in Contexts 16–23 (1993) (on the status of "natural subjection theory" such as Filmer's in the eighteenth century and Locke's aims in countering it).

64. See Robert Filmer, Patriarcha and Other Political Writings (Johann P. Somerville, ed., 1991), in which he writes, "The question is not whether there shall be an arbitrary power, but the only point is who shall have that arbitrary power, whether one man or many?" (The Anarchy of a Limited or Mixed Monarchy, in Patriarcha at 132).

65. See Filmer, Anarchy at 140–41. He wrote of sovereignty: "[N]atural freedom being once granted, there cannot be any one man chosen a king without the universal consent of all the people in the world at one instance, nemine contradicente" (id. at 140). Filmer also argued that if one assumed human beings were naturally free, they would be mad to put themselves under a king, and so to assume natural freedom was to assume the impossibility of political order—an argument akin to those we saw earlier from the conservatives at Putney. See id.

66. See Jeremy Waldron, The Right to Private Property 148–53 (1988).

67. Locke, Two Treatises of Government at 2.5.31.

68. Id.

69. Id.

70. Id.

71. Id. at 2.2.6.

72. Id. at 2.5.31.

73. Id. at 2.5.37, 47–48.

74. Id. at 2.5.46.

75. Id. at 2.5.48.

76. Id.

77. Id. at 2.5.37.

78. Id. at 2.5.32.

79. Id. at 2.5.34 (emphasis added).

80. Id. at 2.5.37.

CHAPTER 3. VARIETIES OF PROGRESS

1. I will use the terms *reversioner* and *remainderman* synonymously in this chapter, as the technical difference between them has no bearing on my argument. The person occupying this position is typically a member of either of two classes: a landlord from whom the tenant rents, or an heir whose inheritance vests fully only at the end of a life term in the tenant.

2. Restatement (Second) of Prop.: Landlords & Tenants § 12.2(1) (1977). I have omitted "leased" twice from the Restatement's characterization simply to avoid confusion because I am discussing both leased property and life estates, which were far more widespread in the nineteenth century than they are today, and thus contributed importantly to the formation of waste doctrine.

3. See id. § 12.2(1) cmt. c.

4. See Richard A. Posner, Economic Analysis of Law § 3.11 71–74 (6th ed., 2003) (discussing different methods for creating an efficient management strategy for divided-ownership estates).

5. See id. at 73.

6. See id. at 71–74.

7. See id. at 72–73.

8. See Pynchon v. Stearns, 52 Mass. (11 Met.) 304, 311 (1846) (stating that action consistently practiced by regional farmers is not waste); Keeler v. Eastman, 11 Vt. 293, 293–94 (1839) (stating that tenant does not commit waste by acting "in a prudent and husbandlike manner"); Owen v. Hyde, 14 Tenn. 334, 339 (1834) (explaining that the tenant did not commit waste "if the proportion of wood land was such as that a prudent farmer would have considered it best to reduce a portion of it to cultivation").

9. Jackson v. Brownson, 7 Johns. 227, 232–34 (N.Y. Sup. Ct. 1810); see Clemence v. Steere, 1 R.I. 272, 274 (1850) (noting that "it is necessary to show that change is detrimental to the inheritance" to prove waste); Davis v. Gilliam, 40 N.C. (5 Ired. Eq.) 308, 311 (1848) ("The tenant may use the estate, but not so as to take from it its intrinsic worth."); Pynchon, 52 Mass. at 312 ("[N]o act of a tenant will amount to waste, unless it is or may be prejudicial to the inheritance"); Keeler, 11 Vt. at 294 (stating that tenant may make changes to the land, but "not so as to cause damage to the inheritance"); Shine v. Wilcox, 21 N.C. (1 Dev. & Bat. Eq.) 631, 632 (1837) ("[T]he cutting down of timber is not waste, unless it does a lasting damage to the inheritance"); Owen, 14 Tenn. at 339 (arguing that the question to ask in a waste case is "did [the tenant] materially injure the . . . estate[?]").

10. See Posner, Economic Analysis of Law § 3.11 at 72–73.

11. See Morton J. Horwitz, The Transformation of American Law, 1780–1860, 54–58 (1977).

12. See John G. Sprankling, The Antiwilderness Bias in American Property Law, 63 U. Chi. L. Rev. 519, 533–36 (1996).

13. See id. at 534–36.

14. See Horwitz, Transformation at 54–62.

15. See Sprankling, Antiwilderness Bias at 533–36.
16. Statute of Marlborough, 1267, 52 Hen. 3, c. 23, § 2.
17. See generally 1 Edward Coke, A Commentary upon Littleton 53a–53b (18th ed., 1823) (detailing the numerous and intricate restrictions on tenants' land use under waste law).
18. See 2 William Blackstone, Commentaries on the Laws of England *283 (1765–69).
19. See 7 W. S. Holdsworth, A History of English Law 278–79 (3d ed., 1925). See generally 3 W. S. Holdsworth, A History of English Law 121–22 (3d ed., 1923) (discussing traditional remedies for waste).
20. 2 Blackstone, Commentaries at *281.
21. 3 William Blackstone, Commentaries on the Laws of England *223 (1765–69).
22. See 7 Holdsworth, History at 277–78 (noting the strictness of the common law rule).
23. See 2 Blackstone, Commentaries at *281–82; 1 Coke, Commentary at 53b.
24. See 2 Blackstone, Commentaries at *281; 1 Coke, Commentary at 53a.
25. See 2 Blackstone, Commentaries at *281–82.
26. See 1 Coke, Commentary at 53a.
27. Id.
28. Id.
29. See 2 Blackstone, Commentaries at *282. This restriction was largely dispensed with in the eighteenth and nineteenth centuries, as it was seen as anachronistic and onerous. See 7 Holdsworth, History at 277–78.
30. See 1 Coke, Commentary at 53a; 2 Blackstone, Commentaries at *282.
31. See 2 Blackstone, Commentaries at *282.
32. As Coke put it, "If the tenant convert arable land into wood, or e converso, or meadow into arable, it is waste, for it changeth not onely the course of his husbandry, but the proofe of his evidence" (1 Coke, Commentary at 53b; 2 Blackstone, Commentaries at *282 [quoting this language from Coke]).
33. 1 Coke, Commentary at 53b.
34. The Provost and Scholars of Queen's College, Oxford v. Hallett, 14 East. 489, 491 (K. B. 1811). In this case, the tenant "erected fences and banks . . . subdivided the same [land] into small inclosures . . . [and] ploughed up and converted great part into tillage" (id. at 490). The plaintiffs did allege that the value of the property was reduced, which was of course material to damages, but it was not the focus of the court's inquiry. See id. at 489–90.
35. See Jones v. Chappell, 20 Eq. 539 (1875). In this odd case, a plaintiff who had no reversionary interest in the property concerned sought to bring an action of waste against the tenant of a neighboring site whose industrial activity had blocked the plaintiff's air and light. See id. at 539–41. Besides noting that such a case could not be brought as a matter of standing, the court held that "to prove waste you must prove an injury to the inheritance" (id. at 541; see also Meux v. Cobley, 2 Ch. 253 (1891) [finding that where a lease explicitly permitted agricultural activity in keeping with that of the neighborhood, and other farmers had built greenhouses, the defendant tenant could not be liable for waste for doing the same]).
36. By "distinct reasons," I mean that the embrace of manufacturing within English law

reflected neither the republicanism nor the imperative to clear wilderness that motivated the change in the United States.

37. See West Ham Cent. Charity Bd. v. E. London Waterworks Co., 1 Ch. 624, 636 (1900)
   ("If the permanent character of the property demised is not substantially altered, as for
   instance, by the conversion of pasture land into plough land, by breaking up ancient
   meadows, or the like, I conceive that the law is that it is not now waste for the tenant to
   do things which within the covenants and conditions of his lease he is not precluded
   from doing."). The case these decisions typically cite, Doe v. Earl of Burlington, 5 B.
   & Ad. 507 (1833), drew on de minimis exceptions to waste law to hold that a tenant's
   tearing down of an ancient and ruined barn was not waste and went on: "[T]here is no
   authority for saying that any act can be waste which is not injurious to the inheritance"
   (id. at 517). Courts continued to treat changes in the course of husbandry as injuries
   to the inheritance but to look to the relevant covenant to avoid finding waste in cases
   of industrial development or improving buildings. See, e.g., West Ham Cent. Charity
   Bd., 1 Ch. at 646; Meux, 2 Ch. at 260–61.

38. See Alan Schwartz, The Default Rule Paradigm and the Limits of Contract Law,
   3 S. Cal Interdisc. L. J. 389, 390 (1993). As Schwartz notes, these defaults were the
   earliest identified by scholars and have been the ones most studied. Id. at 390 n.1.

39. See id. at 390; see generally Ian Ayres & Robert Gertner, Strategic Contractual In-
   efficiency and the Optimal Choice of Legal Rules, 101 Yale L. J. 729 (1992) (introduc-
   ing the concept of an equilibrium-inducing default). Waste law had this character, of
   course, only inasmuch as it averted a less than maximally efficient use of resources;
   simply preventing a transfer of resources from reversioner to tenant is not per se
   equilibrium-inducing (although widespread expropriation would erode the landlord-
   tenant relationship systemically, which might have counterefficiency effects).

40. Schwartz, Default Rule Paradigm at 391.

41. For a discussion of the ways in which complex sets of considerations can enter into
   normative judgments regarding alternative social arrangements, or "social states," see
   Amartya Sen, The Possibility of Social Choice, in Rationality and Freedom 65, 76–97
   (2002).

42. Schwartz, Default Rule Paradigm at 391.

43. Particularly informative on the possibility of meaningful "transformatory" activity in
   the law is Sen's caution against taking people's presently existing views of their own
   well-being as dispositive for the evaluation of their well-being. Those who are severely
   deprived are least likely to regard themselves as such, while those who have some command over resources or social esteem are correspondingly more likely to complain of
   their condition. See Sen, Social Choice at 90–92.

44. The Supreme Court was then the highest court of legal appeals in the state.

45. Jackson v. Brownson, 7 Johns. 227 (N.Y. Sup. Ct. 1810).

46. Id. at 228. The Schuyler manor sat on the eastern side of the Hudson River, about a
   third of the way from Albany to New York City. See Charles W. McCurdy, The Anti-
   Rent Era in New York Law and Politics, 1839–1865, 3 map 1 (2001).

47. Jackson, 7 Johns. at 228.

48. Id. at 227–28.

49. See id. at 227–29.

50. See id. at 229. There was some dispute on these facts, as the plaintiffs claimed that Brownson had entirely cleared his portion of the land. See id. at 228.

51. See id. at 229. The trial court held that the sublease had created a new lease between Brownson and his lessor, severing the old lease, and that his actions since the new lease began did not constitute waste. See id. at 229.

52. For a description of one of New York's largest landholding families, see McCurdy, Anti-Rent Era at 10–15. See also Lawrence M. Friedman, A History of American Law 210–11, 222 (1973) (noting reforms to New York property law in reaction to the estates on the Hudson); Gordon S. Wood, The Radicalism of the American Revolution 109–22 (1992) (discussing the attempts of the American colonists to emulate the social hierarchy of England).

53. See Wood, Radicalism at 271–86 (describing a second, social, revolution against the American aristocracy); Drew R. McCoy, The Elusive Republic 62–70 (1980) (recounting the hopes of Benjamin Franklin and other revolutionaries that Americans would remain a "virtuous" people of farmers, artisans, and other independent laborers); Eric Foner, Free Soil, Free Labor, Free Men 11–39 (1970) (discussing the Republican Party's Civil War–era platform advocating for the nation's laborers, a group that northern society at the time defined to include farmers, small businessmen, and independent craftsmen).

54. See Jackson, 7 Johns. at 227.

55. See id. at 229–32.

56. See id. at 232–35.

57. See id. at 232–33.

58. The advocates of a stricter definition of waste were in the dissent, despite the majority's agreement that waste had occurred in the case at hand, because they agreed with the trial court that the defendant's sublease of a portion of his land to a third party had annulled the original agreement with Schuyler and its provision for forfeiture upon waste. They accordingly contended that there was no basis for a forfeiture action and that the plaintiffs should have sought damages instead. See id. at 235–37 (Spencer, J., dissenting).

59. Id. at 236–37.

60. Id. at 237.

61. Id.

62. Id.

63. Id.

64. Id. Morton Horwitz takes a different view of the dissent's position. In Horwitz's view, the dissenting minority "wanted to go still farther in changing the law to suit the necessities of development" and to sever "entirely the right to property from the right to prevent tenants from completely altering the estate" (Horwitz, Transformation at 55). There is some ambiguity as to just what the dissenters intended to propose. As Horwitz rightly notes, the dissent would have denied the English rule of waste for an action for forfeiture, based on an interpretive principle: "[I]n construing a covenant which is to work a forfeiture, courts adhere strictly to the precise words of the condition, in order

to prevent the forfeiture" (Jackson, 7 Johns. at 235 [Spencer, J., dissenting]). Because the dissenters regarded the majority's standard as vague and unreliable, they would have ruled that waste doctrine could not be invoked in actions of forfeiture or ejectment. See id. In an action for damages, however, the dissenters observed that "then indeed we should have a right to give the covenant not to commit waste a greater latitude of construction" (id. at 237). This suggests that the dissent did not imagine such covenants to be void as to damages but only as to forfeiture. It is in the context of this hypothetical discussion that the dissenters rejected the majority's standard as "fanciful and vague" and praised the clarity of the English common law rule.

   Unfortunately, the nature of *Jackson v. Brownson* makes it difficult to discern what the dissenters believed should be the default rule of waste since the case dealt not with defaults but with the interpretation of a contractual covenant. Although the dissenters praised the clarity of the common law rule and denounced that rule as a basis for forfeiture, they did not say what they regarded as the appropriate default.

65. Pynchon, 52 Mass. at 312 (holding that cutting a new road through land and breaking up a meadow into cropland were not waste as a matter of law, while whether draining and raising a wetland constituted waste was a jury question).

66. Owen, 14 Tenn. at 339 (holding a widow with a dower estate could cut timber for profit, even where it was not necessary to her support, where such cutting did not do a permanent injury to the estate and was consistent with the use a prudent person would make of the land—particularly when certain of the timbering brought land under cultivation to replace cleared land that had been exhausted by cropping).

67. Clemence, 1 R.I. at 274. The court in this case announced adherence to a standard of waste as what "injured the farm, or was such a change as no good farmer would make" (id.). The court ruled that cutting timber for sale from an estate was ordinarily waste but that a jury might find it not so where, as here, the sale was to support a widow with a testamentary life estate. See id. at 275. The court ruled that cutting hoop poles (timber in an early stage of growth) was waste unless it was the ordinary practice of the area; that permitting land to grow up in brush was not waste unless it met the abstract American standard, although it would have been waste in England, where land was at a relative premium; and, perhaps reassuringly, that a tenant could tear down a barn so dilapidated that it threatened to collapse on her cow. See id. at 274–76. The court also noted that a finding of waste could lead to forfeiture, but only of the particular area of the land wasted, such as a woodlot or a meadow. See id. at 276–77.

68. Shine, 21 N.C. at 632 (holding that a widow and her new husband had not committed waste by clearing some seventy acres of forest for cultivation, in light of the expectation that widows should be able to clear land for their support, and because clearing forest to replace exhausted land was customary in the vicinity).

69. Keeler, 11 Vt. at 294 (1839) (holding that clearing timber to open land to cultivation is not waste if it comports with husbandlike behavior because it does no permanent injury to the estate).

70. See Jackson, 7 Johns. at 233–34.

71. Id.

72. Id. at 234.

73. Owen, 14 Tenn. at 339–40.

74. Pynchon, 52 Mass. at 311–12 (observing that adopting the English rule would arrest "the progress of improvement" in the United States).

75. Shine, 21 N.C. at 632.

76. Jackson, 7 Johns. at 234.

77. See id. at 229.

78. See id. at 234.

79. In 1848 the North Carolina Supreme Court made an effort to formulate the standard of "material prejudice" as a general principle. The court found that a widow holding a life estate could sometimes clear timber for cultivation but could not drain turpentine from living pine trees because the tenant "may use the estate, but not so as to take from it its intrinsic worth" (Davis, 40 N.C. at 311). The court held that turpentine production was analogous to mining, which "is not a thing yielding a regular profit in the way of production from year to year from labor, but it would be taking away the land itself" (id. at 312). In either turpentine production or excessive timbering, the tenant does not take "the product of the estate arising in his own time, but he takes that which nature has been elaborating through ages, being a part of the inheritance itself" (id.). This was a kind of usufructuary standard, and it recurred in the jurisprudence of North Carolina, as in the state supreme court's 1888 dictum that "it may be proper to fix a limit to the denudation, that it do not exceed the annual increase from natural growth which replaces that portion of the trees removed" (King v. Miller, 6 S.E. 660, 666 [N.C. 1888] [holding that clearing land for cultivation was not waste where this was the ordinary practice of the neighborhood]). The formula was also quoted approvingly by the Georgia Supreme Court. See Smith v. Smith, 31 S.E. 135, 136 (Ga. 1898) (holding that a widow might not cut timber for sale where this was neither the ordinary practice of local farmers nor necessary to the enjoyment of the homestead). This case appears to be part of the retrenchment of waste doctrine in a conservative form in the later nineteenth century.

80. See, e.g., Owen, 14 Tenn. at 339 ("[I]f the proportion of wood land was such as that a prudent farmer would have considered it best to reduce a portion of it to cultivation . . . such clearing would not be waste").

81. See, e.g., Shine, 21 N.C. at 632 (holding that the question of waste depended partly on "the ordinary use made of the trees in the part of the country where the land is situated").

82. See, e.g., Jackson, 7 Johns. at 233. Although also reciting the standard that waste was whatever was prejudicial to the inheritance, the Massachusetts Supreme Court held that because "it has been the constant usage of our farmers . . . to change the use and cultivation of their lands, as occasions have required," that action could not be waste (Pynchon, 52 Mass. at 311). Vermont's supreme court, while identifying the "permanent injury" standard as law, found no waste where the court was satisfied that a farm had been "managed by the tenant for life, in a prudent and husbandlike manner" (Keeler, 11 Vt. at 293). Tennessee made the standard of "material injury" specific thus: "[I]f the proportion of wood land was such as that a prudent farmer would have considered it best to reduce a portion of it to cultivation," then there was no waste in cut-

ting timber (Owen, 14 Tenn. at 339). In Rhode Island, in contrast to the strict English rule, "it [was] necessary [for waste] to show that the change [was] detrimental to the inheritance and contrary to the ordinary course of good husbandry" (Clemence, 1 R.I. at 274).

83. See, e.g., Jackson, 7 Johns. at 233 (majority opinion) (contrasting the inflexible English rule with the need for adaptability in the race to tame the American wilderness); Pynchon, 52 Mass. at 311 ("That the principle of [the English rule] under consideration was . . . inapplicable to the condition of the country is obvious").

84. See Schwartz, Default Rule Paradigm at 390–91 (discussing a number of defaults, as opposed to immutable rules).

85. See id. at 392.

86. See id.

87. See, e.g., Pynchon, 52 Mass. at 311 (advocating a standard that distinguished between harmful acts of waste and acts that changed the state of the property but did not cause injury to the reversioner's inheritance).

88. See Jackson, 7 Johns. at 237 (Spencer, J., dissenting).

89. Neel v. Neel, 19 Pa. 323, 326 (1852).

90. See id. at 327–29.

91. Id. at 328.

92. Id.

93. Cf., e.g., Eric T. Freyfogle, Land Use and the Study of Early American History, 94 Yale L. J. 717, 738 (1985) (book review) (comparing legally imposed duties on owners of ecologically sensitive land or historic buildings to the "feudal scheme" of land ownership).

94. The Pennsylvania Supreme Court followed this principle two years later in Irwin v. Covode, holding that if tenant use exhausted a mineral deposit, "it would be no more than occurs in every life estate in chattels which perish with the using. So long as the estate is used according to its nature . . . it is no valid objection that the use is consumption of it" (24 Pa. 162, 167 [1854]). The Virginia Supreme Court upheld the right of a tenant for life to exploit without limit a reservoir of salt-impregnated water and, because the salt works required firewood for fuel, to cut as much timber as was necessary. See Findlay v. Smith, 20 Va. 6 (Munf.) 134, 138 (1818).

95. Richard Posner concentrates his economic account of waste doctrine on this explanation. See Posner, Economic Analysis of Law § 3.11 at 72–73.

96. Imagine, for instance, that the improvement involved clearing land of salable timber: even if the reversioner were willing to let the tenant take the profit from the improvement (from a new crop, for instance) during the tenancy, the reversioner might still insist on taking the income from the timber, and the tenant might refuse.

97. Pynchon v. Stearns, 52 Mass. 304, 310 (1846).

98. Id. at 312.

99. See McCurdy, Anti-Rent Era at 10. Lawrence M. Friedman notes that eliminating the "feudal" and "tyrannical" aspects of the English common law from American property law was particularly urgent to New Yorkers because of the presence of the Hudson River valley estates. See Friedman, History of American Law at 210–11.

100. For a discussion of the difficulties faced by Hudson River valley aristocrats among others, in maintaining their social status, see Wood, Radicalism at 113–15. Wood provides a rich description of the aristocratic cast of pre-Revolutionary American society. See id. at 11–92; see also McCurdy, Anti-Rent Era at 1–31 (describing the aristocracies that controlled the Hudson River valley and the political and social forces that would lead to their demise); Eric Kades, The End of the Hudson Valley's Peculiar Institution: The Anti-Rent Movement's Politics, Social Relations, and Economics, 27 Law & Soc. Inquiry 941 (2002) (detailing the social, political, and economic forces that led to the weakening of the Hudson River valley aristocrats' hold over tenants).

101. See Kades, End at 942.

102. See id. at 950.

103. See id. at 942; McCurdy, Anti-Rent Era at 22–23.

104. See McCurdy, Anti-Rent Era at 1. Two legal theories helped sustain this unorthodox form of leasehold. See id. at 24–31. Parliament's act of Quia Emptores in 1290, established the free alienability of freeholders' land and forbade the creation of new feudal obligations upon sale. See id. at 25–27. However, this act had not been in force in New York at the time the lease-in-fee estates were created because New York was won from the Dutch by conquest—thus the law of England did not automatically travel there—and the state legislature did not adopt its own version of Quia Emptores until 1787, when it passed the Act Concerning Tenures. See id. at 27. Under the other theory, which the New York Supreme Court adopted, lease-in-fee deeds took their validity from the principle of freedom of contract, which authorized the deed-making parties to institute whatever terms they saw fit. See id. at 28–31. It is clearly paradoxical that by this account the liberal doctrine of freedom of contract actually legitimated quasi-feudal arrangements and specifically limited the free transfer of land.

105. See id. at 1.

106. Jackson, 7 Johns. at 232 (emphasis added).

107. See McCurdy, Anti-Rent Era at xiii, 1–31.

108. See, e.g., Wood, Radicalism at 95–109 (describing the pervasive, and sometimes hybrid and confused, character of republican ideology in England); Bernard Bailyn, The Ideological Origins of the American Revolution 22–54 (enlarged ed., 1992) (doing the same); McCoy, Elusive Republic at 48–75 (considering the attempts of Americans at the time of the Revolution to reconcile views of republicanism based on classical antiquity with the realities of American society); see also Gordon S. Wood, The Creation of the American Republic, 1776–1787, 65 (1992) (noting that the republicanism of the American Revolution and the time shortly afterward was more the spirit of a political order than its institutions).

109. See, e.g., Wood, Radicalism at 77–92 (describing political order in eighteenth-century America), 95–109 (describing the rise of republican ideas of political authority).

110. See McCoy, Elusive Republic at 32–47, 67–75, Foner, Free Soil at 11–39. An important distinction is present here between the early republican disdain for the craftsman or merchant in favor of the yeoman, a view derived in important respects from feudal values (see McCoy, Elusive Republic at 39–40), and the later celebration of the free

laborer and entrepreneur as the exemplary, independent bearer of modern liberty (see Foner, Free Soil at 11–39).

111. See Wood, Radicalism at 229–43 (describing the uneasy relation of egalitarian ideology and loyalty to ideas of virtue derived from aristocratic ideals); McCoy, Elusive Republic at 48–75 (describing a more robust view of republican virtue).

112. See Wood, Radicalism at 268–70 for a sketch of Kent's conservatism, which included a defense of property qualifications for voters. See also Gregory S. Alexander, Commodity & Propriety: Competing Visions of Property in American Legal Thought, 1776–1970, 127–57 (1997) (examining Kent's contributions to early American property law).

113. Gregory Alexander presents an illuminating and provocative account of Kent's legal, political, and social views in chapter 5 of Commodity & Propriety (at 127–57). I part company with his characterization in one important respect. For Alexander, Kent was a man between worlds, a celebrant of the new commercial order, indebted to Smith's political economy and committed to the principle of the alienability of land. At the same time, Kent was deeply ambivalent about the social churn of commercial society, its tendency to tear down social ranks and traditions and elevate in their place one sole principle of social order: the pursuit of material self-interest. See id. at 130–33. As Alexander presents him, Kent was indebted to a conservative, Federalist brand of republicanism in his traditionalist aspect, but because he embraced the market, he was no republican: "His nonrepublican understanding of property is revealed by his treatment of land as an object of commerce," rather than as the basis of social and political virtue (id. at 148).

For Kent, as a student of the Scottish school of political economy and Smith in particular, this would not have been a sensible opposition. Alexander proposes that on Kent's view, the function of land was "essentially private: the means to create wealth for individual enjoyment"—a quality indicated by Kent's willingness to regard it as a commodity (id.). For Smith, however, the social function of market relations lay precisely in their commodifying nature: by diminishing the prerogative attached to tradition and status and requiring persons to bargain over the terms of their cooperative enterprises, commerce closed the gap between the classes inherent in feudal and courtly hierarchies See Adam Smith, The Theory of Moral Sentiments 120–46 (2000) (1759).

Though one cannot, of course, simply assimilate Kent's thoughts to Smith's, it is important to appreciate that the tradition of political economy which Kent relied on did not presume that *commodity* and *propriety* were opposed but rather treated them as interwoven. I believe that this fairly characterizes the aspects of Kent's thought I am discussing here, as well.

114. Kent explained the significance of the status in what was, for him, fairly fulsome language: "An estate of freehold. . . . denoted anciently an estate held by a freeman, independently of the mere will and caprice of the feudal lord" (4 James Kent, Commentaries on American Law *23 [12th ed., 1873] [1826–30]). He continued, "By the ancient law, a freehold interest conferred upon the owner a variety of valuable rights

and privileges. He became a suitor of the courts, and the judge in the capacity of a juror; he was entitled to vote for members of Parliament, and to defend his title to the land . . . and he had a right to call in the aid of the reversioner or remainderman, when the inheritance was demanded. These rights gave him importance and dignity as a freeholder" (id. at *24). It bears noting that although Kent's definition of a free-holder included a tenant for life, it was precisely the doctrine of waste that threatened to bring such a tenant, in American law, back under "the mere will and caprice of the feudal lord" (id. at *23).

115. As Kent put it, "In England the right of alienation of land was long checked by the oppressive restraints of the feudal system, and the doctrine of entailments. All those embarrassments have been effectually removed in this country" (2 James Kent, Commentaries on American Law *327 [12th ed., 1873] [1826–30]). He explained the political theory of such restraints: "Entailments are recommended in monarchical governments as a protection to the power and influence of the landed aristocracy; but such a policy has no application to republican establishments, where wealth does not form a permanent distinction, and under which every individual of every family has his equal rights, and is equally invited, by the genius of the institutions, to depend upon his own merit and exertions" (4 Kent, Commentaries at *20).

116. See 4 Kent, Commentaries at *20; 2 Kent, Commentaries at *327.

117. See 2 Kent, Commentaries at *328–29 ("A state of equality as to property is impossible to be maintained, for it is against the laws of our nature; and if it could be reduced to practice, it would place the human race in a state of tasteless enjoyment and stupid inactivity, which would degrade the mind and destroy the happiness of social life.").

118. Jean-Jacques Rousseau expressed similarly austere visions in a letter that harshly rejected the idea that Geneva was better off for having a theater and encouraged the citizens of Geneva to eschew aristocratic ways for virtuous ones. See 10 Jean-Jacques Rousseau, Letter to d'Alembert on the Theater (1758), in The Collected Writings of Rousseau 253, 261–352 (Allan Bloom et al., eds. & trans., 2004).

119. See 2 Kent, Commentaries at *329–30 ("The notion that plain, coarse, and abstemious habits of living are requisite to the preservation of heroism and patriotism, has been derived from the Roman and classical writers. They . . . declaimed vehemently against the degeneracy of their countrymen, which they imputed to the corrupting influence of the arts of Greece, and of the riches and luxury of the world. . . . No such fatal union necessarily exists between prosperity and tyranny, or between wealth and national corruption."). Kent cited as evidence the survival of English liberty amid commerce and the arts, and of French patriotism despite "the effeminate luxury of her higher classes and of her capital" (id. at *330).

120. See id. at *329 ("When the laws allow a free circulation to property . . . the operation of the steady laws of nature will, of themselves, preserve a proper equilibrium, and dissipate the mounds of property as fast as they accumulate.").

121. Id. at *328.

122. In this respect, Kent's thoughts parallel Eric Foner's description of the integral role played by "free labor" in the ideology of the early Republican Party. See Foner, Free Soil at 11–39.

123. See 2 Kent, Commentaries at *256. Kent's characterization of the status of slaves reveals something of the intensity of his conviction that property and economic relationships formed much of a person's substance: Slaves, he wrote, "cannot take property by descent or purchase, and all they find, and all they hold, belongs to the master. They cannot make lawful contracts, and they are deprived of civil rights. . . . Their condition is more analogous to that of the slaves of the ancients, than to that of the villeins of feudal times" (id. at *253). These conditions were among those making slaves "property, rather than persons" (id.).

124. See, e.g., John Locke, Second Treatise of Government, in Two Treatises of Government 285, 309 (Peter Laslett, ed., 1960) (1690).

125. See 2 Kent, Commentaries at *329. This is Gordon Wood's account of the significance of Kent's argument for a property qualification for state senatorial election: it made property a mere "interest," to which everyone in principle had equal access, rather than a permanent marker of distinction. See Wood, Radicalism at 269–70. I think, however, that Wood exaggerates the extent to which this was an unintended consequence of a rearguard effort to preserve hierarchy. Indeed, Kent's own language suggests that he regarded equal access to the acquisition of property as the right sort of egalitarian principle for republican America.

126. This characterization may seem somewhat at odds with the earlier contention that the English rule probably played a large role as a bargain-inducing default. In the formulation presented here, I am less concerned with the actual operation of the English rule than with the American perception of that rule, which the great contrast of the republican imagination, the feudal Old World versus the republican New World, helped to power. The question is not what the English rule did for the English, or even what it might have meant expressively to the English, so much as what it meant to Americans whose self-understanding was partly founded on a (partly imagined) contrast with England.

 To understand the difference between the American conception of English law and the actual workings of property law in England, it is helpful to consider Friedman's contention that much of that difference lay in the openness and rapid turnover of the American land market, and the relative lack of sophistication of American lawyers and conveyancers. See Friedman, History of American Law at 206–7. In England, sophisticated legal devices enabled the gentry to circumvent such restrictions on alienation as the fee tail. In the United States, however, such devices were ill understood, and the flurry of transactions that accompanied the westward movement of the population would have overwhelmed the legal system had each one required elaborate consultation and drafting. Thus a formalism that remained tolerable to the parties it affected in England would have severely inhibited American practice. See id. at 210. The difference, however, was not that English property use was static and property relations feudal. Rather, it was that England was rich, sophisticated, and hierarchical, with limited social mobility, thus allowing a relatively small landholding population to operate with the help of a refined bar. A population with considerable mobility and vast new tracts of land constantly entering the market, however, could not negotiate arcane legal forms. See id. at 206–7. Although Friedman does not mention it, I would suggest that this pragmatic consideration became appended to republican ideology and to the caricature of "feudal" England in part because the feudal aspects of English property law represented everything that would have kept most Americans out of that land market: settled wealth, existing claims on land, and legal sophistication. Republican thought, along with its other attractions, provided a vocabulary of status that treated English wealth and refinement as evidence of corruption, and rough-and-ready American initiative as the mark of virtue.

127. 3 James Kent, Commentaries on American Law *386 (12th ed., 1873) (1826–30).

128. Id. at *386–87 (emphasis removed).

129. Jackson, 7 Johns. at 233.

130. Id. at 237 (emphasis removed).

131. Hastings v. Crunckleton, 3 Yeates 261, 262 (Pa. 1801).

132. Shine, 21 N.C. at 632.

133. King, 6 S.E. at 666.

134. Pynchon, 52 Mass. at 312.

135. Winship v. Pitts, 3 Paige Ch. 259, 262 (N.Y. Ch. 1832).

136. 2 Kent, Commentaries at *329.

CHAPTER 4. HAZARDS OF PROGRESS

1. Johnson v. M'Intosh, 21 U.S. 543 (1823).

2. See Joseph William Singer, Property: Rules, Policies, and Practices 3–15 (3d ed., 2002) (opening discussion of property law with Johnson); Jesse Dukeminier & James E. Krier, Property 3–18 (5th ed., 2002) (same); John P. Dwyer & Peter S. Menell, Property Law & Policy: A Comparative Institutional Perspective 69–75 (1998) (beginning discussion of the legal institutions that frame property practices with Johnson).

3. See Johnson, 21 U.S. 543 at 572 ("The inquiry . . . is, in a great measure, confined to the power of Indians to give, and of private individuals to receive, a title which can be sustained in the Courts of this country"), 588 (holding that the unquestioned power of the U.S. government to convey Indian lands to settlers "must negative the existence of any right which may conflict with, and control it," to wit, a right of Native Americans to convey enforceable title).

4. Id. at 591.

5. Id. at 588.

6. Id. at 590–91.

7. Id. at 589.

8. For a concise account of the modes and varieties of imperialism, see Anthony Pagden, Peoples and Empires (2001) (describing the history of imperial institutions and ideas).

9. The major synthetic work on the normative theory of empire in Europe remains Anthony Pagden, Lords of All the Worlds: Ideologies of Empire in Spain, Britain, and France, c. 1500–c. 1800 (1995). An important recent study of the jurisprudence of imperialism, with particular attention to concepts of sovereignty that become important later in this book, is Edward Keene, Beyond the Anarchical Society: Grotius,

Colonialism, and Order in World Politics (2002). On conflicts in English liberalism with regard to the legitimacy of empire, a major advance was Uday Singh Mehta, Liberalism and Empire: A Study in Nineteenth-Century British Liberal Thought (1999), which argued for a relation between liberal universalism and normative self-confidence about empire. A particularly nuanced recent study, demonstrating the subtle and multifarious variation in liberal attitudes toward empire, is Jennifer Pitts, A Turn to Empire: The Rise of Liberal Imperialism in Britain and France (2005).

10. See Mehta, Liberalism and Empire at 77–114; Pitts, Turn to Empire at 3–5. Although an explicit argument about complexity and multifariousness is not the concern of Edward Keene, it emerges in his discussion of imperial jurisprudence. See Keene, Beyond the Anarchical Society at 97–119.

11. For discussions of the Mills' ideas, see Pitts, Turn to Empire at 123–62; Mehta, Liberalism and Empire at 87–114. The essential primary texts are James Mill, The History of British India (William Thomas, ed., 1975) (1820), which evinces staggering disdain throughout for a Hindu civilization which Mill regards as barbaric and in need of thoroughgoing reconstruction; John Stuart Mill, Considerations on Representative Government 415–16 (Geraint Williams, ed., 1993) (1861) ("There are [peoples] which . . . must be governed by the dominant country, or by persons delegated for that purpose by it. This mode of government is as legitimate as any other if it is the one which in the existing state of civilization of the subject people most facilitates their transition to a higher stage of improvement. There are . . . conditions of society in which a vigorous despotism is itself the best mode of government for training the people in what is specifically wanting to render them capable of a higher civilization. . . . The ruling country ought to be able to do for its subjects all that could be done by a succession of absolute monarchs").

12. See Pitts, Turn to Empire at 204–39.

13. See id. at 25–58 (on Smith's theory of history and attitude toward colonialism), 103–22 (on Bentham).

14. On Burke's attitudes, particularly his long campaign against British rule in India, see id. at 59–100 (arguing that Burke's combination of universalism as to essential humanitarian principles and pluralism toward particular cultures lent suppleness and restraint to his cultural and moral judgment); Mehta, Liberalism and Empire at 153–89 (making a similar argument).

15. Diderot wrote in favor of the right of colonized people to resist colonial expropriation and decried colonization of the Americas as the event that had restored the place of slavery in the modern economy after its long decline in Western Europe. See Denis Diderot, Political Writings 175–77 (on the right of resistance), 185–89 (on colonization and slavery) (John Hope Mason & Robert Wokler, trans. & eds., 1992).

16. Throughout this essay, I am dealing with both specifically legal reasoning, especially concerning relationships among types of sovereigns, and the political, historical, and theoretical self-conceptions that accompanied and often lent sense to these. Consequently, I sometimes use this broad but infelicitous pairing of terms to convey my meaning.

17. For a discussion of the conception of sovereignty and culture that supports this sort of

view, see Keene, Beyond the Anarchical Society at 135–50 (discussing an egalitarian conception of states and nonhierarchical conception of cultures).

18. This view, for instance, was a consequence of the Mills' concept of civilization and sovereignty. See J. S. Mill, Considerations at 415–16; James Mill, History of British India (evincing disdain throughout for a Hindu civilization that Mill regards as barbaric and in need of reconstruction); see also Mehta, Liberalism and Empire at 87–114; Pitts, Turn to Empire at 123–62 (discussing the Mills' influence on the development of imperial liberalism in Britain).

19. To appreciate this idea, consider the American conception of the Soviet Union during the Cold War: it was viewed not as a primitive precursor to modern liberty, yet not as a distinct civilization with its own code of values, but rather as another modern society, and a failure by the modern American values of personal freedom and social prosperity. Such a view of China or the Ottoman Empire, for instance, was widespread in early modern Europe.

20. For a pluralist discussion of civilizations, see John Gray, Two Faces of Liberalism (2000) (arguing for a conception of values as genuinely pluralist, articulated in different, incompatible, and mutually irreducible ways in different civilizations).

21. The relation is not perfect, of course. As Jennifer Pitts points out, Adam Smith's broadly universalist theory of history did not lead him to a reductive or patronizing account of non-European societies as primitive little siblings, partly because both his theory of judgment and his account of the history of Europe emphasized flexibility, context, and contingency, rather than consistent and ineluctable principles. See Pitts, Turn to Empire at 43–52 (discussing Smith's thought in this connection).

22. This is roughly Pitt's characterization of Smith. See Pitts, Turn to Empire. In some ways its exemplar is Michel de Montaigne. See Michel de Montaigne, Of Cannibals, in The Complete Essays of Montaigne 150–59 (Donald M. Frame, ed., 1995) (1588).

23. See Montaigne, Cannibals; Diderot, Political Writings at 175–77.

24. For a discussion of Bentham's mistrust of the moral arrogance of imperialism, see Pitts, Turn to Empire at 103–7.

25. Pitts points out that both James and John Stuart Mill were at pains to establish that British rule in India was a net loss for Great Britain and thus was properly regarded as a charitable, humanitarian project. See Pitts, Turn to Empire at 16.

26. Indeed, the defendants in Johnson, arguing against Native American title, marshaled arguments that had been designed precisely to justify colonial expropriation, specifically the accounts of property and sovereignty developed by Grotius, Locke, and Emerich de Vattel. See Johnson, 21 U.S. 543 at 567–71. On the origins and contemporary uses of this line of argument, which rested on the claim that government originated in private property and thus full sovereignty could not exist in nations that lacked private property—meaning that other property by definition could not be legally symmetrical with European-style regimes—see Richard Tuck, The Rights of War and Peace: Political Thought and the International Order from Grotius to Kant 102–8 (on Grotius), 166–96 (tracing development of this theory from Locke through Vattel) (1999); James Tully, An Approach to Political Philosophy: Locke in Contexts 137–76 (on the use of Lockean thought to abridge aboriginal land claims) (1993).

27. See Declaration of Independence (complaining that King George "has endeavored to prevent the population of these States; for that purpose . . . raising the conditions of new Appropriations of Lands" and "endeavored to bring on the inhabitants of our frontiers, the merciless Indian Savages").

28. See Sean Wilentz, The Rise of American Democracy: Jefferson to Lincoln 153 (on the alliance of interest in the War of 1812 between Britain's defense of Canada and the Indians' checking of American westward expansion), 161 (noting the British plan to hand over Michigan territory to Indian allies on the defeat of the American forces) (2005).

29. See id.

30. The Federalist no. 11 (Alexander Hamilton).

31. Id.

32. Id.

33. It was an essential part of Montaigne's irony that an understanding of the frailty and foolishness of the great and the common flawed humanity of all offered a check against the conceits of power. In this respect, his irony served to unsettle self-confidence with the aim of diminishing the motives of unreflective action. See Montaigne, Cannibals.

34. On the importance of the War of 1812 in consolidating a political culture committed to westward expansion and the interests of settlers, see Wilentz, Rise of American Democracy at 175–78.

35. Thus Joseph Singer treats *Johnson* as evidence that "both property rights and political power in the United States are associated with a system of racial caste" and that "property rights in land cannot, for the most part, be traced to a system of individual merit and reward" but rather reflect the use of state power on behalf of favored groups. See Joseph William Singer, Sovereignty and Property, 86 N. W. U. L. Rev. 1, 5 (1991). Singer proceeds to argue that *Johnson* proves that the "historical basis of original acquisition of property in the United States is not individual possession in the state of nature, with government stepping in only to protect property rights justly acquired. Rather, it is redistribution by the government from those who were thought not to need the property or to be misusing it to those who were thought to need it" (id. at 51). See also Liam Seamus O'Melinn, The Imperial Origins of Federal Indian Law: The Ideology of Colonization in Britain, Ireland, and America, 31 Ariz. St. L. J. 1207, 1270 (1999) (terming the "principles" of *Johnson* "the intellectual product of a centuries-old vision [of] a simple native, thought to be in need of imperial instruction, and possessed of valuable commodities to exchange for the blessings of civilization").

36. Philip Frickey has argued that "*Johnson* seemed to establish a rigid dichotomy between power and law. Colonialism, *Johnson* seemed to say, raises almost exclusively nonjusticiable, normative questions beyond judicial authority"—the questions Marshall classed with "natural right and the uses of civilized nations" (Philip P. Frickey, Marshalling Past and Present: Colonialism, Constitutionalism, and Interpretation in Federal Indian Law, 107 Harv. L. Rev. 381, 389 [1993]). In Frickey's reading of the opinion, colonialism was "prior to, and the antithesis of, constitutionalism, which involves justiciable, legal questions about judicially enforceable limits on governmen-

tal action" (id. at 389). Frickey's view that *Johnson* established "a rigid dichotomy" appears to reflect not only Marshall's seeming refusal to give legal effect to "natural rights and the uses of civilized nations" but also Frickey's supposition that if the law endorses colonialism, it must in that measure be lawless. As he puts it, "In a country that prides itself on following the rule of law, the justifications for colonization uttered by those European explorers and recognized by the Supreme Court itself—to impose Christianity upon the heathen, to make more productive use of natural resources, and so on—do not go down easily in the late-twentieth century" (id. at 383). Frickey proceeds to argue that in later decisions concerning the relationship of Native American tribes to the U.S. government, Marshall developed the basic terms of a body of federal Indian law that mediated between constitutionalism and colonialism in much more supple and less quiescent ways than he sees *Johnson* as doing.

37. The exemplar of this approach is Eric Kades, who treats *Johnson* as an exercise in doctrinal reasoning, albeit doctrine for which much of the relevant precedent is the practice of sovereigns. See Eric Kades, History and Interpretation of the Great Case of Johnson v. M'Intosh, 19 Law & Hist. Rev. 67 (2001). Kades's account, much of which is a subtle and richly informed narrative of the land speculation and legal maneuvering that brought the case to the Supreme Court more than fifty years after the first purported sale of the land in dispute, is an apt and precise interpretation of the several pages of the opinion in which Marshall labors to show that no European or settler sovereign has ever acted in North America on any principle other than the one on which he decides the case: the rule of discovery—that the colonial sovereign has the exclusive power to dispose of Native lands. This quasi-doctrinal approach, however, may too readily domesticate *Johnson*, an opinion that continues to fascinate in no small part because of its strangeness: Marshall's embrace of a legal conclusion he apparently concedes to be deeply unjust, the half-disowned apologetics of his dicta, and the unclear relation between the legal conclusion and the historical narrative of the long aside.

38. This reinterpretation has consequences internal to the debate over the meaning of *Johnson*. It also has significance for understanding the relations between the law of that time and the present. In the interpretation of *Johnson*, it stands in contrast to Frickey's account in treating colonialism not as the antithesis of law but as itself an integrally legal episode—albeit, as noted, one whose principles had an ambiguous place in American law. The principle distinguishing full sovereigns from imperfect sovereigns is in fact the keystone of the law of colonialism. By identifying the principles of colonial law operating in Marshall's reasoning, my interpretation adds to Kades's by contending that *Johnson* reflects broader and more diverse sources than Kades identifies.

The significance of my interpretation for Singer's account is somewhat more complicated. The nub of Singer's view is that *Johnson*'s grounds contradict today's conventional conception of property law: rather than meritorious acquisition, the case rests property rights on racial caste and aggressive state redistribution. He argues that these facts should reorient our contemporary conceptions of property in favor of both critical debunking of such justificatory claims and an egalitarian embrace of redistribution. My argument is that a distinct body of legal principles, not just bigotry and power, informed the reasoning Singer condemns; it is not that these principles were much purer than he supposes: they were in fact both racist in certain of their presuppositions and strikingly committed to a purposive and sometimes redistributive conception of property. In this respect, my characterization of the case is akin to Singer's, at least descriptively, but it is more nearly internal to the legal thought of the time. I discuss later the variety of implications that my interpretation might be taken to have.

39. See Jack M. Sosin, The Yorke-Camden Opinion and American Land Speculators, 85 Penn. Magazine of Hist. & Biography 38 (1961).

40. See id.

41. See id. at 38–39.

42. The full text of the redacted version read as follows: "In respect to such places as have been or shall be acquired by Treaty or Grant from any of the Indian Princes or Governments; Your Majesty's Letters Patents are not necessary, the property of the soil vesting in the Grantees by the Indian Grants; Subject only to your Majesty's Right of Sovereignty over the Settlements as English Settlements and over the Inhabitants as English Subjects who carry with them your Majesty's Laws wherever they form Colonys and receive your Majesty's Protection by Virtue of your Royal Charters." Id. at 39.

43. Johnson, 21 U.S. 543 at 599.

44. Marshall quotes the following language: "In respect to such places as have been, or shall be acquired, by treaty or grant, from any of the Indian princes or governments, your majesty's letters patent are not necessary" (id. at 599–600).

45. Id. at 599.

46. Id. at 600.

47. Marshall's other basis of distinction seems grounded in a willful misreading of the Yorke-Camden opinion. He writes, "The question on which the opinion was given . . . and to which it relates, was, whether the king's subjects carry with them the common law wherever they form settlements. The opinion is given with a view to this point" (id.). So far as I can tell, any only fair reading of either version of the Yorke-Camden opinion must recognize the reference to the geographically unlimited jurisdiction of English law over the king's subjects as a proviso to its primary conclusion that private parties may make valid purchases from foreign sovereigns without a grant from the king.

48. *Nation* is clearly the outlier. The *Oxford English Dictionary* notes that the term applies both to an "aggregate of communities and individuals united by factors such as common descent, language, culture, history, or occupation of the same territory, so as to form a distinct people" and "such a people forming a political state" or simply "a political state." The *OED* further notes, "In early examples notions of race and common descent predominate. In later uses notions of territory, political unity, and independence are more prominent." The examples given refer to *nation* in the sense of peoples consistently through 1852 (a citation to Tennyson's "mourning of a mighty nation"). By association with Marshall's other terms, his "nation" is drawn in the di-

rection of "people" or "tribe." Ironically, just two pages later Marshall refers to "grants from the native princes" in quoting from a letter describing the acquisition of land in Narragansett country, "in New-England" (id. at 602). Contemporary evidence comes from an 1828 opinion of the Missouri Supreme Court dealing with enslavement of Indians: "In America, the word nation is not of the same import as in other parts of the globe: here it is applied to small societies or independent tribes or communities, who subsist by hunting over a vast extent of territory; whose ideas of property are limited to the game they catch or kill: amongst whom there is no distinction but what arises from personal qualities, being without government authority, subordination or prescribed duties — whose actions flow from the impulse of their own feelings or passions uncontrolled, unpunished" (Marguerite v. Chouteau, 2 Mo. 71, 1828 WL 2322 at *12).

49. Johnson, 21 U.S. 543 at 591.

50. Id. at 589.

51. "[T]he conquered shall not be wantonly oppressed, and . . . their condition shall remain as eligible as is compatible with the objects of the conquest" (id.). What degree of "eligibility" was compatible with the objects of European colonization in North America is a question I shall shortly reach.

52. Id.

53. James Kent designated three sources of international law, custom among them: "The law of nations is a complex system, composed of various ingredients. It consists of general principles of right and justice, equally suitable to the government of all individuals in a state of natural equality and to the relations and conduct of nations; of a collection of usages and customs, the growth of civilization and commerce; and of a code of conventional or positive law" (1 James Kent, Commentaries on American Law *3 [14th ed., 1889] [1826–1830]).

54. Johnson, 21 U.S. 543 at 573.

55. Marshall concludes after a several-page survey of the history of European acquisition and conflict in North America, "Thus, all the nations of Europe, who have acquired territory on this continent, have asserted in themselves, and have recognized in others, the exclusive right of the discoverer to appropriate the lands occupied by the Indians" (id. at 584).

56. Id. at 591.

57. Id. at 572.

58. Id. at 587.

59. Id. at 573.

60. Id.

61. Moreover, "potentates" is one of the least complimentary terms for rulers, short of an insult: it designates power, not legitimacy or authority, and it carries hints of despotism.

62. Johnson, 21 U.S. 543 at 589.

63. Id.

64. Id. at 591.

65. Id. at 591–92.

66. Id.

67. Id. at 588 (emphasis added).

68. Montaigne, for instance, concludes "Of Cannibals" with a wending and often gripping discussion of the way that judging others "barbarians" obscures both their human traits and our own barbarous qualities, with a despairing suggestion that all his efforts will fall on deaf ears. Having made a case for Native Americans' humaneness and sense of morality and decried Spanish abuses of conquered peoples, he ends with, "[W]hat's the use? They [the Indians] don't wear breeches" (Montaigne, Cannibals at 159).

69. Johnson, 21 U.S. 543 at 589.

70. Keene, Beyond the Anarchical Society.

71. Id. at 98–99. Keene later reports that a "consistent theme in textbooks on international law from the middle of the nineteenth century on was the distinction between the family of civilized nations, which was seen as roughly synonymous with the society of states who had achieved recognition as fully independent sovereigns, and the uncivilized world beyond, of territories and peoples that had not yet achieved such recognition" (id. at 114).

72. Id. at 93–94 (emphasis added).

73. 1 Kent, Commentaries at *21–22.

74. 3 James Kent, Commentaries on American Law *381–82 (13th ed., 1884) (1826–1830).

75. Id. at *381.

76. Id. at *382.

77. Id. at *386.

78. See Francisco de Vitoria, Political Writings 273–85 (Anthony Pagden and Jeremy Lawrance, eds., 1991) (1539). See J. S. Mill, Considerations at 217–34.

79. Mill, for instance, characterized India's peoples as "unfitted for representative government by . . . extreme passiveness and ready submission to tyranny" (J. S. Mill, Considerations at 238).

80. See 2 Lord Cornwallis, Selections from the State Papers of the Governors-General of India 72–126 (George Forrest, ed., 1926).

81. The Moguls emerged from Central Asia and began the conquest of much of India in the thirteenth century. By the time British traders arrived on India's northeast coast, Mogul capitals such as Calcutta, in Bengal, had fallen into profound dysfunction. The British began their eventual conquest of India by contractually undertaking to supplant the Moguls in sovereign activities that those rulers were literally no longer competent to undertake, beginning with tax collection and proceeding rapidly to defense, policing, and the administration of justice. The role, if any, of this experience in giving force to the idea of degrees of sovereign competence would merit investigation.

82. The closest thing to an authoritative study of the Permanent Settlement is Ranajit Guha, A Rule of Property of Bengal: An Essay on the Idea of Permanent Settlement (1996). Guha studies the intellectual and political thought that formed the backdrop to the policy and concentrates on the widely and strongly held belief that property rights would propel Indian economy and society toward commercial modernity. Edward Keene gives a consonant account of the Permanent Settlement in Keene, Be-

yond the Anarchical Society at 88–94. For a fascinating near-contemporary criticism of not the idea but the implementation of the Permanent Settlement, see James Mill, History of British India at 476–93. Mill contended that the reform failed because it placed ownership in the hands of the aristocratic zemindars, to whom he ascribed a class-based taste for arbitrary power over increased wealth. He held this preference responsible for the zemindars' failure to make economically rational improvements in the agriculture in favor of maintaining repressive authority over the ryots. This in turn he blamed on the influence of "the aristocratic ideas of modern Europe" on Cornwallis and others. He argued that a more egalitarian allocation of property rights would have achieved the intended effect: "It is the man of small possessions who feels most sensibly the benefit of petty accessions; and is stimulated the most powerfully to use the means of procuring them. It is on the immediate cultivator, wherever the benefit of his improvements is allowed to devolve in full upon himself, that the motives to improvement operate with the greatest effect. That benefit, however, cannot devolve upon him in full, unless he is the proprietor as well as the cultivator of his fields." (id. at 493).

83. See Guha, Rule of Property at 91–111.

84. As Cornwallis wrote in 1789, "In a country where the landlord has a permanent property in the soil it will be worth his while to encourage his tenants who hold his farm in lease to improve the property; at any rate he will make such an agreement with them as will prevent their destroying it. But when the lord of the soil himself, the rightful owner, is only to become the farmer for a lease of ten years [Cornwallis was commenting on a proposal to freeze exaction rates for a ten-year period], and if he is then to be exposed to the demand of a new rent, which may perhaps be dictated by ignorance or rapacity, what hope can there be, I will not say of improvement, but of preventing desolation? Will it not be in his interest, during the early part of that term, to extract from his estate every possible advantage for himself; and if any future hopes of a permanent settlement are then held out, to exhibit his lands at the end of it in a state of ruin?" (2 Cornwallis at 74).

85. Cornwallis wrote: "I may safely assert that one-third of the [East India] Company's territory in Hindostan [India] is now a jungle inhabited only by wild beasts. Will a ten years' lease induce any proprietor to clear away that jungle, and encourage the ryots to come and cultivate his lands, when at the end of that lease he must either submit to be taxed ad libitum for their newly cultivated land, or lose all hopes of deriving any benefit from his labour, for which perhaps by that time he will hardly be repayed?" (id. at 74–75).

86. See David Arnold, Hunger in the Garden of Plenty, in Dreadful Visitations 81 (Alessa Johns, ed., 1999).

87. Id. at 93.

88. 2 Cornwallis at 75.

89. Id. at 95.

90. Id.

91. Id. at 115.

92. Id.

93. Cornwallis wrote: "In case of a foreign invasion, it is a matter of the last importance, considering the means by which we keep possession of the country, that the proprietors of the land should be attached to us from motives of self-interest. A land-holder who is secured on the quiet enjoyment of a profitable estate can have no motive in wishing for a change. On the contrary, if the rents of his lands are raised in proportion to their improvement; if he is liable to be dispossessed should he refuse to pay the increase required of him; or if threatened with imprisonment or confiscation of his property on account of balance due to Government which his lands were unequal to pay, he will readily listen to any offers which are likely to bring about a change that cannot place him in a worse situation, but which hold to him hopes of a better" (id. at 113).

94. Cornwallis wrote: "Until the assessment on the lands is fixed, the constitution of our internal government in this country will never take that form which alone can lead to the establishment of good laws and ensure a due administration of them. For whilst the assessment is liable to frequent variation, a great portion of the time and attention of the supreme Board, and the unremitting application of the Company's servants of the first abilities and most established integrity will be required to prevent the land-holders being plundered and the revenues of government being diminished at every new settlement; and powers and functions which ought to be lodged in different hands must continue, as at present, vested in the same person; and whilst they remain so united we cannot expect that the laws which may be enacted for the protection of the rights and property of the land-holders and cultivators of the soil will ever be duly enforced" (id.). A passage from Blackstone also aptly illustrates this idea: "Necessity begat property; and in order to insure that property, recourse was had to civil society, which brought along with it a long train of inseparable concomitant; states, governments, laws, punishments, and the public exercise of religious duties. Thus connected together, it was found that only a part of society was sufficient to provide, by their manual labour, for the necessary subsistence of all; and leisure was given to others to cultivate the human mind, to invent useful arts, and to lay the foundations of science" (2 William Blackstone, Commentaries on the Laws of England *8 [1765–69]). One can hardly imagine a more succinct claim for the central necessity of property to civilization.

95. 2 Cornwallis at 74.

96. Id. at 79.

97. Id. at 74 (emphasis added).

98. This is exactly the characterization James Mill gives in the passage quoted in note 82. Mill understood the error in the Permanent Settlement to be the decision to side with the feudal aristocracy rather than the yeomanry, with the concomitant failure to bring about the increasing prosperity and autonomy of the small proprietor—exactly the progress Smith envisioned in Europe.

99. As Guha puts it in a neat summary of the view of Philip Francis, whose plan for Permanent Settlement preceded and largely anticipated Cornwallis's, "Francis had conceived of the agrarian relationship in Mughal India as primarily feudal: he had wanted to replace it by a model derived from contemporary England" (Guha, Rule of Property at 208).

100. Johnson, 21 U.S. 543 at 589.

101. Id. at 590.

102. Blackstone's elaboration of the basis for this view is one of the most famous passages of his *Commentaries:* "As the world by degrees grew more populous, it daily became more difficult to find out new spots to inhabit, without encroaching upon former occupants; and, by constantly occupying the same individual spot, the fruits of the earth were consumed, and its spontaneous produce destroyed, without any provision for a future supply or succession. It therefore became necessary to pursue some regular method of providing a constant subsistence; and this necessity produced, or at least promoted and encouraged, the art of agriculture. And the art of agriculture, by a regular connection and consequence, introduced and established the idea of a more permanent property in the soil, than had hitherto been received and adopted. It was clear that the earth would not produce her fruits in sufficient quantities, without the assistance of tillage: but who would be at the pains of tilling it, if another might watch an opportunity to seize upon and enjoy the product of his industry, art, and labor? Had not therefore a separate property in lands, as well as movables, been vested in some individuals, the world must have continued a forest, and men have been mere animals of prey; which, according to some philosophers, is the genuine state of nature. Whereas now (so graciously has providence interwoven our duty and our happiness together) the result of this very necessity has been the ennobling of the human species, by giving it opportunities of improving its rational faculties, as well as of exerting its natural. Necessity begat property." (2 Blackstone, Commentaries at *7–8).

103. Id. at *7.

104. See Johnson, 21 U.S. 543 at 590.

105. This assertion is not simply an intuition based on something like an analogy between property regimes and systems of grammar or logic. It has been developed in considerable historical detail by William Cronon, who has explained how European ownership and agriculture necessarily excluded the more transient and nonexclusive land uses characteristic of eastern Native Americans. See William Cronon, Changes in the Land: Indians, Colonists, and the Ecology of New England (2003).

106. Johnson, 21 U.S. 543 at 591.

107. As Marshall put it, "The resort to some new and different rule, better adapted to the actual state of things, was unavoidable" (id. at 591). It is at this point that Marshall offers his peculiar history of the displacement of Native Americans as a kind of ecological process: "As the white population advanced, that of the Indians necessarily receded. The country in the immediate neighbourhood of agriculturists became unfit for them. The game fled into thicker and more unbroken forests, and the Indians followed. The soil . . . being no longer occupied by its original inhabitants, was parceled out according to the will of the sovereign power, and taken possession of by persons who claimed immediately through the crown, or mediately, through its grantees or deputies" (id. at 590–91).

    This passage is best understood as elaborating historically on the perception that the two property regimes and their corresponding modes of productive activity cannot coexist, that as the one expands, the other will inevitably give way—whatever the mechanisms of displacement and replacement. It is, of course, also a conveniently agent-free sketch of history, which one could read with the impression that no European ever did anything to a Native American to achieve that displacement. These two interpretations, however, are not entirely incompatible. While the more apologetic version makes the passage plainly, even outrageously, false as a matter of agency, that interpretation might still be right as a matter of the relationship between the two regimes: simply by existing, the one excludes the other. Moreover, precisely because of its dynamic efficiency, the European regime has an expansionist logic: individual participants have an incentive to claim new tracts of land for their own benefit, but with the inevitable consequence of bringing that tract under the terms of the regime.

108. Johnson, 21 U.S. 543 at 591.

109. This is Joseph Singer's concern in his discussion of the case. See Singer, Sovereignty and Property.

CHAPTER 5. MEANINGS OF FREE LABOR

1. Two of the most important and influential treatments of this theme are the very different histories of Charles Taylor and Michel Foucault. See Charles Taylor, Sources of the Self: The Making of the Modern Identity (1989); Michel Foucault, Discipline and Punish: The Birth of the Prison (Alan Sheridan, trans., 1977); 2 Michel Foucault, The History of Sexuality: The Uses of Pleasure (Robert Hurley, trans., 1985). See also Barrington Moore, Jr., Injustice: The Social Bases of Obedience and Revolt (1978) (asking how, historically, inequality and oppression have come to be recognized as "injustice" and how those subjected to them reconceived themselves as competent and entitled to resist and demand a reform of the social order that imposes those conditions); 1 Orlando Patterson, Freedom: Freedom in the Making of Western Culture (1991) (arguing that ideas of freedom developed in the West out of a series of contrasts with slavery that reveal the essential interdependence between freedom and the limits imposed by a need for and vulnerability to others).

2. For discussions of exogenous changes in the value of resources and their relation to the development of property rights, see Harold Demsetz, Toward a Theory of Property Rights, 57 Am. Econ. Rev. 347, 347 (1967) (discussing the effect of the rise of the European market for beaver pelts on rights in land and hunting among Native Americans); Gary D. Libecap & James L. Smith, The Economic Evolution of Petroleum Property Rights in the United States, 31 J. Legal Stud. 589, 589 (2002) (describing exogenous changes in the value of petroleum resources as a fossil fuel–based economy arose); Carol M. Rose, Energy and Efficiency in the Realignment of Common-Law Water Rights, 19 J. Legal Stud. 261 (1990) (exploring changes in water rights that emerged as water became an energy-producing resource with the rise of mills in New England). A methodologically complex view attentive both to changes in the logic of resources with the rise of industrial capitalism and to the internal workings of legal doctrine is Morton J. Horwitz, The Transformation of American Law, 1780–1860 (1977) (describing private law as changing, particularly in its conception of property, to accommodate and facilitate a market-enabling instrumental view of resources).

3. See Demsetz, Toward a Theory; Libecap & Smith, Economic Evolution; Rose, Energy and Efficiency.

4. The great study of the political and legal struggle over slavery in the Anglo-American world is David Brion Davis, The Problem of Slavery in the Age of Revolution, 1770–1823 (1975). Also valuable on these themes is Edmund S. Morgan, American Slavery, American Freedom: The Ordeal of Colonial Virginia (1975). Two scholars whose classic works on the topic represent a sophisticated form of Marxian method, treating ideas and political institutions with full seriousness but assigning ultimate explanatory power to the limits and imperatives of economic relations, are Eugene Genovese, Roll, Jordan, Roll: The World the Slaves Made (1974), and Mark V. Tushnet, The American Law of Slavery, 1810–1860: Considerations of Humanity and Interest (1981).

   Two invaluable resources for appreciating the complexity of the contrast between slavery and free labor are Robert William Fogel & Stanley L. Engerman, Time on the Cross: The Economics of American Negro Slavery (1974) (documenting slaveowners' ready combination of pecuniary inducements and bodily threats to maintain labor discipline, which highlights the complex interaction of these categories in any actual economy), and Robert J. Steinfeld, Coercion, Contract, and Free Labor in the Nineteenth Century 3–38 (2001) (arguing that elements of pecuniary inducement and bodily coercion coexisted in nominally free-labor relations, and documenting some of the forms of coercion prominent in nineteenth-century labor ties).

5. On these issues, see Lawrence M. Friedman, A History of American Law 179–201 (1973) (expounding the law of status in nineteenth-century America, with particular attention to the propertyless, women, and slaves); Rogers M. Smith, Civic Ideals: Conflicting Visions of Citizenship in U.S. History 137–242 (1997) (describing citizenship and status between the adoption of the Constitution and the *Dred Scott* decision); Gordon S. Wood, The Radicalism of the American Revolution 11–94 (1992) (describing social hierarchy and its intersection with political membership and authority in colonial America).

6. As I show, the distinction frequently arose in these terms in judges' language. It also appears in contemporary legal commentary. See Thomas R. R. Cobb, An Inquiry into the Law of Negro Slavery in the United States of America 83 (1999) (1858) ("[T]he negro slave in America, protected . . . by municipal law, occupies a double character of person and property"). The seeming paradox routinely draws observations from historians and commentators. See, e.g., Peter Charles Hoffer & N. E. H. Hull, Editors' Preface, in Mark V. Tushnet, Slave Law in the American South: State v. Mann in History and Literature, at ix (2003).

7. United States v. Amy, 24 F. Cas. 792, 810 (C.C.D. Va. 1859) (No. 14, 445).

8. Neal v. Farmer, 9 Ga. 555, 583 (1851).

9. State v. Jones, 1 Miss. (1 Walker) 83, 85 (1820). Sometimes, however, the matter was put so as to suggest no legal salience in the slave's humanity. Thus, the Kentucky Court of Appeals gave as its opinion that slaves, "although they are human beings, are by our laws placed on the same footing with living property of the brute creation. However deeply it may be regretted, and whether it be politic or impolitic, a slave by our code,

is not treated as a person, but (negotium), a thing, as he stood in the civil code of the Roman Empire. In other respects, slaves are regarded by our laws, as in Rome, not as persons, but as things" (Jarman v. Patterson, 23 Ky. [7 T. B. Mon.] 644, 644 [1828]).

10. Amy, 24 F. Cas. at 810.

11. See id. at 799. Taney ruled that slaves were regarded as legal persons for purposes of enforcing criminal law against them and that where the government's bodily expropriation of a slave was with respect to her as a legal person, the protection of property under the Fifth Amendment did not apply.

12. In *Jones*, the issue was whether it was possible to commit common law murder against a slave; the court found that it was, reasoning in part that "a slave may commit murder and be punished with death; why then is it not murder to kill a slave?" (Jones, 1 Miss. [1 Walker] at 83). In *Neal*, the court found by contrast that the killing of a slave was not a felony under the common law, as the slave relationship was not recognized in common law and thus was not subject to common law regulation (Neal, 9 Ga. at 583).

13. See William W. Fisher III, Ideology and Imagery in the Law of Slavery, in Slavery and the Law 43–85 (Paul Finkelman, ed., 1997) (offering an illuminating portrait of this paternalist approach to justifying the slave relationship, which assimilates it into a broader logic of reciprocal duties up and down the lines of a social and economic hierarchy). Fisher contrasts this approach to a racialist model of slavery that "solves" the problem of the personhood-resource relationship by demoting Africans to a status less than fully human (id.). For a textured discussion of the paternalist attitude, see Elizabeth Fox-Genovese & Eugene D. Genovese, The Mind of the Master Class: History and Faith in the Southern Slaveholders' Worldview 365–82 (2005) (describing the interaction of chivalric ideas of duty with the self-understanding of slaveholders).

14. Commonwealth v. Turner, 26 Va. (5 Rand.) 678 (1827).

15. Id. at 689–90 (Brockenbrough, J., dissenting).

16. Id. at 678 (majority opinion). Andrew Fede presents *Turner* and *State v. Mann* as joint evidence that as slaves, women and men alike were subject to legally sanctioned and effectively unrestricted forms of violence. Andrew T. Fede, Gender in the Law of Slavery in the Antebellum United States, 18 Cardozo L. Rev. 411, 419–24 (1996).

17. Turner, 26 Va. (5 Rand.) at 687.

18. Id. at 687–88.

19. Id. Proslavery legal commentator Thomas R. R. Cobb thus cited *Turner* in his account of the origin and place of the slave's personhood within American law. Cobb, Inquiry at 83–84. Cobb's main point was that the personhood dimension arises only with statutory protection for the slave and is not inherent in the relationship. Id. Cobb wrote: "So long as [the slave] remained purely . . . property, an injury upon him was a trespass upon the master's rights. When the law . . . recognizes his existence as a person, he is as a child just born, brought for the first time within the pale of the law's protecting power" (id.).

20. Turner, 26 Va. (5 Rand.) at 689 (Brockenbrough, J., dissenting).

21. Id. (emphasis added).

22. Id. See also Fox-Genovese & Genovese, Mind of the Master Class for an elaboration of these themes.

23. Turner, 26 Va. (5 Rand.) at 689 (Brockenbrough, J., dissenting).
24. Id.
25. Id.
26. James v. Carper, 36 Tenn. (4 Sneed) 397, 397 (1857). The court was not clear on its view of the scope of the master's power to punish a slave, noting that a parent possessing the status-based "paternal power . . . may not exceed the bounds of moderation" but also suggesting "for the sake of the argument, that the owner of the slave, in virtue of his absolute right of property, might take the law into his own hands, and avenge the crime committed by the slave without appeal to the law" (id. at 401–2). The precise bounds of the master's power were not, of course, at issue in the case.
27. Id. at 401.
28. Id. at 402.
29. See id.
30. Id.
31. Id.
32. Somerset v. Stewart, 98 Eng. Rep. 499 (K. B. 1772).
33. Id. at 505–6.
34. Id. at 505.
35. Id.
36. Id. at 506.
37. Id.
38. See David Brion Davis, Inhuman Bondage: The Rise and Fall of Slavery in the New World 101–12 (2006).
39. Somerset, 98 Eng. Rep. at 505.
40. Id.
41. State v. Mann, 13 N.C. (2 Dev.) 263 (1829).
42. Id. at 263.
43. Id. at 266–67.
44. Id.
45. Mann, 13 N.C. (2 Dev.) at 267.
46. Id.
47. Id.
48. Id. (emphasis added).
49. *Mann* has drawn commentators' interest for well over a century. In a book-length treatment of *State v. Mann*, Mark Tushnet partly rejects this interpretation. See Tushnet, Slave Law at 37. As Tushnet rightly points out, Ruffin not only expresses ambivalence about the moral status of slavery and disapproval of brutality toward slaves. He also suggests that the legislature may in the future choose to govern the master-slave relationship in more humane ways than Ruffin's decision does. Id. In this respect, the decision is concerned with the relative power of courts and legislatures to govern slave relations, not with the "logic of slavery" (id.). Yet, Tushnet concedes, readers of the case who had taken the language I discuss at face value, from the abolitionist novelist Harriet Beecher Stowe to the historian Eugene Genovese, "were not wrong"

because "Judge Ruffin implicitly relied on deep-lying notions about how slavery was embedded in the life of Southern communities" (id.). Indeed, the case does not purport to prohibit legislatures from regulating the institution, and Judge Ruffin appears to look favorably on that prospect, which suggests that he cannot consistently regard his armchair sociology of the master-slave relationship as being as invariant as he elsewhere insists. Nonetheless, his analysis of the reasons for the courts' abstention relies on the "inherent" logic of the relationship, which he presents adamantly. The opinion appears to be divided, as it may be that Ruffin's mind was on the issue. As Tushnet points out, as early as his college years at Princeton, Ruffin seems to have written to his father expressing moral concerns about slavery. Id. at 91–92. The letter his father wrote in return indicated that he regarded slavery as a great evil but could see no way for the South to extricate itself from the institution. Id. This expression of a divided consciousness "bears an uncanny resemblance to the structure of Ruffin's opinion in *State v. Mann*" (id. at 92). This analysis is broadly consistent with Tushnet's 1981 analysis of the case in The American Law of Slavery, where he argues that Ruffin meant to indicate the limits of judicial principle in governing slavery: although humane sentiments might guide the legislature in drawing lines to prohibit certain abuses, a common-law analysis of the relationship had to choose between treating the master's power as absolute and accepting lines of reasoning that would call the institution itself into question. Tushnet, American Law at 54–65. Judicial competence was thus particularly restricted in regard to slavery, on Tushnet's account of Ruffin's analysis. Id.

   Citing Harriet Beecher Stowe, who was "appalled at the legal system's capacity to reduce a man of intellect and insight to a tool for oppression," Robert Cover emphasized the aspect of Ruffin's reasoning that I have been discussing; see Robert M. Cover, Justice Accused: Antislavery and the Judicial Process 78 (1975). He referred with a kind of admiration to "Ruffin's unusual refusal to clothe an exploitative and brutal relationship with the trappings of anything save power," comparing Ruffin in this quality to Oliver Wendell Holmes, Jr. Id. at 77–78. Cover did seem to make an unfounded inference from Ruffin's strong language to "a legislative policy of the utmost brutality," which he believed Ruffin inferred from "the mere existence of slavery" (id. at 78). I believe that Tushnet is right on this point to direct attention to Ruffin's apparently inconsistent declarations, including allowance for legislative reform of slavery, and to the hints of divided consciousness beneath this inconsistency. Eugene Genovese was moved to remark similarly to Stowe on the case: "Never has the logic of slavery been followed so faithfully by a humane and responsible man" (Roll, Jordan, Roll at 35).

   Tushnet's 2003 interpretation is consistent with that of contemporary proslavery commentators. Thomas R. R. Cobb cited *State v. Mann* for the proposition that slavery was not a feature of the common law, and thus "it required municipal law," i.e., statutes, to protect the slave's personhood. Cobb, Inquiry at 83. Cobb, like most southern commentators, stressed the statutory regimes that purported to protect slaves against various specific abuses. See id. at 82–96 (surveying state statutes).

50. A nice formulation of the erasure of slaves' legal personhood comes in Ruffin's opinion: "The slave, to remain a slave, must be made sensible, that there is no appeal from

his master; that his power is in no instance, usurped; but is conferred by the laws of man at least, if not by the law of God" (Mann, 13 N.C. [2 Dev.] at 267). Later Ruffin concluded: "[T]his dominion is essential to the value of slaves as property, to the security of the master, and the public tranquility, greatly dependent upon their subordination" (id.).

51. Somerset, 98 Eng. Rep. at 500.

52. Id. at 501.

53. Id. at 503.

54. Id.

55. Id.

56. I use *feudalism* to designate not just the arrangements of early Norman England or the Europe of the early Middle Ages but, generally, a social and economic order in which stable and marked hierarchy (1) designates fairly specific functions in both the social and economic spheres, which (2) are interdependent, so that occupying a certain economic position will imply playing a corresponding social role, and (3) are hierarchical in the sense that certain prerogatives attach to superior positions in commanding both the economic activity and the social obeisance of inferiors.

57. Richard Hildreth, a prominent campaigner against American slavery, began his discussion of the status of enslavement in Europe with a survey of English and central European villeinage, including both the outright ownership of persons and the ownership of persons appurtenant to land (serfdom). Richard Hildreth, Despotism in America: An Inquiry into the Nature, Results, and Legal Basis of the Slave-Holding System in the United States 177–78 (1970) (1854).

58. For a survey of the major themes and commitments of the free-labor school, see Eric Foner, Free Soil, Free Labor, Free Men: The Ideology of the Republican Party Before the Civil War 1–72 (1970) (commenting on the relation of the ideal of self-ownership and of a commercial society organized on the free sale of labor and talent to the self-conception of northern U.S. society and the Republican critique of southern society in the decades preceding the Civil War).

59. Hildreth wrote: "The relation of master and slave, like most other kinds of despotism, has its origin in war. By the confession of its warmest defenders, slavery is at best, but a substitute for homicide. . . . Slavery then is a continuation of the state of war. . . . The relation of master and slave, as we may conclude from the foregoing statements, is a relation purely of force and terror. Its only sanction is the power of the master; its best security, the fears of the slave" (Hildreth, Despotism in America at 35–38).

60. Smith was concerned to show that relatively poor societies, in which masters worked at the same business as their slaves and might share quarters with them, resulted in more sympathy and less brutality between masters and slaves. Adam Smith, Lectures on Jurisprudence (hereafter "LJ") 172–90 (R. L. Meek, D. D. Raphael, and P. G. Stein, eds., 1982) (1763–63) at 184–85.

61. Describing slavery in the classical world, Smith wrote, "1st, with regard to their lives, they were at the mercy of the master. . . . [H]e might put a slave to death on the smallest transgression. . . . 2dly, as his life, so was his liberty at the sole disposall of his master; and indeed properly speaking he had no liberty at all, as his master might employ him

at the most severe and insupportable work without his having any resource" (id. at 176–77).

62. The psychological significance of the interaction between master and slave also became an important part of the continental tradition of ethical and social thought, specifically the theory of recognition. The seminal discussion is G. W. F. Hegel, Phenomenology of Spirit 111–19 (A. V. Miller, trans., 1977) (1807) (describing the interaction of "lord" and "bondsman" in which the two archetypes, one absolutely powerful, the other absolutely dependent, struggle for survival and recognition). Alexandre Kojève elevated this exchange to particular attention, concentrating on Hegel as a theorist of recognition, in Alexandre Kojève, Introduction to the Reading of Hegel: Lectures on the Phenomenology of Spirit 3–30 (Allan Bloom, ed., James H. Nichols, Jr., trans., 1969) (commenting on the "dialectic of master and slave").

63. Smith, LJ at 186.

64. Smith's account almost perfectly parallels that of James Mill in Mill's account of the motives of "feudal" landholders in India, which he regarded as having thwarted reformist efforts to induce a transition to commercial modernity through reform in land tenure. Despite the incentive the reforms provided to contract free labor rather than maintain feudal relations with dependent peasants, the landholders preserved feudalism, Mill wrote, because "men . . . as education and government have previously moulded their minds, are more forcibly drawn by the love of absolute power, than by that of money, and have a greater pleasure in the prostrate subjection of their tenants than the increase of their rents" (Mill, The History of British India 491–92 [William Thomas, ed., 1975] [1820]).

65. Hildreth, Despotism in America at 143.

66. Id. at 142–57. This theme also emerged in slave narratives. Frederick Douglass, the former slave and abolitionist writer and orator, reflected on the character of his own childhood master: "[H]e was not by nature worse than other men. . . . The slaveholder, as well as the slave, is the victim of the slave system. . . . [T]here is no relation more unfavorable to the development of honorable character, than that sustained by the slaveholder to the slave. Reason is imprisoned here, and passions run wild" (Douglass, My Bondage and My Freedom 32 [John Stauffer, ed., 2003] [1855]).

67. Hildreth writes: "The institution of slavery deprives a large portion of the people of their natural occupation [production]. But as man is essentially an active animal, to supply this deficiency it is necessary to create artificial occupations" (Hildreth, Despotism in America at 154–57). He then describes the respective places of gambling, drinking, and politics in southern culture: "It is impossible to make men virtuous or happy unless by giving them some steady employment that shall innocently engage their attention and pleasantly occupy their time. The most essential step in the progress of civilization, is, to render useful industry, respectable. But this step can never be taken, so long as labor remains the badge of a servile condition" (id.).

68. For a splendid evocation of this idea, see David Bromwich, Lincoln and Whitman as Representative Americans, in Democratic Vistas: Reflections on the Life of American Democracy 36, 47 (Jedediah Purdy, ed., 2004).

69. For a hostile account of the relation between abolitionism and markets, see George

Fitzhugh, Cannibals All! Or Slaves Without Masters 218–19 (C. Vann Woodward, ed., 1960) (1857) ("The whole morale of free society is, 'Every man, woman, and child for himself and herself'").

70. See 1 Adam Smith, The Wealth of Nations 376–427 and passim (R. H. Campbell & A. S. Skinner, eds., 1976) (1776) (laying out comparisons among nations' economic development).

71. See Lysander Spooner, The Unconstitutionality of Slavery (1860) (1845).

72. Hildreth, Despotism in America at 35–38.

73. Spooner, Unconstitutionality of Slavery (1860) (1845).

74. Adam Smith, The Theory of Moral Sentiments 185 (2000) (1759).

75. George Fitzhugh, Sociology for the South; or, The Failure of Free Society 20–22 (1854), available at http://docsouth.unc.edu/southlit/fitzhughsoc/fitzhugh.html.

76. Fitzhugh, Cannibals at 20.

77. Id. at 217.

78. Id. at 32.

79. "Slavery is a form of communism, and as the Abolitionists and Socialists have resolved to adopt a new social system, we recommend it to their consideration" (id. at 223).

80. Fox-Genovese & Genovese, Mind of the Master Class.

81. Fitzhugh gave a particularly conservative view of the American Revolution as a development in national maturity and the global balance of power: "We were only justified in declaring our independence, because we were sufficiently wise, numerous and strong to govern ourselves, and too distant and distinct from England to be well governed by her" (Fitzhugh, Sociology at 183).

82. See Foner, Free Soil at 1–37 (describing the premises and social vision of free-labor ideology). For an exemplary contemporary statement of the outlook, see Abraham Lincoln, Address to the Wisconsin State Agricultural Society, Milwaukee, Wisconsin, in Selected Speeches and Writings 233–37 (Don E. Fehrenbacher, ed., 1992) (1859) (contending for the dignity of labor and the reality of social mobility, and denying that market society implies an opposition between permanent classes of owners and laborers).

    Within legal scholarship, the emphasis on the continuity between antebellum free-labor ideology and the laissez-faire jurisprudence of the Gilded Age marks what is sometimes still called the revisionist view of the *Lochner* era, although there is no longer much to revise of the previously dominant idea. That older idea began in the Progressive critique of *Lochner* jurisprudence as mere dishonesty, a blend of interest-group politics and constitutionally implausible ideology. The Progressives were more interested in changing a recalcitrant Supreme Court than in explaining the intellectual and political origins of its obstructionist attitude to labor legislation.

    Legal scholarship in the revisionist vein was indebted to Foner's Free Soil and the aligned work of Charles McCurdy, who contributed to a renewed understanding of the ideological stakes of the ideas of self-ownership and liberty of contract in the nineteenth century. See Charles W. McCurdy, The "Liberty of Contract" Regime in American Law, in The State and Freedom of Contract 161, 161–97 (Harry N. Scheiber, ed., 1998) (tracing the origins of the free-labor idea in a rejection of the southern slave re-

lation and an ideal of economic independence and exploring its jurisprudential interactions with the Progressive idea of the benefits that "social legislation" should provide to the disadvantaged). The most extensive treatment of the *Lochner* era from this
point of view is Howard Gillman, The Constitution Besieged: The Rise and Demise of
Lochner Era Police Powers Jurisprudence 1–18 (1993) (explaining the historiographic
origins and methodological stakes of the revisionist approach). For a sketch of this
historiographic development, see Manuel Cachán, Justice Stephen Field and "Free
Soil, Free Labor Constitutionalism": Reconsidering Revisionism, 20 Law & Hist. Rev.
541 (2002). For a rich interpretation of the variety of historical narratives, political
visions, and jurisprudential agendas that long placed *Lochner* in the "anti-canon" of
cases that must be wrong on any constitutional theory and have brought it back into
either context-specific or (less plausibly) general validity, see Jack M. Balkin, "Wrong
the Day It Was Decided": *Lochner* and Constitutional Historicism, 85 B. U. L. Rev.
677 (2005).

  A magisterial expression of the "revisionist" position is 8 Owen M. Fiss, History of
the Supreme Court of the United States: Troubled Beginnings of the Modern State,
1888–1910 (1993). Fiss rejects the "strategic" interpretation of the *Lochner* Court's
jurisprudence as "camouflage" for class interests as inconsistent both with what can be
determined of the justices' understanding of their activity and with a view of the law as
a potentially autonomous domain of reason giving rather than a plaything of interests.
Id. at 3–21. In his discussion of the Supreme Court's treatment of labor legislation,
Fiss contends that a particular strength of his interpretive approach is its power to
make sense not just of the cases in which the Court struck down regulations but also
of those in which it upheld them as appropriate exercises of legislative power, particularly *Holden v. Hardy*, 169 U.S. 366 (1898), and *Muller v. Oregon*, 208 U.S. 412 (1908).
Id. at 155–84. I believe that these decisions' harmony with the rest of the labor jurisprudence of the free-labor period indicates the strength of this interpretive approach.

83. See Foner, Free Soil at 11–13, 40–51 (describing the basic tenets of free-labor thought
and its contrast with the slave system of the antebellum South). Free-labor thought in
the United States had its ultimate origin in John Locke's famous declaration, "[E]very
Man has a Property in his own Person. This no Body has any Right to but himself. The
Labour of his Body, and the Work of his Hands . . . are properly his" (Locke, Second
Treatise of Government, in Two Treatises of Government 285, 287–88 [Peter Laslett,
ed., 1960] [1690]). It had its culmination in the passage of the Thirteenth Amendment
to the U.S. Constitution: "Neither slavery nor involuntary servitude . . . shall exist
within the United States[.]"

84. See Foner, Free Soil and other works cited in note 82. This is a corollary of the prohibition on outright ownership of another's labor.

85. See Foner, Free Soil.

86. This is the key characteristic of free labor according to Robert J. Steinfeld, who gives
a helpful and corrective account of free labor as an ideology that has been overdrawn
in its proud contrast with slavery. See Steinfeld, Coercion at 1–2 (noting that what
"was crucial in making free wage labor free was that wage workers were never forced
to perform their labor agreements" either because their employment was terminable

at will or because employers had no meaningful remedy against them for breaching employment contracts by leaving).

87. Foner, Free Soil.

88. See William E. Forbath, The Ambiguities of Free Labor: Labor and the Law in the Gilded Age, Wis. L. Rev. 767 (1985).

89. See id.

90. Id. at 785–94.

91. See id.

92. See id.

93. See id.

94. As noted in the introduction to Part II, the ideal-typical character of this claim is a crucial limit on its descriptive accuracy. For accounts of some of the ways that bodily threats and other forms of nonpecuniary coercion figure into nominally free labor relations both before and after the Thirteenth Amendment, see Steinfeld, Coercion at 3–38, and Eric Foner, Reconstruction: America's Unfinished Revolution, 1863–1877, 155–68 (1988). As Foner notes, although northern laborers often entered contracts under straitened circumstances, southern freedmen from the start struggled with a system in which even the formal liberty of free-labor contracts was at best uncertain and, as Reconstruction crumbled, became almost entirely fictional. Id.

95. A fascinating anxiety about the terms of recruitment and command emerges in the oral arguments of the proslavery side in *Somerset*, 98 Eng. Rep. at 506. The lawyer John Dunning imagines here that, if the slave James Somerset is released, servants will no longer accept orders from their masters.

96. Foner, Reconstruction at 155 (quoting "a Tennessee agent" of Reconstruction), 164 (quoting "a Northern Republican" reporting from New Orleans in 1867).

97. Id. at 155–68.

98. Lochner v. New York, 198 U.S. 45 (1905).

99. Id. at 53.

100. Holden, 169 U.S. at 390–91; see also Forbath, Ambiguities of Free Labor at 777–82 (tracing the appearance of this constitutional vision in Supreme Court jurisprudence to Justice Field's argument for the plaintiff butchers in the Slaughterhouse Cases. Field argued that the Civil War amendments had made economic liberty a part of the Constitution and should forbid interference such as the regulation the majority upheld). Because this chapter is not a history of free-labor jurisprudence as such, I begin my discussion with the fuller and victorious doctrinal formula of *Holden v. Hardy*. For Owen Fiss's discussion of *Holden* as a key to an integrated understanding of the labor jurisprudence of this period, see Fiss, History of the Supreme Court at 172–74.

101. Holden, 169 U.S. at 390.

102. Id.

103. Id.

104. See 2 James Kent, Commentaries on American Law *329 (12th ed., 1873) (1823) ("When the laws allow a free circulation to property . . . the operation of the steady laws of nature will, of themselves, preserve a proper equilibrium, and dissipate the mounds of property as fast as they accumulate"). Alienation and the circulation it facilitated

were thus instrumental to an idea of equality of opportunity. On the role of equality of opportunity in sustaining free-labor ideology, see Foner, Free Soil at 29–33.

105. Holden, 169 U.S. at 397 (internal quotation marks omitted).
106. Lochner, 198 U.S. at 72 (Harlan, J., dissenting).
107. Muller, 208 U.S. at 412.
108. Id. at 421.
109. Id. at 422.
110. Holden, 169 U.S. at 397.
111. Muller, 208 U.S. at 412.
112. Id. at 418.
113. Id. at 422.
114. Id.
115. Lamson v. Am. Ax & Tool, 177 Mass. 144 (1900).
116. Lamson, 177 Mass. at 144–45.
117. Id. at 145.
118. Id.
119. Id.
120. Leary v. Boston & A. R. Co., 139 Mass. 580 (1885).
121. Id. at 586–87.
122. Id. at 587.
123. Id.
124. Robert L. Hale, Freedom Through Law: Public Control of Private Governing Power 15 (1952).
125. For a discussion and economic rationale of the limited number of forms that property rights take, see Thomas W. Merrill & Henry E. Smith, Optimal Standardization in the Law of Property: The *Numerus Clausus* Principle, 110 Yale L. J. 1 (2000).
126. Important exceptions are rife but generally recognized as exceptions: for instance, in real property, implied easements and the right of access in certain circumstances of public officials or medical professionals; and in intellectual property, the right of fair use.
127. For the basic account of allocative efficiency by mutual advantage in the law of property, see Richard A. Posner, Economic Analysis of Law § 3.2. (5th ed., 1998).
128. See Hale, Freedom Through Law at 17 ("[A] manufacturer of goods . . . values his right to prevent their use by others merely as a means of enabling him to exact money from those others. If successful, he will not, in fact, deny to all others the liberty of using his products, but because he may deny that liberty he is in a position to impose conditions with which a person who acquires the liberty must comply").
129. "[A] man who for one reason or another is unable to acquire property by which he can exact a money income from others cannot easily escape the restrictions which other people's property rights place on his freedom. If he is unable to own sufficient property of this type, he may be compelled to accept employment as the only condition on which he can obtain the money essential to purchase the freedom to eat" (id. at 18).
130. See id.
131. See Barbara H. Fried, The Progressive Assault on Laissez Faire: Robert Hale and the

First Law and Economics Movement 47–59 (1998) (discussing Hale's leveling attack on the formal conception of voluntary relations that had been a leading legitimating principle in laissez-faire ideology). Fried's book is an impressively lucid and informative exposition of both Hale's thought and the backdrop of intellectual and jurisprudential disputes against which he and his legal realist contemporaries worked.

132. See id. at 29–33 (describing laissez-faire theorists' "bland self-assurance in describing private economic activity as a bastion of freedom").

133. Fried quotes the Harvard economist Thomas Carver, writing in 1921: "The most important characteristic of the economic life of civilized people is its freedom from compulsion. Nearly every economic act of the average individual is one which he does voluntarily. . . . Among all free people one private citizen is forbidden to exercise compulsion over any other" (id. at 30–31 [quoting Thomas Carver, Principles of National Economy 101 (1921)]).

134. On Hale's efforts to distinguish between acceptable and unacceptable instances of coercion, see id. at 59–70.

135. Dred Scott v. Sandford, 60 U.S. (19 How.) 393, 399–454 (1857).

CHAPTER 6. CHOOSING FUTURES

1. Amartya Sen, The Moral Standing of the Market 1, 13 in Ethics and Economics (Ellen Frankel Paul et al., eds., 1985).

2. One of Arrow's conditions was that any acceptable formula must produce decisions that are Pareto-efficient. This means that if, between two alternatives, the first will be preferred by at least one person in the society while no one would prefer the other, the formula must select the first alternative. The intuition behind this condition is simply that there can be no good reason to choose an alternative that is inferior for one person and superior for no one. Another condition was that the formula must not make one person in the society a dictator. This condition expresses the commonsense idea that the fiat of one person is no way to make social decisions. The third condition is that a social decision should not be affected by alternatives that are not presently in question: that is, a choice between X and Y should not be affected by preferences about Q. Again there is a commonsense idea behind this condition: the social decision should be about what it purports to be about, not about what Arrow called "irrelevant alternatives." (I have left out some other conditions that turned out, in the decades of intense scholarly debate following Arrow's book, not to be necessary to his argument.) The upshot of the proof is that each condition, either by itself or along with one of the others, excludes some alternatives, with the result that no social-choice formula can avoid violating one of the conditions.

3. Kenneth J. Arrow, Social Choice and Individual Values (1951).

4. This discussion draws significantly on Amartya Sen's treatment of the same issues in Sen, The Possibility of Social Choice, in Rationality and Freedom 65, 65–76 (2002) and Rationality and Social Choice 261, 261–74, as well as Opportunities and Freedoms 583, 583–94, both in the same volume.

5. See particularly the discussion in Sen, Rationality and Social Choice at 271–75.

6. See id. For a more accessible discussion of some of the same proposals, see Amartya Sen, Development as Freedom 76–85 (1999).

7. See Robert Cooter & Peter Rappoport, Were the Ordinalists Wrong About Welfare Economics? 22 J. Econ. Lit. 507 (1982).

8. See Sen, Possibility of Social Choice at 71.

9. "[E]conomists came to be persuaded by arguments presented by Lionel Robbins and others (deeply influenced by 'logical positivist' philosophy) that interpersonal comparisons of utility had no scientific basis: 'Every mind is inscrutable to every other mind and no common denominator of feelings is possible.' Thus, the epistemic foundations of utilitarian welfare economics were seen as incurably defective" (id., quoting Robbins).

10. See Lionel Robbins, An Essay on the Nature and Significance of Economic Science 136–58 (2d ed., 1935) (summarizing his attack on the concept of cardinal measurement of utility and insisting, inter alia, on the importance of value-relativism in setting the limits of welfare economics).

11. See id.

12. Robbins also credited William Stanley Jevons, a nineteenth-century Briton, as a predecessor. Jevons, relatively marginal in his day, was a utilitarian skeptic. He believed that subjective pleasure, "psychological hedonism," was the proper measure of well-being, but that there was no way to unify measurement of pleasure across persons because satisfactions were idiosyncratic. See Lionel Robbins, The Place of Jevons in the History of Economic Thought, in The Evolution of Modern Economic Theory and Other Papers on the History of Economic Thought 169, 170–77 (1970). Robbins believed that Jevons's hedonism was theoretically unnecessary but that his skepticism about interpersonal comparison laid the foundation for scientific economic inquiry. See Robbins, Essay at 85.

13. See Cooter & Rappoport, Were the Ordinalists Wrong? at 507, 520–24 (recounting Robbins's critique, on these grounds, of the ambitions to utility measurement of earlier modes of English economics).

14. See C. L. Stevenson, The Emotive Meaning of Ethical Terms, in Logical Positivism 264, 278–79 (A. J. Ayer, ed., 1959) (arguing that evaluative terms make sense only as conventional agreements to name certain states of the world "bad" or "good" and to draw conditional imperatives of action from those descriptions).

15. John Stuart Mill, On Liberty 96 (1993) (1913).

16. Jeremy Bentham, A Fragment on Government 93 (2001) (1776).

17. See id.

18. Jeremy Bentham, A Critical Examination of the Declaration of Rights 496, 497 in 2 Bentham, Works (Richard Doyne, ed., 1837).

19. F. C. Montague, Introduction to Jeremy Bentham, A Fragment on Government 43 (2001) (1891).

20. Id. at 40.

21. For two recent defenses of the method and efforts to adapt it creatively to imposing difficulties, see Cass R. Sunstein, Worst-Case Scenarios (2007) and Richard A. Posner, Catastrophe: Risk and Response (2004).

22. For an example, see Stephen G. Breyer, Breaking the Vicious Circle: Toward Effective Risk Regulation (1993).
23. For a refined and critical account of the method, see Amartya Sen, The Discipline of Cost-Benefit Analysis, in Rationality and Freedom 553, 553–77.
24. For exemplary reformism, see Sunstein, Worst-Case Scenarios. For a critical account, see Lisa Heinzerling, The Accidental Environmentalist: Judge Posner on Catastrophic Thinking, 94 Geo. L. J. 833 (2006); Frank Ackerman & Lisa Heinzerling, Pricing the Priceless: Cost-Benefit Analysis of Environmental Protection, 150 U. Penn. L. Rev. 1553 (2002).
25. Sen, Opportunities and Freedoms at 585.
26. See particularly the discussion in Sen, Rationality and Social Choice at 271–75. For a more accessible discussion of some of the same proposals, see Sen, Development as Freedom at 76–85.
27. Amartya Sen, Rights and Capabilities, in Resources, Values and Development 316–17 (1984).
28. Sen has developed this position in many writings. In addition to those just cited, see Sen, Markets and Freedoms, in Rationality and Freedom 501, 501–30 (analyzing the mechanism of competitive markets using the perspective of individual freedom); Freedom and the Evaluation of Opportunity, in Rationality and Freedom 659, 659, 664–66, 694 (discussing the "opportunity aspect" of freedom, "choice-act valuation," and "option appreciation"); and Sen, Goods and People, in Resources, Values and Development 509.
29. See Sen, Markets and Freedoms at 506 ("[F]reedom gives us the opportunity to achieve our objectives. . . . [I]mportance is also attached to the process of autonomous choice").
30. See id. at 507–8.
31. Sen, Rationality and Freedom, in Rationality and Freedom 1, 36.
32. See Sen, Markets and Freedoms at 512–23.
33. Id. at 515.
34. Sen, Rights and Capabilities at 307, 308–9.
35. For an accessible history of the microcredit movement, see Connie Bruck, Millions for Millions, New Yorker, Oct. 30, 2006.
36. See id.
37. See id.
38. See Nathanael Goldberg, Measuring the Impact of Microfinance: Taking Stock of What We Know 6 (2005).
39. Id.
40. Id. at 7.
41. Hernando de Soto, The Mystery of Capital: Why Capitalism Triumphs in the West and Fails Everywhere Else 54–61 (2000).
42. Syed M. Hashemi et al., Rural Credit Programs and Women's Empowerment in Bangladesh, 24 World Dev. 635, 638–39 (1996).
43. Id. at 641.
44. Id.

45. Sidney Ruth Schuler et al., Credit Programs, Patriarchy, and Men's Violence Against Women in Rural Bangladesh, 43 Soc. Sci. Med. 1729, 1737 (1996).
46. Id.
47. Id. at 1738.
48. Id.
49. Id. at 1738–40.
50. Id. at 1738–41.
51. Sidney Ruth Schuler et al., The Influence of Women's Changing Roles and Status in Bangladesh's Fertility Transition: Evidence from a Study of Credit Programs and Contraceptive Use, 25 World Dev. 563 (1997).
52. See Valerie M. Hudson & Andrea M. Den Boer, Bare Branches: The Security Implications of Asia's Surplus Male Population 58–66 (2004) ("In 1990 . . . more than 100 million women were missing nationwide.").
53. There is considerable debate on the relative proportions of gender disproportion caused by each of a variety of factors. One class of factors reveals a preference for sons over daughters, exercised at different points in the cycle of conception and childhood: sex-selective abortion, infanticide, and preferential caregiving and medical expenditures resulting in higher levels of childhood mortality in girls than in boys. For an outline of the debate over proportions among these causes, see Chu Junhong, Prenatal Sex Determination and Sex-Selective Abortion in Rural Central China, 27 Population & Dev. Rev. 259, 259 (2001) (noting that many Western observers were skeptical that sex-determination technology was widely available in China, while Chinese scholars resisted the suggestion that postnatal sex discrimination or infanticide caused the sex disparity).
54. For an introduction to the dispute, see Hudson & Den Boer, Bare Branches at 112–13. One study of a hospital in Punjab in the 1980s and 1990s found that 13.6 percent of mothers of boys admitted—with a reticence which may suggest underreporting—having undergone prenatal sex-selection; the comparable figure was 2.1 percent for mothers of girls. The other female fetuses presumably were not carried to term. See id. at 112.
55. See Sen, Development as Freedom at 197 ("[V]ariables that relate to the general level of development and modernization either turn out to have no statistically significant effect, or suggest that modernization . . . can even strengthen, rather than weaken, the gender bias in child survival").
56. Naila Kabeer, Gender Mainstreaming in Poverty Eradication and the Millennium Development Goals 129 (6.1) (2003), available at www.idrc.ca/openebooks/067-5/.
57. See Sen, Development as Freedom at 192–93 (describing "decision making in the family" as a "form of pursuing cooperation with some agreed solution . . . of the conflicting aspect"). For a particularly helpful discussion and elaboration of Sen's model, see Bina Agarwal, A Field of One's Own: Gender and Land Rights in South Asia 53–81 (1994).
58. See Sen, Development as Freedom at 192–93; Agarwal, Field of One's Own at 53–81.
59. As Agarwal points out, the variables that figure here are not just control of resources

but also cultural ideas of which issues are at stake in negotiation and which are so clearly settled as to be off limits. See Agarwal, Field of One's Own at 73–75. Another important variable is which conditions women perceive as "problems" bearing on their well-being or that of their children and which are accepted as untroubling. The philosopher Martha Nussbaum emphasizes the importance of an idea of false consciousness in this connection, suggesting that experience of empowerment reveals interests that were previously obscure to the interest holder. See Martha Nussbaum, Charles Taylor: Explanation and Practical Reason in The Quality of Life 232, 232–41 (Martha Nussbaum & Amartya Sen, eds., 1993). So does Sen, Development as Freedom at 65, 90–92. Others argue that the poor are always in some measure aware of their disadvantage and simply require practical opportunities, not enhanced insight, to challenge it. See, e.g., James C. Scott, Weapons of the Weak: Everyday Forms of Peasant Resistance (1985) (explaining class relations using insights of the peasants).

60. Families, that is, pool resources for relative prosperity and provide forms of protection that increase bodily security and integrity. Just as important, they provide intimacy and forms of complex and ongoing interpersonal recognition—which may be on terms ranging from quite reciprocal to highly nonreciprocal.

61. See Alaka Malwade Basu, Culture, the Status of Women, and Demographic Behaviour: Illustrated with the Case of India 160–81 (1992) (surveying and interpreting findings to this effect from India and elsewhere, including Latin America and sub-Saharan Africa). Basu notes that although sex ratios in childhood survival improve with both variables, maternal employment is sometimes associated with reduced overall rates of childhood survival, most likely because of the sacrifice of direct caregiving implied by the decision to work outside the home, particularly for families on the edge of survival. See id. at 170–73.

62. See Albert O. Hirschman, Exit, Voice, and Loyalty: Responses to Decline in Firms, Organizations, and States (1970). For his part, Sen notes "considerable evidence that when women can and do earn income outside the household, this tends to enhance the relative position of women even in the distributions within the household" (Sen, Development as Freedom at 194). He also suggests that literacy and education make women aware of alternatives and give them some confidence in insisting on the legitimacy of their desires. Id. at 198–99. The phenomenology of these suggestions is of mixed voice and exit, which seems right.

63. This is a kind of moral-psychological corollary of the growing recognition that women's agency is a critical factor in economic and social development, not merely in the passive sense that it makes women bearers of greater quanta of well-being but in the active sense that women's empowerment contributes to development processes that affect both women and men. This thesis is the thrust of the discussion in Sen, Development as Freedom at 189–203. For a recent summation of arguments and data supporting this view, see Isobel Coleman, The Payoff from Women's Rights, Foreign Aff., May–June 2004, at 80, 83 ("Educated women have fewer children; provide better nutrition, health, and education to their families; experience significantly lower child mortality; and generate more income than women with little or no schooling. Investing to educate them thus creates a virtuous cycle for their community").

64. See Agarwal, Field of One's Own at 421–66 (describing theoretically and in several case studies how struggles over resources are also "struggles over meanings," that is, over what women's and men's interests are and how they should count). "Struggles" should be underscored: women's increasing control of resources has often resulted in both violence and a recrudescence of male-supremacist politics. See id. at 271–76.
65. Kabeer, Gender Mainstreaming at 152.

CHAPTER 7. SOCIAL VISION FOR
THE NEXT ECONOMY

1. This sketch of the issues draws heavily on Robert Shiller, The New Financial Order 1–68 (2003).
2. See id. at 107–13.
3. See id. at 110–20. Milton Friedman sharply criticized schemes of this sort as invasions of freedom. See Milton Friedman, Capitalism and Freedom 103 (1962) (describing a similar plan for education, in which the lender would "buy" a share in the student's future earning prospects, as "economically equivalent to . . . partial slavery"). To my mind, this emphasis on the first, libertarian, dimension of freedom may be misplaced here, as the character of the interference with economic liberty is not clear, while the contribution to opportunity freedom is straightforward.
4. Consider Abraham Lincoln's praise of the free-labor ideal as a fitting premise for democratic citizenship because of its recognition of the dignity of each person, to which he added, "If any continue through life in the condition of the hired laborer [rather than become a proprietor], it is not the fault of the system, but rather because of either a dependent nature which prefers it, or improvidence, folly, or singular misfortune" (Lincoln, Address to the Wisconsin State Agricultural Society, Milwaukee, Wisconsin, in Selected Speeches and Writings 233–37 [Don E. Fehrenbacher, ed., 1992 1859]). Ronald Dworkin, in particular, has done heroic work in seeking ways of reconciling these considerations into an account of distributive justice. For a recent statement, see Ronald Dworkin, Is Democracy Possible Here? Principles for a New Political Debate 102–26 (2006).
5. On the origins and ambiguities of the invisible hand metaphor, see Emma Rothschild, Economic Sentiments: Adam Smith, Condorcet, and the Enlightenment 116–56 (2001).
6. See Robert C. Ellickson, Property in Land, 102 Yale L. J. 1315, 1322–35 (1993) (discussing the concept of externalities and legal responses thereto).
7. According to the United Nations' 2006 estimate, global population was a bit over 6.5 billion in 2005 and is estimated to reach just over 6.9 billion in 2010. Readers can view the latest forecasts at United Nations Population Division, World Population Prospects: The 2008 Revision, http://esa.un.org/unpp/index.asp?panel=1 (last visited July 30, 2009).
8. See Ellickson, Property in Land at 1322–35 (discussing property regimes as instruments for managing externalities).
9. See Jedediah Purdy, People as Resources: Recruitment and Reciprocity in the

Freedom-Promoting Approach to Property, 56 Duke L. J. 1047, 1085–89 (2007) (discussing the prohibition on enslavement as a premise of the modern property regime).

10. For a sketch of the respective mechanisms and their advantages and disadvantages, see William Chameides & Michael Oppenheimer, Carbon Trading over Taxes, 315 Science 1670 (March 23, 2007).

11. For an argument that such a policy would ultimately prove cost-effective, see Richard A. Posner, Catastrophe: Risk and Response 155–65 (2004).

12. See Jonathan B. Wiener, Think Globally, Act Globally: The Limits of Local Climate Policies, 155 U. Penn. L. Rev. 1961, 1966–73 (2007) (setting out the functional disadvantages of any subglobal effort to control climate change).

13. I base this on the share of the United States (300 million) of the world population.

14. See Cass R. Sunstein, Worst-Case Scenarios 71–117 (2007).

15. See Jonathan B. Wiener, Designing Global Climate Regulation, in Climate Change Policy: A Survey 151, 160 (Stephen Schneider, Armin Rosencranz, & John O. Niles, eds., 2002).

16. See id. at 161–62, 166–67.

17. See id. at 169.

18. On competing approaches to international distributive justice in connection with climate change, see Peter Singer, One World: The Ethics of Globalization 14–51 (2002); Stephen M. Gardiner, Ethics and Global Climate Change, 114 Ethics 555 (2004). On the relevance of ideas of fairness to the American political debate over the Kyoto Protocol, see Frank Luntz, The Environment: A Cleaner, Safer, Healthier America 137 (strategy memo for Republican Party candidates that notes, "The 'international fairness' issue is the emotional home run.").

19. For a survey of the range of potential impacts, see Climate Change 2007: Impacts, Adaptation, and Vulnerability: Summary for Policymakers (Report of the Intergovernmental Panel on Climate Change, Fourth Assessment Report) (2007).

20. See id. For treatments of some of the disastrous scenarios associated with climate change, see Posner, Catastrophe at 43–58; Peter Schwartz and Doug Randall, An Abrupt Climate Change Scenario and Its Implications for United States National Security (2003) (unpublished paper commissioned by U.S. Department of Defense, on file with author).

21. See, e.g., Wiener, Think Globally; Sunstein, Worst-Case Scenarios at 101–4. Recognizing the difficulty presented by climate change under a static analysis, Sunstein has expressed increasing interest in the role of moral considerations and dynamic analysis. See Cass R. Sunstein, The World vs. the United States and China? The Complex Climate Change Incentives of the Leading Greenhouse Gas Emitters, 55 U. C. L. A. L. Rev. 1675, 1696–98 (2008).

22. See Anatol Lieven, The End of the West as We Know It? International Herald Tribune (Dec. 28, 2006); Albert Gore, Nobel Prize Lecture (Stockholm, Dec. 10, 2007) ("Indeed, without realizing it, we have begun to wage war on the earth itself. Now, we and the earth's climate are locked in a relationship familiar to war planners: 'Mutually assured destruction.'").

23. See Sunstein, Worst-Case Scenarios at 109–11.

24. On the moral considerations attending discounting, see id. at 244–74; Daniel Farber, From Here to Eternity: Environmental Law and Future Generations, 2003 Ill. L. Rev. 289; Frank Ackerman & Lisa Heinzerling, Pricing the Priceless, 150 U. Penn. L. Rev. 1553 (2002).

25. See Sunstein, Worst-Case Scenarios at 54–60.

26. See id. at 43.

27. See id. at 54–63.

28. See id. at 59–60.

29. An Inconvenient Truth (Lawrence Bender Productions 2006).

30. See Paul Slovic, "If I Look at the Mass, I Will Never Act": Psychic Numbing and Genocide (unpublished paper, on file with author) (2006).

31. See id.

32. See id.

33. See id.

34. See id.

35. While frequently attributed to Stalin, this remark cannot be reliably traced to him. See http://en.wikiquote.org/wiki/Joseph_Stalin#_note-statistics (last visited February 7, 2008).

36. A distinct but related phenomenon is the extra importance people frequently assign to problems identified with concrete and easily envisioned villains like Osama bin Laden. See Sunstein, Worst-Case Scenarios at 65 (on the "Goldstein effect").

37. See Thomas L. Brewer, Public Opinion on Climate Change Issues in the G8+5 Countries 4 (reporting movement in the share of respondents identifying climate change as a "very serious problem" from just over 30 percent to just under 50 percent between 2003 and 2006) (paper on file with author). In 2006, 41 percent of U.S. respondents said they believed climate change was caused by human activity. See Little Consensus on Global Warming (report of Pew Center on People and the Press, July 12, 2006), available at http://people-press.org/reports/display.php3?ReportID=280 (last visited February 7, 2008). In January 2008, a CNN/Opinion Research Corporation poll found 78 percent of U.S. respondents claiming global warming would be "extremely," "very," or "moderately" important in their choice of candidates. Poll summary available at http://www.pollingreport.com/prioriti.htm (last visited February 7, 2008).

38. Global warming did not show up in responses to an open-ended poll conducted by CBS News in January 2008, while only 6 percent of respondents to an NBC News–Wall Street Journal poll in the same period chose "environment/global warming" as the most important of a list of issues. Poll summaries available at http://www.polling report.com/prioriti.htm (last visited February 7, 2008).

39. See Dan. M. Kahan, The Logic of Reciprocity: Trust, Collective Action, and the Law, 102 Mich. L. Rev. 71, 102 (2003) (making this observation).

40. See Lawrence Summers quotes, BrainyQuote, http://www.brainyquote.com/quotes/authors/l/lawrence_summers.html (last visited February 13, 2008).

41. See David Brion Davis, Explanations of British Abolitionism, in Inhuman Bondage: The Rise and Fall of Slavery in the New World 231, 231–49 (2006).

42. See id.

43. See David Barron & Martin S. Lederman, The Commander in Chief Power at the Lowest Ebb—A Constitutional History, 121 Harv. L. Rev. 941, 944–55 (2008) (so stating, noting that the historical fact contradicts much commonplace supposition).

44. See Ted Nordhaus & Michael Shellenberger, Break Through: From the Death of Environmentalism to the Politics of Possibility 22–24 (2007).

45. See John Muir, My First Summer in the Sierra (1911); Rachel Carson, Silent Spring (1962).

46. On the Romantic roots of John Muir's work, see Roderick Nash, Wilderness and the American Mind 122–140 (2001). On Carson's debt to the apocalyptic tradition in literature and rhetoric, see M. Jimmie Killingsworth & Jacqueline S. Palmer, Millennial Ecology: The Apocalyptic Narrative from *Silent Spring* to Global Warming, in Green Culture: Environmental Rhetoric in Contemporary America 21, 21–45 (Carl G. Herndl & Stuart C. Brown, eds., 1996).

47. I discuss this point in greater detail in Jedediah Purdy, The Promise (and Limits) of Neuroeconomics, 58 Ala. L. Rev. 1, 21–40 (2006).

48. See Singer, One World at 150–60.

49. For a discussion of moral identity as a motivational factor, see Jonathan Glover, Humanity: A Moral History of the Twentieth Century 26–30 (2001).

50. See Davis, Explanations of British Abolitionism at 245–47.

51. See Purdy, Promise (and Limits) at 10–13.

52. See Davis, Explanations of British Abolitionism at 246–49.

53. See Eric Foner, Free Soil, Free Labor, Free Men: The Ideology of the Republican Party Before the Civil War 1–37 (1970) (describing the premises and social vision of free-labor thought).

54. See id. at 11–13 (describing the basic tenets of free-labor thought and its defining contrast with the slave system of the antebellum South).

55. See Gordon S. Wood, The Radicalism of the American Revolution 205–6 (1992) (on the idea of civic honor as a motive in George Washington's decisions in the early republic).

56. See Kahan, Logic of Reciprocity at 75–85.

57. See id. at 73–74.

58. See id. at 75–99.

59. See Engel & Orbach, Micro-Motives at 3–7 (setting out local climate initiatives).

60. For a list of cities that have (at least nominally) committed to meeting Kyoto Protocol goals locally, including Salt Lake City, see U.S. Conference of Mayors, Mayors Climate Protection Center, http://www.usmayors.org/climateprotection/Climate Change.asp (last visited February 13, 2008).

61. See Luntz, Environment.

62. For a discussion of this issue in international distributive terms, see Singer, One World at 27–34. For an account of developing-country perspectives on the question, see Lavanya Rajamani, Differential Treatment in International Environmental Law 216–36 (2006).

63. See Yochai Benkler, The Wealth of Networks: How Social Production Transforms

Markets and Freedom (2007); Yochai Benkler, Freedom in the Commons, 52 Duke L. J. 1245, 1254–60 (2003); Lawrence Lessig, Free Culture: How Big Media Uses Technology and the Law to Lock Down Culture and Control Creativity (2004) (criticizing the expansion of intellectual property rights at the expense of the public domain); James Boyle, The Public Domain: Enclosing the Commons of the Mind (2009).

64. See Robert S. Boynton, The Tyranny of Copyright? N.Y. Times Mag. 40 (Jan. 25, 2004).

65. As James Boyle presents the question, "The assumption is that [with appropriate reform] we will return to a norm of freedom, but of what kind? Free trade in expression and innovation, as opposed to monopoly? Free access to innovation and expression, as opposed to access for pay? Or free access to innovation and expression in the sense of not being subject to the right of another person to pick and choose who is given access, even if all have to pay some flat fee? Or is it common ownership and control that we seek, including the communal right to forbid certain kinds of uses of the shared resource?" (Boyle, The Second Enclosure Movement and the Construction of the Public Domain, 66 L. & Contemp. Probs. 33, 58 [2003]).

66. The term is attributed to the cultural theorist John Fiske and is now in wide currency in discussions of intellectual property and politics. See Jack M. Balkin, Digital Speech and Democratic Culture: A Theory of Freedom of Expression for the Digital Age, 79 N.Y. U. L. Rev. 1, 3 (2004) (arguing that digital technologies alter the social conditions of speech and therefore the focus of free-speech theory should shift from protecting the democratic process to a larger concern with protecting and promoting a democratic culture). For a critical view of such theories of the public domain from a postcolonial perspective, see Anupam Chander, The Romance of the Public Domain, 92 Cal. L. Rev. 1331, 1334–35 (2004): "By presuming that leaving information and ideas in the public domain enhances 'semiotic democracy'—a world in which all people, not just the powerful, have the ability to make cultural meanings—law turns a blind eye to the fact that for centuries the public domain has been a source for exploiting the labor and bodies of the disempowered—namely, people of color, the poor, women, and people from the global South."

67. See Abraham Lincoln, Address at Cooper Institute, New York City, in Abraham Lincoln: Speeches and Writings, 1859–1865 111 (Don E. Fehrenbacher, ed., 1989).

68. See Jim Rutenberg, The Ad Campaign: Kerry Invokes Bush's Carrier Landing to Emphasize Points, N.Y. Times A18 (Nov. 11, 2003).

69. See Frank Rich, How Kerry Became a Girlie-Man, N.Y. Times sec 2 at 1 (Sept. 5, 2004).

70. Patrick E. Tyler, The 2004 Campaign: Global Reaction; As the World Watched the Debate, Some Saw a New Race, N.Y. Times sec 1 at 34 (Oct. 3, 2004).

71. See Bush Blair Endless Love, www.youtube.com/watch?v=nupdcGwIG-g (last visited July 30, 2009).

72. See Bush v. Bush, http://www.thedailyshow.com/watch/mon-april-28-2003/bush-v—bush (last visited August 11, 2009).

73. See David Armitage, The Declaration of Independence: A Global History 103–38 (2007).

74. The text of the Declaration of Sentiments is available at Modern History Sourcebook, http://www.fordham.edu/halsall/mod/senecafalls.html (last visited Nov. 17, 2008).

75. I give some discussion of Douglass's role as a constitutional interpreter in Jedediah Purdy, A Tolerable Anarchy: Rebels, Reactionaries, and the Making of American Freedom 25–32 (2009).

76. See generally Jürgen Habermas, The Structural Transformation of the Public Sphere: An Inquiry into a Category of Bourgeois Society (Thomas Burger and Frederick Lawrence, trans., 1989) (describing the development and decline of "the public sphere"); Amy Guttmann and Dennis Thompson, Democracy and Disagreement (1996) (outlining ways in which fractious democratic societies deliberate complex and divisive issues).

77. Boyle, Second Enclosure Movement at 58.

78. Lessig, Free Culture at 8, 192–93.

79. See generally Benkler, Freedom in the Commons (discussing the social transformations resulting from the "networked information economy"); Yochai Benkler, Sharing Nicely: On Shareable Goods and the Emergence of Sharing as a Modality of Economic Production, 114 Yale L. J. 273 (2004) (discussing the emergence of social sharing in the technology industry and its capacity to decrease transaction costs and increase efficiency).

80. See Benkler, Freedom in the Commons at 1247–48 ("An underlying efficient limit on how we can pursue any mix of arrangements to implement our commitments to democracy, autonomy, and equality . . . has been the pursuit of productivity and growth. . . . [W]e have come to toil in the fields of political fulfillment under the limitation that we should not give up too much productivity in pursuit of these values").

81. See id. at 1248 ("Efforts to advance workplace democracy have . . . often foundered on the shoals—real or imagined—of these limits, as have many plans for redistribution in the name of social justice. Market-based production has often seemed simply too productive to tinker with").

82. See Benkler, Sharing Nicely at 275–81 (designating as "lumpy" those capital goods that typically come in packages that include excess capacity and as "mid-grained" those whose scale encourages widespread personal ownership).

83. See id. at 281–89 (describing carpooling as a form of social sharing resulting from this excess capacity of automobiles).

84. See id. at 289–96 (describing the efficiency advantages of distributed computing).

85. See Benkler, Freedom in the Commons at 1256–60 (discussing voluntary, loosely collaborative "peer production").

86. See id.

87. Benkler goes so far as to say, "Capturing the potential for human action that could be motivated by the exchange of love, status, and esteem, a personal sense of worth in relations with others, is the strong suit of social production. . . . Social production rewards action either solely in these forms or, if it adds money, organizes its flow in such a way that it at least does not conflict with and undermine the quantum of self-confidence, love, esteem, or social networking value obtained by the agent from acting" (Benkler, Sharing Nicely at 328).

88. See Benkler, Freedom in the Commons at 1252–54 (discussing the character of information as "nonrival," a quality now attaching to cultural goods that can be electronically reproduced and transmitted as mere information); Benkler, Sharing Nicely at 349–51 ("[I]n displacing industrial distribution, peer-to-peer distribution is thought both by its critics and by some of its adherents to be likely to undermine the very possibility of industrial production of music").

89. For a discussion of this idea, see Ian Shapiro, Resources, Capacities, and Ownership: The Workmanship Ideal and Distributive Justice, in Early Modern Conceptions of Property 21, 21–42 (John Brewer & Susan Staves, eds., 1995) (describing the workmanship ideal of ownership as centering around "the conviction that so long as the resources with which people mix their productive capacities are justly acquired they may legitimately own the product of that conjunction").

90. See generally, Benkler, Freedom in the Commons.

91. Aristotle, Nicomachean Ethics 18–19 (D. P. Chase, trans., 1911).

92. See http://slashdot.org (last visited Nov. 17, 2005) (hosting a collaborative news site maintained by hundreds of thousands of volunteers).

93. See Adam Smith, Lectures on Jurisprudence 181 (R. L. Meek et al., eds., 1978) (1762–63) (stating that feudalism in Europe is a form of slavery).

94. This point follows Hale's observation that the market actor who succeeds in accumulating a good deal of productive capital thus achieves a significant advantage in bargaining position over one who does not have the same success in accumulation. See Robert L. Hale, Freedom Through Law: Public Control of Private Governing Power 17–18 (1952) (discussing the bargaining advantage of the factory owner).

95. I discuss the significance of the creation, appropriation, and subversion of brand identity in cultural politics and in the politics of global economic regulation in Jedediah Purdy, Being America: Liberty, Commerce, and Violence in an American World 221–40 (2003). In that discussion I draw attention both to the historical continuity between Adam Smith's idea of commerce as persuasion and the contemporary politics of branding and to the way the latter politics has shaped the fight over sweatshop regulation in poor countries. Id. at 232–40.

96. See id. at 223–30 (discussing the self-conceptions that branding campaigns appeal to and seek to shape).

97. See generally Benedict Anderson, Imagined Communities: Reflections on the Origins and Spread of Nationalism (1991) (investigating the relation between nation-building projects and the media); David Bromwich, A Choice of Inheritance: Self and Community from Edmund Burke to Robert Frost (1989) (arguing that the tension between self and community—between individualism and public-mindedness—was a motive for great writing from the end of the eighteenth century to the beginning of the twentieth); Alasdair Macintyre, After Virtue: A Study in Moral Theory (1984) (arguing that the abandonment of Aristotelian teleology has rendered moral discourse and practice hollow in the modern world).

INDEX

acquisition of property: and Due Process Clause, 103; by occupation, 2; original, 2, 40, 41–42; right of, and Locke, 40–41; right of, and Marshall, 74; and right of contract, 102

alienation, power of, in legal imagination, 17–18

anti-instrumental tradition, 24

appropriate use, 51, 53

appropriative artist, 148

Arrow, Kenneth, 117–18, 121; impossibility theorem, 117–18, 124, 126; and Sen, 124

Bacon, Francis, 30

Bangladesh and microfinance. *See* microfinance

bargaining: in American waste law, 54–56; bound by right of exit, 100; as circumstances of recruitment, 88; conditions for, in *Johnson* dissent, 51; in English waste law, 48–49, 54; fairness in, 49; and free labor, 104–7; Hale's view of, as system of mutual coercion, 107–9; hierarchical, induces efficient use of resources, 57; key to Adam Smith's social vision of free labor, 12–13, 15; and market pricing, 152; power affects sex asymmetry, 133–34; and reciprocity, 154–55; transforma-

tory, 49; and women's empowerment, 130, 133–34. *See also* contract; default rules; free labor

Bengal. *See* East India

Benkler, Yochai, 146, 149–53; and collaborative production (*see* collaborative production); and cultural production's capital structure, 149; on new technologies and productivity, 151–52; on property regimes and interdependence, 152–53; and recruitment via self-realization, 149; and sharing of excess capacity, 149–50; and Shiller, 149

Bentham, Jeremy: and imperialism, 69–70; and property's aspects, 19–20; and realists, 159; and utilitarianism, 120–23; and welfare analysis, 123, 124; and welfarists, 158

Berlin, Isaiah: and negative liberty, 19; and positive liberty, 20

bilateral monopolies, 56–58

Blackstone, William, 1–4; and four-stages theory of history, 38–39, 85; and grounds of ownership, 2; and imperialism, 68; and *Jackson*, 50; and *Johnson*, 86; and law of waste, 47; and libertarians' view of ownership, 2; and original acquisition of property, 2; and personhood view of

Index 223

thought; welfarist property thought
Proudhon, Pierre, 1
Public Domain (Boyle), 146
Pufendorf, Samuel, 10, 37
Putney Convention, 29–36; and anarchy,
29, 33–34, 87; and definition of property,
31–32; and English legal imagination, 32;
and natural rights, 29, 33–34; and voting
rights, 30–32
Pynchon v. Stearns, 56–57

Radin, Margaret Jane, 20
Rainborough, Thomas, 29, 33, 36, 37; and
self-sovereignty, 111
realist property thought (realism), 21
reciprocity: and climate change, 145–46;
and consent, 154; and cultural production, 154–55; society of, key to Adam
Smith's social vision, 15; as value of economic order, 112–13
recruitment: basic features of, 96, 112;
circumstances of, 88; and coercion in
next economy, 154; and peer production,
152–53; rules of, 88; terms of, 88
reform: arc of, related to property, 155;
three elements of successful, 155
republican property thought, 22, 57–61
responsibility, as value of economic order,
112–13
reversioner: in American law of waste,
45–46, 53–57, 60–61; and bilateral
monopolies, 56; in English law of waste,
47–49, 60; in *Jackson*, 53, 57–58; and
Kent's commercial-republican ideas, 60;
in *Pynchon v. Stearns*, 56–57. *See also*
bargaining; *Jackson v. Brownson*; waste
right of acquisition, 41–42
Robbins, Lionel, 119–20
romantic property thought, 21–22; and
moral and aesthetic perfectionism, 24
rule of discovery, 74–75
rules of recruitment, 88; and free labor,
101. *See also* recruitment

salience, 140–41
Schwartz, Alan, 49
Scottish Enlightenment, 12–16; integration of values in, 25–28. *See also* Smith,
Adam
self-interest: and British abolition of
slavery, 142, 143; and climate change,
138–40; Fitzhugh's attack on Adam
Smith over, 99; and institution of property, 3–4, 9; and Locke's theory of rights,
40; in Putney Convention, 29–30; in
Adam Smith's economic view, 10, 12
self-realization (flourishing), as value of
economic order, 112–13
self-sovereignty, 40, 111
semiotic democracy, 146
Sen, Amartya: and Arrow's impossibility
theorem, 124; cooperative conflict, 132–
33; and dimensions of freedom, 124–26;
and economic development, 132–33; and
market mechanism as incomplete, 116;
"negative" protections, 124; and Pareto
efficiency, 118; "positive" entitlements,
124; and Adam Smith, 26–27; and welfare economics analysis, 26–27, 123–27
sex asymmetry, 131–32
Shiller, Robert, 136–37
slavery: anomaly model, 89; analogy with
servitude, 92–93; and common law
arguments, 89, 90–91, 92–94; conciliatory model, 89, 93; English abolition of,
142–44; English positive law silent on,
92; and feudalism, 13, 95–96; Fitzhugh's
view of, 98–100, 109; and free labor,
95–100; Hale's view of, 108–9; Hildreth's
view of, 96–98; judicial decisions, 90–
95; Kent's view of, 59–60; and normative tradition, 24; paradox of, jurisprudence, 101–2; permissible discipline of
slaves, 91–95; and personhood in U.S.
history, 89–95; reconciling with other
relations, 92–94; rejection of, as cultural
arrogance, 93; Ruffin's anomalist view
of, 93–94; Adam Smith's view of, 12–16,